FOUNDATI SPORT DEVELOPMENT

Offering a complete introduction to sport development policy and practice, this book covers key theory, themes, issues, and debates in sport development, without assuming any prior knowledge on the part of the reader. It outlines the organisational landscape of sport in the UK and explains important differences across England, Scotland, Wales, and Northern Ireland, as well as the global context.

Examining both community and elite sport, it covers public, private, and third sectors, including national and local government and national governing bodies, and considers change – cultural, managerial, social, and political – as an element of sport development policy, strategy, and operations. Every chapter includes an in-depth case study around which a seminar or tutorial can be based, as well as definitions of key concepts and terminology that students and practitioners are likely to encounter during their studies or professional practice. Questions at the end of each chapter encourage the reader to reflect on their own work, and useful guides to further reading make the book an ideal jumping off point for further study.

This is the perfect foundation textbook for any sport development course taken as part of a degree program in sport development, sport management, or sport coaching.

Chris Mackintosh is a Senior Lecturer in Sport Development at the Department for Sport and Exercise Sciences at Manchester Metropolitan University, UK. He is Chair and Founder of the United Kingdom Sport Development Network (UKSDN) and currently has research interests in public policy of sport, development, and delivery systems in national governing bodies, local government, and the role of the voluntary sector. He has advised the Tokyo 2020 Olympics, Department of Digital, Culture, Media and Sport (DCMS), Sport England, Sport Scotland, the Sport and Recreation Alliance, and undertaken over 100 industry-facing research projects.

Foundations of Sport Development

CHRIS MACKINTOSH

Routledge
Taylor & Francis Group

LONDON AND NEW YORK

First published 2021
by Routledge
2 Park Square, Milton Park, Abingdon, Oxon OX14 4RN

and by Routledge
52 Vanderbilt Avenue, New York, NY 10017

Routledge is an imprint of the Taylor & Francis Group, an informa business

British Library Cataloguing-in-Publication Data
A catalogue record for this book is available from the British Library

Library of Congress Cataloging-in-Publication Data
Names: Mackintosh, Chris, author.
Title: Foundations of sport development / Chris Mackintosh.
Description: First Edition. | New York : Routledge, 2021. | Includes bibliographical references and index. |
Identifiers: LCCN 2020035953 | ISBN 9780367345839 (Hardback) | ISBN 9780367345846 (Paperback) | ISBN 9780429326707 (eBook)
Subjects: LCSH: Sports. | Sports administration. | Sports--Social aspects. | Physical education and training--Social aspects.
Classification: LCC GV713 .M332 2021 | DDC 796.06/9--dc23
LC record available at https://lccn.loc.gov/2020035953

ISBN: 978-0-367-34583-9 (hbk)
ISBN: 978-0-367-34584-6 (pbk)
ISBN: 978-0-429-32670-7 (ebk)

Typeset in Sabon
by SPi Global, India

This book is dedicated to my wonderful wife, Laura, and tremendously fun nieces, Niamh and Orla, who have been my inspiration to refocus on having a go at writing a research-led teaching and learning textbook. Their constant nagging to get onto this section has spurred me on to complete it. I'd also like to thank my mum, dad, and brother for their support in the highs of life and the parallel challenges of academia.

CONTENTS

PART III CONCLUSIONS, FUTURE DIRECTIONS, AND DEBATES 191

FIGURES

TABLES

CASE STUDIES

PREFACE

This book is aimed at providing an entry level year 4 level undergraduate text-book to understanding policy and practice in sport development. In particular, it will provide an insight to the importance of UK sport development for students in a range of global settings. However, it is also meant as a point of reference from level 4 to level 6 as a reference textbook for those students studying the management, development, and delivery of community sport. It covers key areas of subject content and approaches to the study of sport development including government policy, national governing body, local government, charity, and voluntary sector sport provision. In a period of increasing uncertainty in the UK with devolution contexts and associated political fragility, it offers a vehicle for learning and teaching in this complex domain. It also aims to act as a bridge for undergraduate students that may have difficulty with traditional academic 'entry' texts. It is aimed at you, the undergraduate student, not at the purest form of complex academic language. It will offer simplified learning exercises to help explain highly complex social phenomenon in the world of sport, physical activity, and, increasingly, 'wellbeing'. Knowledge, understanding, and skill development around the delivery and implementation of 'mental and physical health interventions' are now central to the undergraduate student's future employability.

Likewise, the central government drivers of policy are shaping what agencies and organisations do over the next 10 to 15 years. This book will aim to embrace the new landscape of social policy agendas that have re-emerged under this policy and associated strategies. Crucially, it will also consider them in the UK context as England, Scotland, Wales, and Northern Ireland, which, whilst closely connected, are also highly unique socio-political sport development contexts. Never before has a book attempted to unpick these four national contexts within the wider context of the UK amidst the shifting sands of changes at 'supra-national' (or EU governance level). Put simply, Brexit, devolution, and the role of sport development and management will never look the same post exit from the EU. As the book is written it will be a further point in the long history of books that draw a line in the sand. But, it is hoped that it can provide a useful update on many of the texts that preceded it in the field of sport development (Eady, 1993; Harris et al., 2012; Houlihan and White, 2002; Houlihan and Lindsey, 2013; Houlihan and Green, 2005; Hylton, 2013; King, 2009; Wilson and Platts, 2018). Many of these provide hugely useful contexts, historical detail of strategies and contexts that current policy and practice emerged through. But, as with many books, the level of change in political democracy, post-9-11, and commercial shifts in society now leave aspects of these books as more of a historical legacy than a useful introductory text for new students entering the contemporary landscape of working in, studying, and undertaking placements in community sport development. Indeed, some in the more market-orientated element of industry have argued for how sport development is itself a 'dead term'. More on this later.

This is the definitive undergraduate entry textbook that provides an accessible and informative introduction to the study, analysis and understanding of sport development policy and practice in the UK. The book has the following five key pillars of learning:

- To outline and explain the key policies, strategies, organisations that operate within sport development policy and practice
- To establish an introductory curriculum for staff and students in this field in a highly changeable policy and practice environment that can be updated in future editions.
- To explore key issues, topics for analysis and contemporary debates in UK and global sport development
- To introduce key concepts, theories and academic terms used in the global study of sport development policy and practice
- To provide an introductory text for future texts that examine this field in more academic detail/depth as part of a series.

In order to meet these aims the book has several objectives that are also to be read in some ways as values that underpin the philosophy of approach in this landmark textbook. These include:

- To offer students an accessible, richly informative, and easily understandable text that can support their first-year studies on sport development, management, and policy undergraduate degrees
- To provide academic staff a clear point of reference for introductory texts on BA (Hons) sport development, sport coaching, sport management degrees for yearlong modules that are introducing sport development policy and practice
- To outline key theoretical ideas, ideological meanings and values, conceptual terms, debates, and issues that can be a point of departure for background reading in 'one place'
- To offer clear reading list support for students in this field and make the development and of learning more engaging for new and experienced staff
- To be the core textbook of choice in this field for undergraduate level 4 students and build an underlying understanding of global difference, otherness, social justice, and equality to underpin sport development practice in the UK context.

The textbook will principally have accessibility and bridging between further education and school and your first-year studies at its heart. It will also provide an overview of the UK context, as opposed to England, or regional bias as other books tend to focus on. This will make it useful for understanding the entire UK market as opposed to those universities solely in England. It will also open up employability for English students in other countries in the UK and vice versa. In an era of Brexit and devolution, it is increasingly important that we are all more mobile and flexible in an era of austerity. It will also offer the foreign (non-UK) market an opportunity to teach this academic field in non-UK educational settings by providing an 'introduction' text' for the foreign student wishing to explore the UK. It will use research-informed text, but will provide this in an accessibly written format for students that have entered HE with the potential 'technical' subject literacy that can come with this. I believe this is a growing issue amongst HE teaching staff concerns and this book will support addressing this issue. Most importantly, I hope that you enjoy using the book, not just reading passively. I hope this book goes some way to challenging the notion that sport is a subject not to be researched 'for real' or is not a valid subject to read for at university. I also hope in some small way my 12 years of involvement as a researcher and chair at the UKSDN, advisor to UK and other governments can be successfully distilled down into a research-led book, which has my own passion for teaching and learning at its core. For this, I will be judged by the interest in the book by staff and students.

Dr Chris Mackintosh
Chair and Founder, UK Sport Development Network (UKSDN)
Senior Lecturer in Sport Development, Manchester
Metropolitan University
January 2021

References

Eady, J. (1993) *Practical Sport Development*, Essex: Longman Group.

Harris, S., Bell, B., Adams, A., and Mackintosh, C. (2012) *Sport for Sport? Practical and Theoretical Insights into Sports Development*, Brighton: Leisure Studies Association.

Houlihan, B. and White, A. (2002) *The Politics of Sports Development: Development of Sport or Development Through Sport?*, London: Routledge.

Houlihan, B. and Lindsey, L. (2013) *Sport Policy in Britain*, London: Routledge.

Houlihan, B. and Green, M. (2005) *Elite Sport Development Policy Learning and Political Priorities*, London: Routledge.

Hylton, K. (ed.) (2013) *Sport Development* (Third Edition), London: Routledge.

King, N. (2009) *Sport Policy and Governance*, Oxford: Butterworth-Heinemann.

Long, J., Fletcher, T., and Watson, B. (2017) *Sport, Leisure and Social Justice*, London: Routledge.

Medcalf, R. and Mackintosh, C. (eds.) (2018) *Researching Difference and Otherness in Sport and Physical Activity*, London: Routledge.

Mackintosh, M. and Dempsey, C. (2017) The British Asian Muslim male sport participation puzzle: An exploration of implications for sport development policy and practice, *Journal of Youth Studies*, 20:8, 974–996.

Wilson, R. and Platts, C. (2018) *Managing and Developing Community Sport*, London:
Routledge.

ACKNOWLEDGMENTS

It would be remiss for me not to say a big thank you specifically to a few lovely people in academia and industry that have supported my 12-year journey with the UK Sport Development Network (UKSDN) since we founded it in 2008. So, in no order, James Allen, Dr Richard Medcalf, Chris Cutforth, Dr Gerald Griggs, Dr Helen Ives, Dr Mat Dowling, Matt Bloor, Dr Kate Mori, Abbie Lench, Dr Claire Jenkins, Dr Spencer Harris, Dr Verity Postlethwaite, and Lou Morby. Also, Prof Joyce Liddle, Prof Rosie Meek, and Prof Mark James for their individual nudges of intellectual insight along the way that a practice and policy focused book is needed.

Finally, a huge thanks to all my undergraduate students and doctoral researchers that constantly inspire me to keep teaching and writing. I hope the book helps shape future employability and critical thinking in sport development, and ultimately builds better practice and experiences in for those that first come to study community sport at university. However, I hope most crucially it has a small impact on future generations of critical community sport development practitioners and the people and places they serve.

PART I

Introducing the sport development landscape

This section of the book is intended as a precursor to answering the many requests and queries I have had over 20 years of teaching sport development. The central challenge is to help bridge the gap between a student arriving at a university needing explanation and support and what we as staff offer them in terms of accessibility of a single text. This also is related to the reality they often face with books and journals that are hard to read and, hence, disempowering. Part I in this book is designed specifically as a toolkit for bridging this gap. It first provides a foundational set of ideas and historical background to the study of the subject area that many students will go on to look at in much more detail over the next three years. Further to this, it is worth exploring key myths in this overview. There is no neat definition of a fluid, complex, and often debated term and set of professional practices. Sport development has in some ways never been so well positioned politically; government is asking officers and staff in these areas to deliver ever more nuanced and complicated projects hopeful of meeting sensitive and challenging policy outcomes. You may well want to be coach, manager, football community trust leader, or chief executive of a national governing body (NGB) or local authority. What is clear is that the skills, knowledge, and assumptions of when sport development leapt onto the platform of 1980s England are very different now in the post-2020 UK. Sport occurs in a global setting – funding, social conditions, and economic trends are ever more hyper-global in their occurrences. Interactions between and through organisations can occur more quickly. However, equally as we experienced with the COVID-19 pandemic, a small health issue can now rapidly be spread globally to have catastrophic implications on sport and physical activity.

In establishing the foundations of sport development, the book clearly outlines sections of the sector in Part II of the book and then goes on to impress upon the reader the changing and future landscape of sport development in Part III. Foundations of sport development are themselves an interesting idea. In this part of the book, we also explore the bridging ideas that underpin these foundational aspects of a profession, of policy ideas, and principles of why we do what we do. First, there is a consideration of how, why, and where we examine

1

certain types of sport development sector organisations. These vary from the lowly sport club in a voluntary setting through to a major provider such as a local government provider. At one time in the heyday of the 1980–1990s UK, they held the majority of posts and resourcing. But the landscape has moved, shifted to now encompass new types of organisations in new sectors that are part of what might be termed a more 'mixed economy'. The understanding and examination you will get from knowing these sectors and sub-sectors within sport development is critical to the spine of learning in this book. You have to know these agencies and settings and how they start to offer a spring-board for your learning as they carve out your own professional learning. Indeed, many students say to their respective university staff they didn't know about the scope and reach of sport development until they spoke to their university tutors and began their degree. What it might now mean to be employed in sport development is so different to even five years ago. The emergence of the private sector, social enterprises, decline of local government sport development functions, and growth in devolved government expenditure in Northern Ireland, Wales and Scotland as they are more free from centralised English control all give a good indication of significant tremors at play in the landscape.

After outlining the organisational approaches and landscapes that will be examined in Part I, the book then begins to lay out an accessible chapter on theory. Theory must be the word that sends most fear through the veins of my students. Instead of dispelling the myths of theory, we as academics can be tempted to make it a veiled complex and confusing 'tool'. In fact, what this book will do is set out in simple and plain English terms how you can start to take very different theoretical approaches to studying sport development. Business management will be compared to sociology and other areas of the social sciences. It is then down to the reader to start their own journey in reading and exploring these new parts of their degree. What is clear is that ten years ago theory was less relevant to practice, but as sport development moves into the realms of motivation, organisation culture, strategy, behaviour change, and crime prevention a field that is 'atheoretical' would be like a surgeon operating without an understanding of the body. In our case, sport development's 'lab' space is society, communities, individual perceptions, and decision making. The interventions we design as students, future practitioners, and when on placement years are underpinned by theory, concepts, and ideas. However, we also now need to be able to react to an NGB that comes to us with an idea and be able to explore theory. If a coaching company wants to do coaching better there is theory there to help us better use digital resources. Theory effectively is a frame or lens to help us understand, improve, and shape practice better. Then there is also theoretical work just for its own sake. But I would argue there is less place for this on a sport development degree as employability and future career choices are so central to your learning.

CHAPTER 1

Introduction

This chapter will provide an outline introduction to the emergence and evolution of the professional field of sport development. It will also cover an introductory set of definitions, and debate about the origins, and changing concept of sport development. For the reader new to the study of sport development (beyond level 3 FE, England or college in Scotland/Northern Ireland/Wales), it will begin to set foundations for understanding key pillars of the subject area, profession, and processes involved in sport development and, in particular, in community-facing sport. As a scholar of this subject, many of the terms will be new. As a student, many of the ideas and ways of studying will be foreign to you, and some of the 'big concepts', philosophies and ideologies of what government do and don't do will be hard to grasp initially. However, it will provide a scaffolding for your learning, and a book you can return to time and time again if you are unsure of some the harder terms we as academics and practitioners draw upon. Just talking about government, national sport 'agendas', and the difference between evaluation, implementation, and project management is a false division of what are closely interwoven, highly debateable ideas. For one sport development professional in Wales, compared to a more senior strategist of policy in this same field of say mental wellbeing and sport in England, the operational environment is very different. This is in part the challenge for you studying this subject, but also the aim of the book. Sport development at its heart is simplistic. It can be condensed down to guiding principles, but the political and social environment that professionals, students, and academics operate is now very different to when it started evolving as an 'industry'. I will draw the distinction between elite sport, medal-winning goals of policy and talent development. However, at the same time I will aim to provide clear linkages with the pathways for participation, barriers to participation, and introduce sectoral philosophies in sport development that have been present historically and that are emerging in current policy contexts (sport for all, sport for social good, mass participation era, austerity in Britain and the modernisation of sport development systems). The final, most recent, phase of sport development's evolution is the most fascinating in my opinion as the very subject, discipline, and what was a profession is under attack. The political and ideological forces of government, the big ideas – or what some call philosophies of the day (neo-liberalism, conservatism, social democracy, environmentalism, Brexiteer-ism) – are fundamentally changing the landscape of what was always a non-statutory, loosely connected body of individuals. Hylton and Hartley (2012) argue in their examination of the sport development 'profession' that the realm of this area back in 2012 was not structured, lacked the professional 'body', membership organisation, and definitional pillars that might make sport development such a 'profession'. Moving forward a number of years, sport development as a concept and imagined sphere of professional practice, and domain of government activity has shifted in all areas of the UK fundamentally. Recent assessments of UK sport development have focused on its 'UK' nature, attempted to define it according to previous parameters such as the philosophy of the government. However, it is my assertion that the very definition of sport development needs to shift.

Defining sport development

At its heart, sport development has always been about the provision, delivery, and planning of policy and practice of community sport. It may be useful to not draw a distinction between elite and local community sport, but instead consider all sport on a spectrum without a hierarchy from 'bottom' to 'top' from community sport participation up to elite medals. Other academics have framed this more as a contested debate around the 'public value' concept of sport and sport development (Brookes and Wiggan, 2009; Collins, 2010a, b). Here, the central tug-of-war in sport policy has been between notions of 'sport-for-sports sake' and sport for a role in delivery of 'social good'. Brookes and Wiggan (2009) provide a powerful research case study leading up to London 2012, suggesting that the period of long-term legacy is where government will be judged. We will return to these debates throughout the book. If anything, the way that recent government has repositioned sport development is on a far more thematic level in the new Department of Culture, Media and Sport (DCMS) (2015) strategy document. In my own professional practice working with national governing bodies (NGBs), local government(s) (read councils at various municipal levels), and charities, few ever stop to define this most complex of terms. For many, whilst the term may be long 'dead' (Macdonald, 1995), in decline, and new, more neoliberal, managerial terms have more appeal, there is a strong workforce of individuals that contest this and align with a sport development professional identity.

However, it is useful to think of this central term of your studies as a 'conceptual construct', or idea, a set of inter linked interpretations that have emerged over time and have come to now form an imagined set of management practices and policy documents and decisions. This can be very complex to the new student of sport development. Here we are using wider ideas from politics, sociology, geography, and the wider social science to help us in our toolkit to understand a 'messy term'. It is, I find, far better to acknowledge a concept or idea as theoretically hard to understand then look for theory and practical ways of examining it rather than assuming it is a simple straight definition. Indeed, what the industry needs is critical managers that will constantly question, come up with new 'ways of seeing' (Berger and Luckman, 1976) and employ their own sociological imagination (Wright Mills, 1959). Often, the definition of sport development as a student is driven by the theoretical way we study 'it'. A geographer will look a time, space and place(s) of sport and leisure as a starting point (Bale, 1989; Bale, 2003). Political science researchers will look at the State, government, and how different views and ideas of political parties shape the sport policy and practices in community and elite sport (Houlihan and White, 2002; Houlihan and Lindsey, 2013). Sociologists will look in a multitude of ways at people, communities, and individuals in society, and the beliefs and norms that are present within sport development and how involvement in sport shapes beliefs. It is also likely that, increasingly, your sport development course will also cover aspects of business management and marketing. These philosophies are resisted in some areas of sport development, particularly where the commodification of community amateur sport enters a more professionalised set of products and brands. Herein lies our second major lesson – we can disagree. Whether we are in class, on the sport pitch or in meetings as sport development professionals, there are a diversity of ideologies, perspectives and preferred approaches. Later in the book, we will look at the challenges around multi-agency partnership working in the sector where the issue of disagreement appears frequently.

Perhaps, in defining sport development, it is most critical to understand that today's practice, management, and development of sport is historically, politically, and socially situated. By this we mean, it is 'positioned'. So, what we see as sport development has changed over time from 1960 to 2020 or from Wales to Scotland, or, between different political parties during the same electoral period. This can be very hard for new students to understand. But, it is a fundamental of learning to study that we embed criticality in our study from as soon as possible in our scholarly practice. In embracing a consideration of sport development in the UK across different home nations, this in itself is relatively novel for an undergraduate text where the majority lean strongly towards England and its policy landscape.

A starting point for conceptualising

The places and people involved in community sport development a the starting point for the conceptual definition in this book. Think of this as the who and where sport development occurs, but, also how, when and in what ways. Considering some of these most basic of questions allows us to build a basic framework around a field of study. Some authors have questioned the existence of a sport development profession (Hylton and Hartley, 2012). Likewise, others have acknowledged the increasing professionalisation of coaching (Dowling, Edwards, and Washington, 2014; Taylor and Garrett, 2010; Gale and Ives, 2019) and sport development (Bloyce et al., 2008). To some, this is part of a historical movement away from the origins of community sport development which lies in the oft cited Wolfenden Report of 1960 (Houlihan and White, 2002; Houlihan and Lindsey, 2013). Why this report is cited as the foregrounding document of sport development is also important. Indeed, it is perhaps due to the focus of scholarly attention in sport development being largely driven by political and sociological academics. As a geographer, I am also interested in why we focus on the very UK-centric 'origins' of a discipline. For many other countries, the term and field of sport development has grown in recent years but through the use of the term 'sport-for-development' or sport-in-development' (Coalter, 2007). These terms must also be clarified as they offer a newer, fresh more globally outward-facing definitional starting point that may now be far more useful than a historical political reference point that existed before Brexit, devolution, and many of the global shifts we have experienced in the last 20 years.

Eady (1993) is seen by many in the field and academia to be a founding father of the study of sport development, after which a number of text books emerged that shaped the next generation of the discipline. This was led by Hylton (2007) who has produced three editions of his standard 'core' text with colleagues at Leeds Beckett University sport development team and their *Centre for Sport and Social Justice* launched in 2020. This book and its various formats and editions provide ample background to the foregrounding to this text. However, what I aim to do is offer an alternative updated standpoint on what sport development is, who is now involved, and how it has emerged since the first draft of this text back in 2006–2007. Much has happened since then, including multiple government changes and far wider global shifts such as the economic crisis, strengthening of Brexit politics in the UK, and the rise of far-right ideas, extremism, and racism in Europe as well as islamophobia in part as a reaction to the 9/11 attacks. The definitions by Eady of 'sport development' in 1993 and those of the government agencies at the time of the home nation Sports Councils (Sports Council, 1982; Scottish Sport Council, 1990; Audit Commission, 1989) and NGBs made no reference to wider societal conditions or determinants of health and wellbeing. The role focused on the 'process', I would argue a linear pathway from primary school to elite participation. The model that this centred upon was the sport development continuum. This, in fact, was not a model, had minimal empirical evidence, and has now firmly been critiqued as little more than a guiding set of ideas with minimal evidence underpinning or theoretical orientation (Green, 2005). Regardless, multiple references continue to be made to this within industry whether it is in NGB posters around swimming pools, or textbook references to the 'original theory'. I question the theoretical foundations of this, and you, as students, should too. Theory is meant as an explanatory tool, to help us understand complex ideas and we should ask hard questions about assumptions, empirical evidence, and wider constructs it draws on. The power of the article is in the coherent unpicking of the assumptions of an upwards pyramid model in sport, aspects such as whether mass participation leads to more players at elite standard; differences in 'the model' by sport, region, and country context; and lack of any empirical evidence underpinning the original model (Green, 2005). A useful and powerful point of acknowledgement is in her statement "it is a measure of the analogy's cultural power that it is common parlance among sport administrators and policymakers but lacks any sustained empirical or conceptual integrity" (Green, 2005: 234). In a more recent study in Holland, sports clubs membership figures for one region were compared with national figures to identify the common trends. Analysis across 20 sports revealed no consistent relationship between membership levels and success (De Boscher, Sotiradou, and Van Bottenburg, 2013). The study also supported a questionable relationship between mass participation and elite success. Simplistic notions of sport developmental pyramid pathways must be critically questioned. This is without any consideration of complex societal factors around disability, ethnicity, gender, and social disadvantage.

Houlihan and White (2002) undertook a comprehensive review of sport development origins and political and ideological foundations since the 1960s. However, Houlihan and White's book does have a leaning towards political science and policy analysis. It is a suggestion that the very subject of the book has also now changed fundamentally from 18 years ago when the book (a classic of our field) was written. Hylton and Bramham (2008) suggest, in contrast to this, that sport development can be considered a contested process that is the responsibility of a multiplicity of different partners, not just those with perhaps a headline 'sport development' label in a neat job description. They identify conflict and disputes within partnerships and central processes as core within sport development.

Such typical definitions are usually UK focused, as indeed is my own attempt to define the area (Mackintosh 2011: 47) where I argue that it can be defined as something that:

> embraces the dual goals of increasing community sports participation linked to the aspiration to improve standards of elite sports performance. Furthermore, the work of the sports development officer (SDO) could embrace varied aspects of community sport including voluntary sports club development, community event planning, volunteer recruitment and retention, and coach education and development activities.

For other academic authors, definitions remain elusive, and in supporting students on an introduction to their degree subject, this can be unhelpful at best or confusing and unsettling at worst. This is not to mean that definitions such as the one I provide above are to be reified (made 'concrete' in our minds, writing, and professional practice). Instead, I suggest we need a starting point to study, something to evaluate and set our contextual learning against. For example, whilst largely avoiding providing a unified definition Bloyce and Smith (2010: 8) suggest

> despite the uncertainty that surrounds the jobs of sports development professionals and the often vague, contentious definitions of sport development and the roles and responsibilities of SDOs, it may nevertheless be said that more or less the key aspect of sports development is getting more people involved in sport.

This was written ten years ago, before Sport England's latest strategy (Sport England, 2020), and a ten-year lag since the home nations have responded to Brexit, devolution, and developing their own approaches to sport development. The question I would pose on the back of this quote, is whether infrastructure is increasingly driven now by social policy and social good – not by the 'main aim of getting more people playing'. Arguably, for example, there are still targets to be achieved on this agenda (more women, disability participants, coaches, and so on), but my question is: is it not now that sport in the UK, in some countries more than others, is aiming to address social issues through sport and physical activity more than just growing a mass participation base?

TABLE 1.1 An adaption of Houlihan's (2011) conceptualisation of sport development aligned to UK policy in 2020

	Elite sport development	Sport for sports sake	Sport-for-development
Where	English Institute of Sport Welsh Institute of Sport Regional Centres (e.g. Plas Y Brenin) Professional clubs	Amateur sports clubs Playing fields Open spaces/parks Leisure centres	Prisons, young offender institutions, mental health project spaces, Abroad locations (e.g. Africa, India; Coalter, 2007)
Who	NGBs, athletes, elite coaches, elite support staff, sponsors, global agencies (world anti-doping agency, IOC)	Club volunteers, NGBs, general public. (Hylton and Totten, 2013)	Varied non-sport sector partners (e.g. NHS, charity, social enterprise)
How	Funding partnerships from UK Sport, Sport England and NGBs Delivery plans, KPIs, whole sport plans (Thompson, Bloyce, and Mackintosh, 2020)	'Traditional sport development' pathway working/ construct Local organic agenda setting	Partnerships and cross-agency funding relationships Programme design to deliver social outcomes
Why	Political mega events (Grix, 2010) Mass participation argument (Grix and Carmichael, 2012)	Sport as a leisure time activity 'serious leisure' (Stebbins, 1982; Sport Scotland, 2019)	Policy direction and funding alignment (DCMS (2015; Sport England (2016)

Houlihan (2015) set the scene neatly when he suggested that sport development was now following a three-tier area of practice in terms of elite sport development, community sport for sport's sake and sport-for-development (social good). If we then go back to our frame for beginning to understand this vast area of academic interest, you can map across those three areas who, where, how, and why organisations and individuals are connected to sport development by spaces and places. For example,

However, it is important to look beyond the UK for wider reference points in an increasingly globalised policy environment where organisations beyond the national, regional, and even international influence sport, the time to reconsider sport development fundamentally is now. Defining sport development has, at its heart, various common components. As a 'constructed term' we could refer to a false dichotomy, or a binary (think 'two-way') way of thinking (Collins, 2010a, b). For some, it is where the two aspects stand opposite each other's, so it becomes a case of medals or participation, or serious or fun sport (Grix and Carmichael, 2012). Or, even more fundamentally, we are forced to classify professional or organisational 'work streams' as development of sport, wellbeing or physical activity. In recent times, this has, however, become incredibly blurred. A good example of this is the DCMS (2015) strategy, which cites wellbeing, physical activity, and sport quite interchangeably. Likewise, the new England Coaching Strategy (Sport England, 2017) has a far broader conceptual understanding of what coaching consists of. It fundamentally blurs the previous division between tiers of elite and localised social coaching. Who is to say the very highest level of elite sport should not be fun, and that the most local, or 'micro' activities in a local hockey club are not incredibly serious (Figure 1.1). Figure 1.2 below offers a new way of examining this breakdown of just how I have historically defined sport development in Table 1.1, above. Here it is this 'third' space where we need to not be focusing on mass or elite as they are now too closely connected. Likewise, sport for development arguably cuts across elite sport (child protection through to coach-athlete neglect and poor mental health systems within NGBs) and mass participation

Community	Elite	Continuum of opportunities
Grass roots	Medals	Progression and pathways
Enjoyable/fun sport	'Serious' sport	Ideology, ethos and values
Local facility	performance venues	Multi-use (flexible) space
Local event	Mega events/national competitions	multi-tier event hosting
Unregulated	Explicit governance/legal systems	governance
SDO	Elite coach/support/scientist	sport development professional

FIGURE 1.1 The false dichotomy of elite-community sport

(abusive coaches). This way of considering a new third space for sport development gives greater fluidity and offers opportunities to re-examine the original grounds of what was at one time a more narrowly defined occupational domain.

Original foundations and new directions

Inherent within Figure 1.2 is the notion that the participant (think 'mass participation') can, does, and will move through a neat system. It is not a messy, disjointed misaligned and complex system which sport by sport, space by space, differs in its nuances. It is actually perhaps most useful for acting as a starting point for thinking about how this could work in a conceptual landscape of theory alone. Arguably, its origins lie with Tungatt and MacDonald (1991), English Sports Council Officers that emerged from the National Demonstration project work they were involved with as policy and researchers. The concept was then taken as a policy idea and transferred into regional projects, plans, and visions (Collins, 2010a, b), and also the first textbook teaching the subject of sport development (Eady, 1993). However, as Green (2005) argued in her consideration of a normative theory of sport development the pyramid model as it is also known in America and Europe is conflicted with issues. In particular, she identifies how it varies between different sports (e.g. bobsleigh versus soccer), and how the shape of model would differ by sport in terms of some sports recruiting later than others and others younger. Gymnastics, for example, in the UK recruits very young to feed into elite programmes and coaching, as it does internationally. Thus, the idea of this model having a primary school 'level' and secondary school that then feeds into clubs and regional centres of excellence and 'elite' is a myth. Some primary school gymnasts will already be identified as elite 'track' by entry into secondary school. Green is not alone in her critique (Bloyce and Smith, 2010; De Boscher et al., 2013; Hill, 2007). But as the title of this book is *Foundations of Sport Development*, it is important we consider the original foundations before

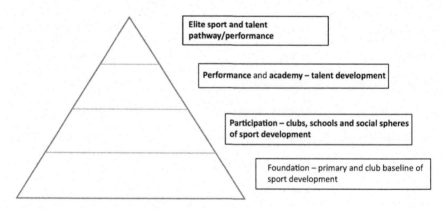

FIGURE 1.2 The sport development pyramid

looking at how they have shifted, drifted, and emerged in a new climate that is very different to where it originally was. Figure 1.2 is probably one of the most commonly taught staple components of mainstream sport development degree courses. Students constantly refer to this, and its multiple derivative formats and reference points as the definitional starting point for studying the subject. However, it has been 14 years since Christine Green wrote her seminal article examining the normative theory of sport development. It is here that for the first time we saw a non-UK academic clearly evaluate, critique, and unpick the so-called theory of Tungatt and MacDonald (1991) as taught through the text of Eady (1993) that had taken on the almost mystical power of the sport development continuum myth. It was grounded in the era when it was an industry that had the priority of developing athletes and athlete pathways from early or pre-school through to secondary school systems and clubs and into regional and national development squads (Hill, 2007; Houlihan and Green, 2005). This 'model' was based on very little policy research, minimal if any empirical evidence, and instead gained traction to support most NGB performance and participation policies and funding approaches. Numerous articles in academia have since built strong debates to evaluate the thinking behind this (Chalip, 1996; De Boscher et al., 2013; Green, 2004; Sotiradou, Shilbury, and Quick, 2008). What is fundamental to the new era of community sport development policy and practice is that such ideas are now useful as a historical reference point but not as a lever for meeting the needs of the industry or training the next generation of new professional graduates that will be employed by NGBs, Active Partnerships (formerly CSPs), coaching consortiums and the plethora of other diverse agencies now engaged in the sector across the UK.

The sector is in need of new theory, new ways of seeing and doing sport development. It is uncomfortable to step outside the ivory tower of textbooks that we know. But, as the challenges we get asked to examine are more complex, so we need more nuanced, subtle specific training, and ideas and theory to support project development. Too often at present, the default setting is simply to a commercial business, or what agencies refer to as a 'customer focused' rhetoric of products to meet needs. What if this was the wrong overarching discourse? It is the intention of this book to clearly map out the emergent new landscape as a starting point for better understanding what is a brave new world for community sport in the UK that lies a far cry from that of the 1960s Wolfenden Report, 1970s golden era of facility expansion, early days of 1982 Action Sport responses to urban riots across England, or even the 2002 Game Plan document of DCMS and the Cabinet Office.

CASE STUDY 1.1

How do we conceptualise sport development?

The notion that sport development is contested is not new (Hylton, 2013; Houlihan and White, 2002). This essentially means that people, organisations, institutions, and different realms of society have different expectations and interpretations of what this professional domain means. If there are alternative visions for what it means, this obviously has an impact upon how it is operationalised by, say, an NGB or a local authority body. It is also the case that each of the home nations is now, post-devolution, setting its own agendas around what sport development can and should deliver. This will be discussed in more detail later. In this section, we want you to consider how you understand sport development at this stage of your studies, unit you are engaged with, and potential career. In particular, it is important to consider the different lenses you are looking at this through. Is it historical, for example? How has sport development altered between different governments' period of political control? At different societal periods of historical context, where were people 'doing' sport development and what for? Second, we could look to sociological theory to help us conceptualise sport development and very specific theorists would consider sport development having different actual and potential roles. In more recent times, for example, Marxist theorists might look at the commercialisation of community sport, through the use of sponsors as a vehicle to sell more trainers, kit, and alter attitudes of young people and their families. Sociological theory could also examine the potential emancipatory potential of sport development officers to address issues of gender inequality through feminist theory. Different strands of theory such as feminism use key concepts, one being patriarchy. Students often worry about the more theoretical side of subjects. Sport development students will be exposed to theory; it is simply crucial to engage and try to understand these more abstract ideas. Staying with feminist theory's conceptual tool of patriarchy, this refers to the principle that masculinity and men dominate systems of power and thus exploit females and create and advance greater levels of gender inequality. They would argue this applies to society, but also specifically sport development and communities engaging with projects and initiatives relating to it.

In this case it is therefore useful to explore the issue of gender inequality in sport and what role sport development might play. There are many examples of initiatives established by numerous sporting bodies in the UK and beyond set up to deal with different components of such inequality. This includes supporting females into positions of leadership in sport development and onto executive boards overseeing NGBs, targeting of coaching projects at girl-only sessions in specific Black and Minority Ethnic (BAME) participant groups, and media campaigns such as *This Girl Can*.

Seminar questions

1. How do you understand sport development?
2. If we were to think of sport development as having values and principles, what might some of these be?
3. What are the boundaries of sport development? (Where does it stop being sport development and become 'something else'?)

Suggested group activity

In a group, share your understanding of what you individually understand by sport development. Beyond this, use the framework above to research the where, who, how, and when of your different understanding(s). In this way, build a peer-led picture of a starting point for what you are studying and potentially working towards a career in.

Further reading

Cutforth, C. (2018) Understanding the landscape of community sport, in Wilson, R. and Platts, C. (eds) *Managing and Developing Community Sport*, London: Routledge, 15–29.

Houlihan, B. (2015) Introduction, in Houlihan, B. (ed.) *International Handbook for Sport Development*, Routledge, London, 1–4.

References

Audit Commission (1989) *Sport for Whom?* London: Audit Commission.

Bale, J. (1989) *Sports Geography*, London: Routledge.

Bale, J. (2003) *Sports Geography (2nd edition)*, London: Routledge.

Berger, P. L. and Luckman, T. (1976) *Social Construction of Reality*, London: Penguin Books.

Bloyce, D. and Smith, A. (2010) *Sport Policy and Development*, London: Routledge.

Bloyce, D.. Smith, A., Mead, R., and Morris, J. (2008) 'Playing the game (plan)': A figurational analysis of organizational change in sports development in England, *European Sport Management Quarterly*, 8:4, 359–378.

Brookes, S. and Wiggan, J. (2009) Reflecting the public value of sport: A game of two halves? *Public Management Review*, 11:4, 401–420.

Chalip, L. (1996) Critical policy analysis: The illustrative case of New Zealand sport policy development, *Journal of Sport Management*, 10, 310–324.

Coalter, F. (2007) *A Social Role for Sport: Whose Keeping the Score?*, London: Routledge.

Collins, M. (2010a) From 'sport for good' to 'sport for sport's sake' – not a good move for sports development in England? *International Journal of Sport Policy and Politics*, 2:3, 367–379.

Collins, M. (2010b) *Examining Sport Development*, London: Routledge.

De Boscher, V., Sotiradou, P. and Van Bottenburg, M. (2013), Scrutinizing the sport pyramid metaphor: An examination of the relationship between elite success and mass participation in Flanders, *International Journal of Sport Policy*, 5:3, 319–339.

Department of Culture, Media and Sport (DCMS) (2015) *Sporting Future a New Strategy for an Active Nation*, London: DCMS.

Dowling, M., Edwards, J. and Washington, M. (2014) Understanding the concept of professionalisation in sport management research, *Sport Management Review*, 17:4, 520–529.

Eady, J. (1993) *Practical Sport Development*, Essex: Longman.

Gale, L. and Ives, B. (2019) Emotional struggles and troubled relationships, in Gale L. A. and Ives, B. (eds) *Sports Coaching in the Community: Developing Knowledge and Insight*, Manchester: Manchester Metropolitan University.

Green, M. (2004) Changing policy priorities for sport in England: The emergence of elite sport development as a key policy concern, *Leisure Studies*, 23:4, 365–385.

Green. C. (2005) Building sport programs to Optimize athlete recruitment, retention, and transition: Toward a normative theory of sport development, *Journal of Sport Management*, 19, 233–253.

Grix, J. (2010) The 'governance debate' and the study of sport policy. *International Journal of Sport Policy*, 2:2, 159–171.

Grix, J. and Carmichael, F. (2012) Why do governments invest in elite sport? A polemic, *International Journal of Sport Policy*, 4:1, 73–90.

Hill, M. (2007) *In Pursuit of Excellence*, London: Routledge.

Houlihan, B. (2015) Introduction, in Houlihan, B. (ed.) *International Handbook for Sport Development*, London: Routledge, 1–4.

Houlihan, B. and Green, M. (2005) *Elite Sport Development Policy Learning and Political Priorities*, London: Routledge.

Houlihan, B. and Lindsey, I. (2013) *Sport Policy in Britain*, London: Routledge.

Houlihan, B. and White, A. (2002) *The Politics of Sports Development: Development of Sport or Development Through Sport?*, London: Routledge.

Hylton, K. (ed.) (2007) *Sports Development: Policy, Process and Practice (1st edition)*, London: Routledge.

Hylton, K. (2013) (ed.) *Sport Development: Policy, Process and Practice*, London: Routledge.

Hylton, K. and Bramham, P. (2008) *Sport development: Policy, Process and Practice*, London: Routledge.

Hylton, K. and Hartley, H. (2012) Sports development: A profession in waiting? in Harris, S., Bell, B., Adams, A. and Mackintosh, C. (eds) *Sport for Sport? Theoretical and Practical Insights into Sports Development*, Brighton: Leisure Studies Association, 4–22.

Hylton, K. and Totten, M. (2013) Developing 'sport for all', in Hylton, K. (ed.) *Sport Development: Policy, Process and Practice*, London: Routledge, 37–79.

MacDonald, I. (1995) *Sport for All-'RIP'. A Political Critique of the Relationship between National Sport Policy and Local Authority Sports Development in London*, Brighton: Leisure Studies Association, 55, 71–94.

Mackintosh, C. (2011) An analysis of county sports partnerships in England: the fragility, challenges and complexity of partnership working in sports development, *International Journal of Sport Policy*, 3:1, 45–64.

Scottish Sports Council (1990) *Sports Development Groups and Plans*, Report OP1, Edinburgh: Scottish Sports Council.

Sotiradou, P., Shilbury, D. and Quick, S. (2008) The attraction, retention/transition, and nurturing process of sport development: Some Australian evidence, *Journal of Sport Management*, 22:3, 247–272.

Sports Council (1982) *Sport in the Community: The Next Ten Years*, London: Sports Council.

Sport England (2016) *Towards an Active Nation*, London: Sport England.

Sport England (2017) *The Coaching Plan for England: Two years on*, London: Sport England.

Sport England (2020) *Shaping Our Future*, London: Sport England.

Sport England (2019) *The Sport Scotland Business Plan 2019–2021*, Glasgow: Sport Scotland.

Stebbins, R. A. (1982) Serious leisure: A conceptual statement, *Pacific Sociological Review*, 25:2, 251–272.

Taylor, B. and Garrett, D. (2010) The professionalisation of sports coaching: Relations of power, resistance and compliance, *Sport, Education and Society*, 15:1, 121–139.

Thompson, A., Bloyce, D., and Mackintosh, C. (2020) 'It is always going to change' – managing top-down policy changes by sport development officers working in national governing bodies of sport in England, *Managing Sport and Leisure: An International Journal*, iFirst, 1–20.

Tungatt, M. and MacDonald, D. (1991) *National Demonstration Projects – Major lessons and Issues for Sports Development*, London: Sports Council.

Wright Mills, C. (1959) *The Sociological Imagination*, Oxford: Oxford University Press.

CHAPTER 2

Historical and political context of the United Kingdom

For very detailed profiles of the contested history of sport development, the role of government, and the changing shape and landscape of practice, no better source can be highlighted than the analysis undertaken by Houlihan and White (2002), and more recent work by Houlihan and Lindsey (2013). Both texts provide a detailed year-by-year, policy document-by-document account of the complex interweaving of policy development from a political science perspective. However, this is just one academic position to undertake and this book is intentionally critical of solely political, sociological, or geographical analyses. It embraces an interdisciplinary position of the analysis of history. Indeed, many students ask why do I do need to even study history. Sport development is what we do now, today, and maybe for the next six months, then it all changes. So, my argument in this foundational text is that a sound broad historical foundation of what happened, when, and why is critical to understanding today's practice and policy. It also allows us as social scientists of a subject that has undergone constant change to see the layers of meaning that lie at the heart of the delivery, implementation, and planning of projects. It also allows us to consider why trends may be present such as specific approaches to talent development and elite athlete mega events are offered as a solution to increasing mass participation. In more recent times in the UK, and further afield in countries as diverse as Sweden, USA, and Australia, sport development processes and programmes have been identified as a vehicle for delivery of social policy goals such as crime prevention. This is not new. History and analysis of past government policies shows that countries have played in these areas.

This chapter will provide the historical timeline of the sport development field in the United Kingdom from pre-Wolfenden report (1960) through to 2020. Given that most students disengage with the historical context of policy and practice, it will try to use engaging and accessible examples from government, community sport, and national governing bodies (NGBs) in the UK (not just England) to shape the context for the professional field. Other books provide an exhaustive document-by-document historical analysis (see Houlihan and Lindsey, 2013; Houlihan and White, 2002). The England-centric focus of past books on sport development will also be addressed by introducing background information on all four home nations. But, it will try to provide a condensed synthesis of some key dates pertinent to community sport development up until current day. Crucially, the chapter needs to persuade the reader as to the importance of history in understanding the most contemporary of policies and ways of day-to-day working. Table 2.1 and Table 2.2 below provides a timeline for tracking sport development policy and strategy over time between 1960 and 2020.

The role of government

In the UK, it is worth first explaining the machinery of government. For those students new to this subject area in the UK, we did have a democracy built on the united four home nations and a centralised parliament in London represented by an elected government that then controls the State. The State is different to the government. For example, the machinery of the state and nation are the geographical, military, and economic tools, and administrative functions such as the army, NHS, local government, and social services (to name but a few). Every five years (typically) there is an election and from this a political party, or in more recent times (in 2010) a coalition of several parties, effectively controls parliament and decisions, public policy, and strategy. For many in the realm of politics and political analysis, this has focused on economics, health, welfare, and military budgets and strategy. But sport and physical activity, as well as education, and therefore physical education, has an equally valid place at this table. In this book, it will become apparent that whilst you may have interests in sport development practice, coaches, managers, or youth inclusion advisors have very varied and divergent job roles. Many of the budgets and ideological visions for the role of sport change with different governments. Equally, in more recent times there has been, at least on the surface, elements of continuity across huge governmental (between political parties) and even State defining infrastructure change such as devolution in 1998.

So, with a political or societal change comes change in sport development policy and practice. National agencies such as NGBs and charities such as Street Games can see income fall or rise. With this, the community coaches that work in elite sport or grass-roots provision for excluded youth see their financial and human resources shift dramatically. Not all of these changes are within the remit and control of our national government either as we are part of a global economy. The recent Covid-19 pandemic and earlier 2008 financial crash, which arguably led to a ten-year period of austerity in the UK (Widdop et al., 2017), are good examples of where local, regional, and national sport development policy suffer from a complex mix of political ingredients. This section of the book will provide an overview, intended to be brief for students to grasp the headlines, broad timeline of events in the UK sport development evolution, and provide a much-needed simple starting point. It is expressly not intended to be comprehensive, extensive, and exhaustive. Such a task is for a whole volume of another book. Further reading on this matter has also been pointed out based on three additional book chapters listed below. This is an educational tactic. It is meant to avoid the approach of asking a very new student to read a whole book, accessing over 300–600 pages on a topic they have low motivation for. Instead, I ask you to read this chapter as a start, but then focus in on what appeals to you as a learner next. You can also use this as a point of reference for more complex work in levels 5 and 6. It will, in addition, offer an update of what the key policies are from 1998 to 2020 in relation to devolution (when Scotland, Northern Ireland, and Wales got their own Assemblies) and from around 2012–2020 in England to cover the new Sport England and DCMS strategies that several of the core readings do not make reference to in depth.

Table 2.1 shows the key policies, documents, and strategies in England from 1960 to 2020. For the student being introduced to sport development, it is essential to be aware of the historical documents, pathways, and narratives that have shaped current policy and practice. Also, how the paths of policy and realities of daily sport development practice have become interwoven through history between the publication of the Wolfenden Report in 1960 and the latest iterations of each country's approach to elite, community, and social policy ventures through sport is far beyond the scope of this textbook. What is key is that in this section of the book you begin to understand starting points for using other textbooks that have shaped policy understanding from 1960 to, say, 2012 (Collins, 2010; Devine, 2012; Houlihan and Lindsey, 2013) and more recent texts to give sense of what new issues for sport development were emerging from 2012 to 2019 (Brunton and Mackintosh, 2017; Harris and Houlihan, 2016; Mackintosh and Dempsey, 2017; Mackintosh, Griggs and Tate, 2019). Indeed, the principal shifts in the post-London 2012 games era in England have been the publication of the DCMS (2015) Strategy for sport and physical activity in the UK *Sporting Future*. This strategy centred upon the delivery of five core outcomes of sport policy, so where sport development was to argue it had a role, it had to position itself around economic development, individual development, social and community development, physical wellbeing, and mental wellbeing. For the first time ever, it also used a genuinely cross-government approach to developing the strategy with implementation covering departments as diverse as economics and business, local government, education, the environment, and DCMS.

Following the publication of this vision, the sport development agency for England, Sport England, published its own national strategy in 2016, followed by new approaches to coaching and volunteering. This tripartite vision and system for implementing change is the ground under which many NGBs, charities, and local government operators have operated since 2016. A return to emphasising the social outcomes of sport and physical activity is evident. This is not to say that a considerable and sizeable market of sport development professionals and agencies have not been inhabiting this space since New Labour's presence in 1997.

TABLE 2.1 Key policy landmarks in sport development in England, 1960–2020

Title	Organisation	Year
Sport England (2020) Shaping Our Future consultation document	Sport England	2020
Volunteering in an Active Nation	Sport England	2016
Coaching in an Active Nation	Sport England	2016
Towards an Active Nation: 2016–2021	Sport England	2016
Sporting Future	HM Government	2015
Creating a Sporting Habit for Life: A New Youth Sport Strategy	DCMS	2012
Sport England Strategy 2008–2011	Sport England	2008
Shaping Places through Sport	Sport England	2008
2012 Legacy Action Plan, Before, During and After: Making the Most of the London 2012 Games	DCMS	2008
Playing to Win	DCMS	2008
Review of National Sport Effort and Resources	Sport England	2005
The Sport England Delivery System	Sport England	2005
The Framework for Sport in England	Sport England	2004
Game Plan: A Strategy for Delivering Government's Sport and Physical Activity Objectives	Cabinet Office	2002
A Sporting Future for All	DCMS	2000
The Sport England Lottery Fund Strategy 1999–2009	Sport England	1999
England the Sporting Nation	English Sports Council	1997
Sport: Raising the Game	Department of National Heritage	1995
Sport in the Nineties: New Horizons	Sports Council	1993
Sport and Active Recreation	Department of Education and Science	1991
Sport in the Community: Into the 90s A Strategy for Sport 1988–1993	Sports Council	1988
Sport in the Community: The Next Ten Years	Sports Council	1982
Sport For All	Sports Council	1981
Sport and Recreation (White Paper)	Department of the Environment	1975
Sport and the Community: The Report of the Wolfenden Committee on Sport	CCPR	1960

A devolved view of sport development

But, the issues above and the shape of sport development are also important to examine in a country-by-country basis where, for example, post-devolution has seen Wales, Scotland, and Northern Ireland develop their own positions on sport, physical activity, and community-elite sport development dualistic tensions. Table 2.2, for example, shows Scotland, Wales, and Northern Ireland's key sport development related policies embedded within a unique approach to sport development. It should also be noted that earlier historical political period from 1960 saw statements made that the United Kingdom sport development needs highlighted directly equated to those of the individual home nation countries (Jefferys, 2017).

Table 2.2 illustrates the development of Northern Irish, Scottish, and Welsh sport development policy and practice context over time. They have been integrated for a reason. Analysis has shown that their paths as countries stem from their origins closely tied to what the UK, and English Sport Council positions were back in the early 1960s. Furthermore, with devolution in 1998, they occupy a unique position as a sport development policy vehicle that were for their first 20 or so years led very closely by the UK. Even post-devolution, several authors have argued that, with the exception of PE and school sport, most areas of sport development policy remain very closely aligned to the UK government (Bairner, Kelly and Lee, 2017; Houlihan and Lindsey, 2013; Jefferys, 2017). This is not to say that UK-wide policies such as mega-events, global decisions around sport-for-development, or elite sport do not affect sport in Wales, Northern Ireland, and Scotland.

Equally, devolution has allowed Wales and Scotland, in particular, to shape their own future in terms of sport development policy. Houlihan and Lindsey (2013: 80) identify that Sport Scotland expenditure on sport was a 300 per cent increase and 216 per cent increase excluding the 2014 Commonwealth Games. Reid (2009) supported the notion that sport has climbed up the political spectrum of importance. As Table 2.2 shows, Scotland has developed its own policies post-devolution, although in reality they do not vary considerably from that of England and the other home nations (Jefferys, 2017; Houlihan and Lindsey, 2013; Reid, 2009; Reid, 2017). The key exception to this was a move away from sport, towards concerns around physical activity and health. Locating this within a UK-wide policy debate, all three other home nations had this as a pivotal policy concern at around the time of devolution. It was seen by authors such as Houlihan and Lindsey (2013) as following a somewhat parallel track looking towards major events to stimulate sport participation and establishing 245 Active Schools coordinators in Scotland in a uniquely similar vein to School Sport Partnerships in England. There is a useful metaphor by these authors in their rich analysis where they argue that sport policy in Scotland is more of a 'temporary lodger' than 'permanent resident'.

Since the devolution project in Wales, and the publishing of the Wales Act 1998, a further development has been seen in the embedding of the Well-being of Future Generations (Wales) Act 2015 in wider sport policy such as the new

TABLE 2.2 Key policy document in Wales, Northern Ireland, and Scotland, 1960–2020

Title of strategy or policy document	Organisation	Year
Operational Plan Outcomes 2019–2020	Scottish Sport Association	2019
Sport For Life: A Vision for Sport in Scotland	Sport Scotland	2019
The Vision for Sport in Wales	Sport Wales	2019
Facilities for Future Generations: A Blueprint for Sport and Active Recreation in Wales	Sport Wales	2016
Programme for Cohesion, Sharing and Integration Consultation	Northern Ireland Executive	2015
Well-being of Future Generations (Wales) Act 2015	Welsh Assembly	2015
Sporting Future	HM Government	2015
Creating a Sporting Habit for Life: A NEW YOUTH SPORT STRATEGY	DCMS	2012
Sport Matters (2009–2019)	Sport NI	2009
2012 Legacy Action Plan, Before, During and After: Making the Most of the London 2012 Games	DCMS	2008
Playing to Win	DCMS	2008
Reaching Higher: Building on the Success of Sport 21	Scottish Executive	2007
Sport in Our Community	Sport NI	2006
Physical Education and Sports Provision in Primary Schools	Sport Wales	2005
Sport NI Community Sport Impact Review (2005–2008)	Sport NI	2005
Sport 21 2003–2007: The National Strategy for Sport	Sport Scotland	2003
Sport 21 1998–2003	Sport Scotland	1998
Climbing Higher	Welsh Assembly	2003
Devolved Assembly Legislation in Wales, Northern Ireland and Scotland	Devolved Governments	1998
Sport in the Community: Into the 90s a Strategy for Sport 1988–1993	GB Sports Council	1988
Young People and Sport in Wales: Moving On	Sport Council for Wales	1996
Sport Council for Wales (SCW) and Scottish Sports Council Granted Royal Charter	Royal decree	1972
Recommended 100 Grants to GB Sports Council for Welsh Sport Facilities and Development	Sports Council for Wales	1969

Title of strategy or policy document	Organisation	Year
Advisory Sports Council Formed in Wales and Scotland	GB Sports Council	1965
Sport and the Community: The Report of the Wolfenden Committee on Sport	CCPR	1960

Vision for Sport in Wales (Sport Wales, 2019). Prior to 2015, Sport Wales had parallel policies published around its elite sport development processes, pathways, and plans for elite success. But, there is a dominant narrative around education, health, and social policy roles for sport and increasingly physical activity at present. Again, it is worth acknowledging that between 2000 and 2012 the sport budget of the Welsh Assembly increased by 250 per cent (Houlihan and Lindsey, 2013). This is obviously prior to the period of super austerity and London 2012 onwards to 2020. However, it did parallel Scottish increases in expenditure on sport budgets seen over a similar period post-devolution.

Sport and politics in Northern Ireland is invariably bound up with a complex religious, social, and political history dating back centuries. Again, for clarity and detail on the specific cases of this unique country, it is worth reading widely and shaping a discrete understanding of very subtle nuances of this context. This chapter will set the scene for your springboard into understanding of the context of sport development policy and practice. Useful starting points, alongside those listed below include Hassan and Telford (2013) who offer a useful and clear overview of the period from devolution through to 2013. As with other Sports Councils in the UK, Sport Northern Ireland (Sport NI) is the lead agency implementing the work of government. A key feature of the history of the sector in this country, aside from the religious, social, and political dynamic, is that sport development has a fairly compressed operational history. In the 1960–1970s, due to the public disorder and in some cases civil unrest and riots, sport was often used a quasi-tool for 'getting kids off the streets'. It was only in 1996 that Sport NI appointed their first sport development officer with a remit and 'special responsibilities' for community relations (Bairner, 2004). Herein lie the strong roots in the country's sport development work in the sport for development and sport-for-peace sector. With devolution in 1998 came change in many areas; in sport development governance, for example, this can be seen in how Rule 21 was removed from the Gaelic Athletic Association (GAA) constitution. This was essentially a clause forbidding British Security Forces from joining the GAA. No starker reminder of the boundaries and borders in sport participation in Northern Ireland can be offered.

Post devolution and setbacks around the time of devolution saw a number of schemes and policies emerge following on from the GAA style integrative and socially inclusive approach to sport. A roll out in 2000 of the Irish FA (IFA) 'Football for All' saw various projects and initiatives targeting the countries youth. Sport NI publish strategic spending reviews (Sport NI, 2006), investment outlines (Sport NI, 2006), and, most recently, an ambitious ten-year vision for elite, community, and sport for development (Sport NI, 2009). Whilst these policy documents show us expenditure in focused projects at key points in time of around £4m across 34 projects (Sport NI, 2006), they fail to show the subtle emergence of a real expertise in sport-for-peace.

It is apparent that across numerous sports, multiple previous, and, in part, still divided communities, sport can, and does, play a role in developing individuals, communities, and families. Those sport development staff stemming back to the first officially appointed officer by Sport NI in 1996 perhaps do not reflect the long-standing contested history and religious context of such work in youth and community settings. Again, deeper analysis of this is beyond the scope of this chapter. Local context is important, and this is an important theme we will return to in the book. Many of the ideas and concepts for programmes in Northern Ireland are perhaps not new. Projects that have attracted attention include: *Midnight Soccer, Belfast Urban Sports*, and *Bridging Urban Skate Park*. Origins of such schemes exist globally; ownership of the ideas are globalised features of sport development now. What is unique to Belfast and other communities of Northern Ireland are the ever changing and richly complex historical landscape that underpin sport development provision, policy, and goals. Commenting six years after devolution and the Good Friday Agreement, (Bairner, 2004: 283) argued

> one peculiar and no doubt unintended consequence of the peace process would appear to be the creation of a society in which politicians are actively encouraged to demarcate their ideological distinctiveness while in civil society, arguably and most noticeably in the world of sport, citizens are being asked to set aside cultural difference in the interests of social inclusion and cross community integration.

Unlike any other context perhaps of the other three home nations, authors are exploring how sport can play a role in community integration (Hassan and Telford, 2013). But the critical point above that seems to still resonate is wheather the public sport development past religious, cultural, and community dividing points approaches can operate through past. Design of projects and delivery of initiatives is part of this complexity, but even elite sport development, choice of cultural sports to be involved in (GAA, boxing, football, and so on), together with who you will 'represent' as 'your team' remains highly political.

What role for history in understanding today's landscape?

This chapter has offered a springboard as opposed to a tablet of stone with all the answers. History and policy background are large subjects for any student setting out on a journey of learning at university. As already stated, this chapter gives a balanced starting point for all student starting to examining the background to sport development. But, there is no single history. Instead, you should focus on the idea that there are multiple contested histories. How one academic or one practitioner 'presents' you history is likely to conflict with others. Your view and interpretation of a document will vary based on perhaps when you read it (levels 4, 5, and 6) and how you read it (theoretical lens, philosophical, or political standpoint). What are the important documents around a policy theme might be the ones that government produce, but, what if not one of the 151,000 voluntary sports clubs read it all? In these cases, perhaps we need a new way of looking at public policy and how we consider history. For other authors, local context and local history offer real insights as they are what individuals and communities draw upon for their interpretation of policy (Bevir and Rhodes, 2016; Wagenaar, 2011). The local sports club historical policies on male and female membership, coaching and governing the club will inevitably shape actor experiences and journeys in sport development. Or, how sport development officers in a NGB interpret policy change becomes less about the national policy document and more about lived experience (Thompson, Bloyce, and Mackintosh, 2020). Consider your own experience of national policy in recent times. How much of this is even present in your understanding of, say, coaching and community sport development? But, if probed, the new coaching plan from Sport England has clearly moved to a more recreational and active lifestyle coaching definition. From here, providers, coaching companies, and those earning money through delivery of government targets will, with time, maybe change. Will a level 2 badge become more or less relevant? How does this affect NGBs, clubs, and other providers? Might this offer unintended consequences? To conclude, this is a learning and teaching space that you should want to engage with. It offers the context for all you will do in the sector, whether managing, coaching, developing, or working with volunteers. Without the historical policy context, it is unlikely we learn the lessons of the past or see potential from the past for tackling the sport development needs of the present.

▰▰▰▰▰▰ CASE STUDY 2.1 ▰▰▰▰▰▰

The historical evolution of a policy field

The Wolfenden Report produced in 1960 marked a landmark position in UK sport policy, and that of the home nations. On its sixtieth-year anniversary, certain themes have, to a point, been addressed. Others policy agendas remain fresh and fully in need of being addressed today in 2020 as much as they did 60 years earlier. This case study, however, is about identifying a policy agenda and trying to map its presence through key historical documents and academic texts that discuss and analyse the sport development theme, and come to a point where you can, as a level 4 student, provide an overview. This is not about being a historian. This is not, at this stage of your academic career, about being an expert on hundreds of articles, their ideas, and the standpoints of the different authors. This is, perhaps, something you will progress to at level 6, and certainly if you study postgraduate analysis and evaluation of sport development.

Three obvious policy agendas in sport development to look for are:

- Elite sport development pathways and talent identification;
- Community sport development 'for sport's sake';
- Sport for development.

In this task, identify one of these agendas. First, be clear what this means, in terms of policy definition (see Houlihan, 2015; Wilson and Platts, 2018). Be aware that no single definition will be present, but starting to conceptualise what you are looking at is key, in those first few analytical steps that move beyond description. Second, identify a home nation country; this could be where you live, study or a country you'd like to explore because you don't know so much. Use Tables 2.1 and 2.2 above as a starting point to explore the key themes and the additional sources listed below to get other academics views on the original landmark policies. The first step to undertake is then to produce a timeline of the key sport development policies, strategies, and documents. Your second task is to write a short 200-word commentary around this timeline, about your chosen agenda.

The key here is to understand that you might need to refer to main strategies that provide national context, but it is in the specific detail on a specific topic that you can identify the aspects that matter. Ultimately, this is a writing task that is meant to see how you use this book alongside two to three other books, e-books and journals. The best way of learning is to do, reflect, and discuss in class. The skills in this activity will come in useful as a practitioner when you are asked to review policy and strategy documents in sport development. They will also develop your academic skills in research, critical reading, critical description, analysis and writing concisely.

Supporting academic sources (annotated list)

Collins, M. (2010) The development of sports development, in Collins, M. (ed.) *Examining Sports Development*, London: Routledge, 14–32.

Concise review of sport development policy of early Sports Council and later focus on English sport development policy. Analysis and outline of many policy documents and their impacts. A great starting point for reading, note-taking, and seeing where 1960–1998 non-devolved policy came from.

Houlihan, B. and Lindsey, I. (2013) *Sport Policy in Britain*, London: Routledge.

Highly comprehensive overview of sport development policies in all home nations. Specific chapter dedicated to devolution and impact on sport development in Wales and Scotland post-1998. This should be a more in-depth point of reference for those interested in knowing more about the three strands of policy identified above.

Houlihan, B. and White, A. (2002) *Sport Politics and Development*, London: Routledge

For a long time, this was the only text leading the historical policy analysis of sport development in the UK. It remains a seminal (or 'classic') of the field and shows a rigorous and thorough chronological path from origins of a field to a point in 2001–2002 mid-New Labour government. Specific insights around 'original' infrastructure, project types and the movement and values of a profession can provide a critical cross-sectional point of reference for contemporary times.

Jefferys, K. (2017) Sport and politics in Great Britain, in Bairner, A., Kelly, J and Lee, J. W. (eds) *Routledge Handbook of Sport and Politics*, London: Routledge, 259–271.

Provides a rich account of the post-devolution case of sport development context in Scotland and Wales. The account in this book that focuses on Northern Ireland focuses on NGB and complex government infrastructure around the Good Friday agreement. There is minimal reference to the role of, or indeed presence, of government sport departments, strategies, or Sport Northern Ireland.

Bloyce, D. and Smith, A. (2010) The emergence and development of sport policy, in Bloyce, D. and Smith A. *Sport Policy and Development: An Introduction*, London: Routledge, 29–55.

A historically rich and succinct account of UK sport policy between 1960 and 2010. Limited reference to devolution due to the timing of publishing, but relevant historical strands around the themes set in this task. If interested in extension learning, Chapters 3 to 6 provide narrow further secondary research into policy on topics of school sport and PE, community sport development and elite talent development.

Guided seminar reading questions

1. How has a historical reading of sport development helped your understanding?
2. Do you see any emerging trends within the chosen policy agenda you wanted to look at?
3. What do you notice about the time line for sport development policy?

References

Bairner, A. (2004) Sport Policy in Northern Ireland, *Sociology of Sport Journal*, 3:1, 270–286.

Bairner, A., Kelly, J. and Lee, J. S. (2017) *Routledge Handbook of Sport Politics*, London: Routledge.

Brunton, J. and Mackintosh, C. (2017) Interpreting university sport policy in England: Seeking a purpose in turbulent times?, *International Journal of Sport Policy and Politics*, 9:3, 377–395.

Bevir, M and Rhodes, R. (2016) *Interpretive Policy Analysis*, London: Routledge.

Collins, M. (2010) *Examining Sports Development*, London: Routledge.

Department of Culture, Media and Sport (DCMS) (2015) *Sporting Future*, London: DCMS.

Devine, C. (2012) London 2012 Olympic legacy: A big sporting society? *International Journal of Sport Policy and Politics*, 5:2, 257–279.

Harris, S. and Houlihan, B. (2016) Implementing the community sport legacy: The limits of partnerships, contracts and performance management, *European Sports Management Quarterly*, 16:4, 433–458.

Hassan, D. and Telford, R. (2013) Sport and community integration in Northern Ireland, *Sport in Society*, 17:1, 89–101.

Houlihan, B. (2015) *The Government and the Politics of Sport*, London: Routledge.

Houlihan, B. and Lindsey, I. (2013) *Sport Policy in Britain*, London: Routledge.

Houlihan, B. and White, A. (2002) *The Politics of Sports Development*, London: Routledge.

Jefferys, K. (2017) Sport and politics in Great Britain, in Bairner, A. Kelly, J., and Lee, J. S. (eds) *Routledge Handbook of Sport and Politics*, London: Routledge, 259–271.

Mackintosh, C. and Dempsey, C. (2017) The Muslim male youth sport participation puzzle: An examination of the role of identity, religion and ethnicity in determining involvement in sport, *Journal of Youth Studies*, 20:8, 974–996.

Mackintosh, C., Griggs, G. and Tate, R. (2019) Understanding the growth in outdoor recreation participation: An opportunity for sport development in the United Kingdom, *Managing Sport and Leisure: An International journal*, 23:4, 315–335.

Reid, G. (2009) Delivering sustainable practice? A case study of the Scottish Active Schools programme, *Sport, Education and Society*, 14:3, 353–370.

Reid, G. (2017) A fairy tale narrative for community sport? Exploring the politics of sport social enterprise, *International Journal of Sport Policy and Politics*, 9:4, 597–611.

Sport NI (Sport Northern Ireland). (2005) *Sport NI Community Sport Impact Review (2005–2008)*, Belfast: Sport NI.

Sport NI. (2006) *Sport in Our Community*, Belfast: Sport NI.

Sport NI. (2009) *Sport Matters (2009–2019)*, Belfast: Sport NI.

Sport Wales. (2019) *A Vision for Sport in Wales*, Cardiff: Sport Wales.

Thompson, A., Bloyce, D. and Mackintosh, C. (2020) 'It is always going to change' – managing top-down policy changes by sport development officers working in national governing bodies of sport in England, *Managing Sport and Leisure: An International Journal*, iFirst 1–20.

Wagenaar, H. (2011) *Meaning in Action: Interpretation and dialogue in policy analysis*, London: Routledge.

Widdop, P., King, N, Parnell, D., Cutts, D. and Millward, P. (2017) Austerity, policy and sport participation in England, *International Journal of Sport Policy and Politics*, 10:1, 7–24.

Wilson, R. and Platts, C. (2018) *Managing and Developing Community Sport*, London: Routledge.

CHAPTER 3

Locating and defining sport development in a global context

It is important to acknowledge how sport development is located within the global landscape of community sport policy, provision, and practice (Green, 2005; Sherry, Schulenkorf, and Phillips, 2017). It will also pick up on the introduced theme of Brexit/EU issues and how this relates to the context of the UK in areas such as immigration, social integration, and sport, and illustrate the political nature of sport. The second half of the chapter will introduce UK Sport as an agency and some of the wider sport development agencies of relevance and discuss how sport development moves into sport-for-peace, for/in-development. Again, other books cover this well (see Sherry, Schulenkorf, and Phillips, 2017), but it is important even at level 4 to set national/regional and local sport in a global curriculum. Increasingly, this is a theme that many more HEIs are asking staff and their students to consider. Globalisation whilst a wide-ranging, extensive, and complex issue, must be embedded within the text. Globalisation is a potential complex and multifaceted term but we need an academic starting point for our understanding. Thus, Jarvie (2003: 93) defines it as "the process by which interaction between humans, and the effect of that interaction, occurs across global distances with increasing regularity, intensity and speed". He goes on to state that, in agreement with Maguire (1999; Maguire et al., 2002), the processes themselves are not new. In this sense, we can begin to consider how aspects of sport development provision need to be located in this space. Global competition is a good starting point, such as the Olympics and mega-events in single sport disciplines. However, it is also part of a growing discourse and set of ideas that, for example we assume they can deliver a participation legacy in and across national boundaries.

Media is also a second area of increasing significance of student of sport development, where we can connect with, share ideas, and build virtual communities at a very fast pace. This is all tracked through an ever-expanding diverse and powerful range of platforms such as Instagram, Twitter, and Facebook. For example, refugee communities in Britain can build an online presence in Glasgow that supports not only the development of their sporting heritage (in Britain) but also their identities, culture, and the principle vehicle for this could be Facebook and online tools. In this sense, sport development has already changed. Professionals of the future need to keep up to date with their own communities and learn from them. Globalisation is a powerful force and has already changed a profession beyond where it was when it emerged post-Wolfenden report in 1960 and even as recently as Game Plan (DCMS, 2002).

This chapter provides a point of reference for UK sport development students in one easy location. It will be pitched at those that have no prior knowledge of sport development beyond the UK. The chapter will end with a return to how and why this matters to those studying and training to work in sport development. For many students, sport development has historically been taught as a subject or degree that is UK focused and defined by the geographical parameters of the overarching policies or strategy of UK government of the time. However, it is important to acknowledge the increasingly globalised world that we now operate in. Even with the briefest time spent on a search engine or exploring social media, we can find agencies, organisations, and individuals working in the professional domain of sport development. What then becomes of interest to those studying in the UK are the similarities and differences between provision in different countries. There is no simple explanatory tool for why countries undertake activities in the way they do, but it is a clear that there are significant factors that shape what we might call their 'sport development systems'. This said, even assuming there is one 'system' within a country is an oversimplification of what will usually be fractured and dynamic ways of community and elite sport operating alongside each other.

If we consider our definitions of sport development across different countries, this often shows how certain domains of activity work better conceptually in some countries. Factors including, but not limited to history, culture, traditions, political orientation, and ideology are powerful forces that can determine this 'fit'. In some ways, the best way of exploring such systems is to do so yourself as a student and seek academic papers, government strategy documents, and secondary information on other countries. In this information era we are well placed to source such information. However, it is necessary to understand other sport development systems from their perspective. This is particularly relevant where global comparisons start to be made between what we call the Global North and Global South. Previously, these would have been termed developed and 'developing' with the sense of economic aid and humanitarian requirements needed. Indeed, the language, expectations, even local delivery of sport development here, will often be vastly different. For you as a future practitioner in these areas, there are considerable gaps in our understanding of how to work across these nuanced and very different boundaries. This book does have a UK focus but it is critical to acknowledge the complex difference within the UK, and beyond our borders.

So, understanding sport development in a global setting and globalised context is useful for a number of reasons. First, all students and staff co-produce knowledge in the learning they are engaged within and around their degree that is now located globally. We frequently ask, or should do, students to be able to research other countries, incidents and policy factors, and case studies from abroad. Second, it is important as students that we are global citizens, looking far beyond our narrow regional hub of our local authority we study in. Finally, the globalisation processes (Jarvie, 2003; Maguire et al., 2002) that are so incredibly powerful are deeply embedded within all we do in sport development. I will now consider each of these in more detail.

A global community of sport development students

Sport development does have a range of broad definitions, and indeed its interpretation from England to Scotland is different. If we then extrapolate this out from the UK to the EU and its member states, we see vastly divergent constructs of the domain. Much of the definitional and conceptual variation comes from the ideology of country and the associated government and state regime present. For example, in Scandinavia there is a strong association between 'active recreation', encouraging mass participation for its own sake, and prioritising this as part of the engine of government sport policy. Equally, such work is not directly labelled 'sport development' policy, although voluntary clubs, schools, and a variety of other agencies in community provision would be implicated in a similar way to the UK. Thus, whilst these variations exist and are very real for policy and practice, it is the meanings, values, and beliefs around such practices that come to distinguish across national boundaries. So far, these examples are all in what can be termed the 'Global North'. It is fundamental to also recognise that sport development also exists and, indeed, thrives in the 'Global South' and very different global contexts set in deep contrast to the polarised world of developed countries with their income, infrastructure, and long-established history and policy backgrounds in sport development.

It is equally important to not look at such settings and practices in binary, divergent ways. There is an easy trap to fall into to assume that what happens in 'The North' or 'West' (themselves complex terms to be aware of) leads what should happen in 'The South'. Indeed, an African community, city, township, or suburb is as different as any is across the UK might be. Likewise, the approaches, models, theories, and ideas we use to work in such settings must vary. Languages are different; culture will be similar in parts but also distinct and have multiple challenges. The staff that work in other countries may all be volunteers; paid staff may be a thing of the imagination yet to be experienced. Notions of a 'sport development' model and profession or pathways in development structures or even national governing bodies may not exist. We therefore must not make assumptions. Understanding the culture of a region, national setting, and the multiple layers of meaning that come to be the context of the sport development practices is fundamental.

Acknowledging this in your practice as a sport development officer in the UK is also important for the work you engage with day to day here. If you are on placement and are asked to engage with a group of refugees from a war-torn country such as Syria, positioning yourself and your potential project participants needs a different 'global outlook'. Compassion, care, political awareness, and an ability to empathise with human rights now locate sport development in a very new nexus. Likewise, as sport development in the UK is increasingly being asked to work in policy fields such as mental health, social development, and youth engagement (DCMS, 2015; Sport England 2016, 2020), students need to be aware of global policy in such areas. It is now well established that the World Health Organisation (WHO) acknowledges mental health problems as one of the world's major diseases affecting our global population (WHO, 2013). Students, by studying sport development in a university anywhere in the world, are indirectly buying into a global community of practitioners, researchers, and body of learning, and teaching knowledge that is being shared across national and regional boundaries. Good practice in the UK is shared as quickly as a downloaded report in Australia. Likewise a placement year in an Australian national governing body or university sport department allows students to return to their course and replicate ideas and policy learning.

A global reach of sport development research enquiry

At the heart of all degrees sits academically robust research in sport development. Whether we are undertaking a placement project, a final-year thesis or dissertation, or opting into master's level or PhD research in sport development, it is a growing area of practice. In part, such skills are about the response of higher education institutions (HEIs) to 'what works' and evidence-based-practice narratives (Cairney, 2016; Nutley, Walter, and Davies, 2007). Such evidence and need to research and evaluate sport development projects are unquestionably important in a modern professional setting. The quality of evidence in areas of the UK sport development system has been questioned (Ives, 2014; Smith and Leech, 2010). As a level 4 student, you are entering a field that has never been so data driven, evaluation-heavy, and reliant upon research to shape policy. When engaging with any topic of enquiry, as I have explored elsewhere, there is a fairly standardised research process that is increasingly stated (Bryman, 2004). But in our assessment of researching sport and physical activity in different and 'Othered' populations, as is increasingly common in sport development policy, we identified a new set of factors to consider (Medcalf and Mackintosh, 2019). In this revisiting of the generic research process we more centrally located a 'globalised lens' in design and implementing research. For example, if being asked to recruit and retain BAME sport participants in a rugby club, we may wish to undertake baseline research. It is critical to have a global outlook on this and not simply employ a standard set of thinking to a highly contested set of cultural labels, identities, and sporting behaviours. Or, as a swimming NGB, we need to look at working with non-participants in a community that we may need to understand through research how religious and faith factors shape engagement with pools and swimming lessons and this may also be layered with gender, too. For further exploration of this see Chapters 1, 2, and 13 of Medcalf and Mackintosh (2019).

Finally, the research activities of students should no longer be limited to the UK and the city you study in. Staff and students should be endeavouring to explore global policy and practice in sport development. Indeed, there has been a recent sizeable expansion in core texts and reading in this area (Henry and Ko, 2014; Houlihan and Green 2013; Bergsgard et al., 2007). These texts provide useful overviews of the key readings and information on the 'systems' you may wish to explore. Some are also country specific such as Australia (Sotiriadou, Shilbury, and Quick, 2008), Canada (Sam, 2011), and New Zealand (Piggin, Jackson, and Lewis, 2009). Other global sport development research studies have been cross-comparative in their nature (Bergsgard et al., 2007; Green and Collins, 2008). It is likely that at level 4 people will ask 'what is sport development?', 'what is the sport development process?', and similar broad questions. It can be useful to explore these questions outside the UK. If we are truly global citizens, engaged in global lessons around humanitarian decisions that underpin national football, rugby, and daily sporting issues, then this is critical.

Alongside core texts that provide part of your diet, the shrinking size of the global development distances between country-specific systems means we can learn, engage with, and research policy and practice elsewhere. The processes thorough which we do this are different to only a few years ago. We can now set up minute-by-minute direct message queries and exchange of research and policy on sport development through Twitter. Conversations and friendships can be built through live streaming, FaceTime, Zoom meetings, and Skype. As software changes and improves, so our abilities and skills as sport development professionals must also alter. Likewise, it can also mean that the 'flows' and information points can affect us in yet to be understood ways. Will we as sport development staff of the future be recruited by the Norwegian government (global workforce) to work on a sport-based project in a former war zone (global issue) around a WHO and *Medicines Sans Frontiers* (global health agencies)?

Globalisation impacts on sport development policy and practices

A large part of this book covers the agencies and organisations within the UK that specifically drive sport development policy and practice. This section of the chapter explains how these organisations connect to far wider global organisational issues and decisions. For a specific organisation that you will study (NGB, local authority, national agency), often an issue might be considered and in unpicking why things are how they are we start and stop at the local or regional level with perhaps a measure of national context thrown in. In reality, there is always a global position, context, and set of forces at play that underpin the sport development processes, impact and delivery. A good example is the recent decline in sport development provision at local government level (Mackintosh, 2012; Mackintosh and Liddle, 2015; Widdop et al., 2017). At first glance, this may be due to the political decisions of the transition between the New Labour government (1997–2010) into Coalition (Lib-Conservative) in 2010 and then movement into a full Conservative government from 2015 onwards. However, this has been suggested as being more closely underpinned by a range of conflicting a contested global 'driving forces' such as the 2007–2008 banking crisis, interwoven with period of austerity and other fluctuating earlier factors that led to global instability, which stem from overstimulation of financial markets in the USA that then unravelled across the globe. How a small district council loses a SDO or a NGB receives less money and can't employ a regional development officer in a minority sport is linked to such financial global crises is at first two totally separate issues. But, by locating our understanding from day one in a more global lens, we can start to consider things critically as global students.

Other examples relate to the staging of major sport events and how such decisions are taken in closed board rooms often years and years ahead of the 'main event'. Unquestionably, global decisions, global scale and global impacts have fundamental influence on local and regional sport development policies and practices. For example, a national decision by a global body such as FIFA on mixed gender participation would significantly shift sport development practices in all local football participation. Global world championships in, say, gymnastics can heavily shape local club participation, membership recruitment and inculcate local latent demand in activities. But many of these programmes have sport development participation programmes inherently linked to them (Mackintosh and Liddle, 2015; Weed et al., 2015). They rely on the principle of 'trickle down' (Misener et al., 2015) and assumptions of legacy in local community but how this actually plays out at London 2012, Rio 2016, or Tokyo 2021 will vary considerably. Global events implemented in regional/local settings rarely consider such local cultural drivers as a facet of their potential success. Likewise, the global event is also driven by private sponsors supporting such schemes (or not), a multitude of highly political global organisations and their individual committees, leaders, and biases. Finally, as a student in sport development of the event, context, or process, it is becoming increasingly crucial that you understand and can navigate this global context. Some view this as a level 6 issue to be explored. Given the ubiquitous, wide-ranging and fast-paced nature of the presence of globalisation within sport development, I consider it something to introduce at level 4. It will inevitably be a theme to return to in more detail as you progress through levels 5 and 6.

▉▉▉▉▉▉▉▉▉▉▉▉▉▉▉▉▉ **CASE STUDY 3.1** ▉▉▉▉▉▉▉▉▉▉▉▉▉▉▉

Leveraging community sport participation from global events – Rugby League World Cup 2021

Mega-events are a global phenomenon by their definition and conceptualisation (Frawley, 2016). However, how they are utilised more locally often has strong undertones of community sport development principles and processes. It is, however, heavily contested as to whether such events actually deliver 'legacy' (Weed et al., 2015). By legacy, we mean an enduring and sustained impact beyond the lifespan of the event itself. Mega-events can be positioned as a good example for us as sport development students exploring the themes presented in this chapter. Are they events that can capture 'wellbeing', a sense of pride, a desire to volunteer, change behaviour, bring inactive populations to existing sports clubs, or give a 'shock' to a system where a specific sport has lacked engagement? The Olympics is the most commonly cited example of a mega-event in sport, probably alongside the Rugby World Cup, FIFA World Cup, Cricket World Cup and majors in golf and tennis. However, not all such events have a sport development programme that aims to harness the so-called 'power' through specific community and individual mechanisms. Indeed, a number of longstanding pieces of academic research have suggested that events as diverse as Sydney 2000 and London 2012 (Mackintosh and Liddle, 2015; Misener et al., 2015; Weed et al., 2015) had limited impacts on coach recruitment, volunteering, and participation beyond an initial positive rise. Indeed, the processes around these are somewhat misunderstood and remain complex and nuanced at best, at worst, significantly misunderstood and built into mythical narratives and rhetoric of government sport development policy.

If we take the case of the Rugby League World Cup 2021 (RLWC2021) in England, this is an event that aims to have a positive social impact on communities, individuals, volunteering, sport clubs, and a whole host of other wider government targeted policy outcomes such as individual development, economic development, and community development (DCMS, 2015; Sport England 2016; Sport England 2020). Rugby League is not a top five 'big player' NGB, it is very regional in bias towards specific areas of the north of England. Thus, to develop the sport and sport engagement is different. It is a sport that is not ubiquitous across the globe like others such as football and Rugby Union. Viewing figures and globalisation processes attached to, and interlinked with, the sport are different (TV rights, sponsorship packages, player wages, income in the game, and number of development officer staff). The event does have men's, women's, and wheelchair Rugby League tournaments being run in parallel. This in itself is a change and contrast to many other sporting mega-events where such events are not equal, but separate and distinct in identity, timing, and delivery. In 2020, the RLWC2021 development team were engaging in activities in Warrington, a very localised, passionate Rugby League community, to generate further interest in the sport and its clubs. Specifically, they were using materials that "includes a 6-week lesson plans, fixtures templates, certificates and video messages from RLWC2021 ambassadors to help inspire pupils" (RLWC, 2020; Online).

This began in 2019, two years before the delivery of the major event. Tracy Power, Legacy Director for RLWC2021, said:

> Our education programme plays a key role in inspiring the next generation of Rugby League players and fans. We are delighted to be reinvesting money back into local communities rather than into external providers and it's great to see four Warrington-based schools working together to create the next phase of our education resources.

(RLWC2021; 2020; Online)

As a potential development officer working alongside this programme in Warrington across primary and secondary schools on behalf of the 'legacy department' of RLWC2021, this task is for you to consider how sport development is becoming increasingly globalised in its position.

Seminar questions

1. As a student in sport development, how does studying a global event and associated sport development issues, themes, and ideas affect you and your understanding of the area?
2. What are the global influences on the RLWC2021 that could impact on the community sport development programme?
3. Taking the case of a complex issue like Brexit or austerity how might this shape involvement in the mega-event, legacy programmes, and 'assumed' simplistic results of the tournament like social impact, sport participation increases and volunteering?

Reflective task

Take time to consider the challenges of engaging with a group of primary school-aged refugee children from diverse countries in the RLWC2021 who have only been in the UK for one month. How might you as a professional SDO working in the RLWC2021 offices have to consider your *positionality* (Mackintosh and Medcalf, 2019) when researching and planning a series of legacy sessions at a local level in Warrington? By positionality, we refer to who you are, in relation to aspects of your social identity (gender, sex, sexuality, background in sport, social class, and so on). Second, how might this shape your practice and outlook in sport development?

Further reading

Mackintosh, C. and Liddle, J. (2015) Emerging school sport development policy, practice and governance in England: Big Society, autonomy and decentralisation, *Education 3-13: International Journal of Primary, Elementary and Early Years*, 43(6), 603–620.

Mackintosh, C. and Medcalf, R. (2019) Researching difference and otherness: next steps and challenges in sport and physical activity, In R. Medcalf and C. Mackintosh (eds) *Researching Difference in Sport and Physical Activity*, London: Routledge, 148–154.

Sherry, E., Schulenkorf, N., and Phillips, P. (2017) What is sport development? In Sherry, E. Schulenkorf, N., and Phillips, P. (eds.) *Managing Sport Development: An International Approach,* Routledge, London, 3–11.

References

Bergsgard, N., Houlihan, B., Mangset, P., Nodland, S.I. and Rommetvet, H. (2007) *Sport Policy: A Comparative Analysis of Stability and Change,* Oxford: Butterworth-Heinnemann.

Bryman, A. (2004) *Social Research Methods (2nd edition),* Oxford: Oxford University Press.

Cairney, P. (2016) *The Politics of Evidence-Based Policy Making,* London: Palgrave MacMillan.

DCMS. (2002) *Game Plan,* London: Cabinet Office/DCMS.

DCMS. (2015) *Sporting Nation,* London: DCMS.

Frawley, S. (2016) *Managing Sport Mega Events,* London: Routledge.

Green, C. (2005) Building Sport Programs to Optimize Athlete Recruitment, Retention, and Transition: Toward a Normative Theory of Sport Development, *Journal of Sport Management,* 19:19, 233–253.

Green, M. and Collins, S. (2008) Policy, politics and path dependency: Sport development in Australia and Finland, *Sport Management Review,* 11, 225–251.

Henry, I. and Ko, L.-M. (eds.) (2014) *Routledge Handbook of Sport Policy,* London: Routledge.

Houlihan, B. and Green, M. (eds.) (2013) *Routledge Handbook of Sports Development,* London: Routledge.

Ives, H.M. (2014) The social construction of physical education and school sport: Transmission, transformation and realization. PhD thesis, University of Bedfordshire.

Jarvie, G. (2003) Internationalism and sport in the making of nations, *Identities: Studies in Global Culture and Power,* 10:4, 537–551.

Maguire, J. (1999) *Global Sport: Identities, Societies, Civilizations,* Cambridge: Polity Press.

Maguire, J., Jarvie, G., Mansfield, L. and Bradley, J. (2002) *Sport Worlds: A Sociological Perspective,* Illinois: Human Kinetics.

Mackintosh, C. (2012) The shifting dynamics of local government sports development officer practice in England: New identities and hazy professional boundaries, in Harris, S., Bell, B., Adams, A. and Mackintosh C. (eds) *Sport for Sport? Theoretical and Practical Insights into Sports Development,* Brighton: Leisure Studies Association, 113–130.

Mackintosh, C. and Liddle, J. (2015) Emerging school sport development policy, practice and governance in England: Big Society, autonomy and decentralisation, *Education 3–13,* 43:6, 603–620.

Mackintosh, C. and Medcalf, R. (2019) Researching difference and otherness: next steps and challenges in sport and physical activity, in Medcalf, R. and Mackintosh, C. (eds) *Researching Difference in Sport and Physical Activity,* London: Routledge, 148–154.

Medcalf, R. and Mackintosh, C. (2019) *Researching Difference in Sport and Physical Activity,* London: Routledge.

Misener, L., Taks, M., Chalip, L. and Green, C.B. (2015) The elusive 'trickle-down effect' of sport events: Assumptions and missed opportunities, *Managing Sport and Leisure: An International Journal*, 20:2, 135–156.

Nutley, S.M., Walter, S., and Davies, H.T.O. (2007) *Using Evidence: How Research Can Inform Public Services*, Bristol: Policy Press.

Piggin, J., Jackson, S.J., and Lewis, M. (2009) Knowledge, power and politics: Contesting 'evidence-based' national sport policy, *International Review for the Sociology of Sport*, 44:1, 87–101.

Sam, M. (2011) Building legitimacy at Sport Canada: Pitfall of public value, *International Review of Administrative Sciences*, 77:4, 757–778.

Sherry, E. Schulenkorf, N., and Phillips, P. (2017) What is sport development? In Sherry, E., Schulenkorf, N., and Phillips, P. (eds) *Managing Sport Development: An International Approach*, London: Routledge, 3–11.

Smith, A. and Leech, R. (2010) 'Evidence. What evidence?': Evidence-based policy making and school sport partnerships in North West England, *International Journal of Sport Policy and Politics*, 2:3, 327–345.

Sotiriadou, K., Shilbury, D., and Quick, S. (2008) The attraction, retention/transition, and nurturing process of sport development: Some Australian evidence, *Journal of Sport Management*, 22, 247–272.

Sport England. (2016) *Towards an Active Nation*, London: Sport England.

Sport England. (2020) *Shaping Our Future*, London: Sport England.

Weed, M., Coren, E., Fiore, J., Wellard, I., Chatziefstathiou, D. Mansfield, L. and Dowse, S. (2015) The Olympic Games and raising sport participation: A systematic review of evidence and an interrogation of policy for a demonstration effect, *European Sports Management Quarterly*, 15:2, 195–226.

Widdop, P., King, N., Parnell, D., Cutts, D. and Millward, P. (2017) Austerity, policy and sport participation in England, *International Journal of Sport Policy and Politics*, 10:1, 7–24.

World Health Organisation (WHO). (2013) *Mental Health Action Plan 2013–2020*, Geneva: WHO.

CHAPTER 4

Exploring organisations, policy, and practice

This chapter will provide the theoretical context for exploring sport development as a subject and offer some of the existing paradigms through which the subject has been examined. Principally, sociological, political, geographical, and management are the dominant theoretical domains used to explore the subject area. This chapter will use an introductory language to bridge new students to this area. For example, it is often assumed that we know what theory, concepts, typologies, tautologies, and frameworks are without explaining them. We will come to explain what these terms mean themselves later. You can refer back to the book when reading other texts that make reference to such 'technical' academic language. This chapter will use existing theories to illustrate the inter-disciplinary and wide-ranging nature of the subject and how advancement in the subject is changing what theories we draw upon and why. Second, the chapter will show how each of the dominant subject areas considers organisations, policy, and practice. What is needed for students at level 4 is not a complex often-cited highly academic theoretical discussion about 'what is policy?'. Instead, the chapter will provide some introductory ideas that bridge learning that will be developed through the book's later chapters. Finally, the chapter will end with a return to what this means for studying sport development as a student. I believe that this is what staff and students will find most useful as a discussion point in class, and the student audience will engage with as opposed to extensive text defining policy, practice, and organisations. For most students, this will be a complex new set of terms and the chapter must play a pivotal role in engaging learners, not putting them off a subject.

What is the need for this bridging chapter?

Ultimately, this is about supporting learning, engaging with what students in sport development, coaching, and management need. It is well established that sport development is a complex and emerging profession (Mackintosh, 2018), if a distinct profession at all (Hylton and Hartley, 2012). Collins suggested an estimated 5000 individuals were at the time of his analysis ten years ago working in sport development (Collins, 2010), although the realities of this 'definition', its scope, and the process behind it are questionable. In any matter, the estimate is now out of date by two UK government strategies for sport and nearly 20 years of professional practice.

More recently, Sport England (2014) have identified in their research and strategy on the workforce in an Active Nation for England that 400,000 people are actively employed in the sport and physical activity sector. This encompasses coaches, the private sector, and the public sector, and doesn't discriminate and delineate for a sub-group in 'sport development'. In addition to the paid staff comes a sizeable sector of sport-specific volunteers, the majority of which work in sport development. The student market shows that around 27,000 students study a sport-related qualification at school or further education (FE); from this research in 2014, 72,000 students are studying sport and physical activity related qualifications (Sport England 2014). Herein lies a key workforce challenge for today's sport development students, which is that this is a busy and growing market.

Theory is more and more relevant to the profession as there are calls for evidence-based practice (Sport England, 2014; Sport England, 2019; Sport Wales, 2019). What we mean by people using theory can be reduced in its simplest form to having an abstract idea that is a conceptual thread of a set of ideas to breakdown a process, set of relationships, or aspect of practice or management. For sport development, as it moves into its new era, this has to be closely focused on theory from other areas than it has previously been embedded in. For example, physical activity and health and the benefits of an active lifestyle are a well-worn track. In contrast, mental health and community and individual wellbeing and development move the professional towards new areas of academic theory. Indeed criminology (Meeks, 2018), youth justice and engagement (Mackintosh and Dempsey, 2017; Morgan and Batlle, 2019), and evidence-led evaluation (Davies, Nutley, and Smith, 2007) move the profession into exciting but new domains. Likewise, implementing projects and developing funding regimes in these domains of professional practice have implications for what managing sport development looks like and, again, the theory and concepts that it draws upon. As students of sport development, theory allow us to understand, explain, and interpret activities. You can move beyond common sense and into a more critical graduate level understanding of your subject. One thing is for sure, sport development and the theory it needs to support the work it may touch on and the graduates that emerge alongside the profession it was, say, ten years ago is now a very different space. There is not sufficient room in this book to embed all this new theoretical and conceptual work in the future professional workforce. But, as a bold goal it is hoped that future endeavours can start to really shape a dialogue between student–higher education (HE) and researcher–practice–policymaker. Only in this way can we then embrace the demands of industry and also let the advances in thinking in HE sport look beyond the status quo. If we ask hard questions, such as why has sport remained so white, so male, so heterosexual, can we begin to unpick where new theories may come from and how other disciplines may help us to challenge orthodoxy in our studies as students so when we enter the workplace we are well placed to challenge the status quo and orthodoxy, and offer genuine insights and innovations. Indeed, many of the current fresh approaches to sport development have been born firmly outside of the sport sector.

Organisations, policy, and practice – the what, who and where of sport development

For most students that study sport development, a good starting point is to orientate yourself with complex web that is this area (Hylton and Hartley, 2012; Mackintosh, 2012; Wilson and Platts, 2017). By this, I mean to map out who is doing what, when and how across the sector. Indeed, it is the purpose of this book to help do this. Sport development organisations and individuals have changed their role in the field of management practice in the last 20 years. Alternatively, in what Bloyce et al. (2008) refer to as a movement from 'tracksuits to suits' sport development has seen a shift to a more managerial and office-led role for an industry that previous was delivery and project led. The implication of this seminal study in 2008 was that many sport development professionals have experienced a move away from 'doing' and delivery towards a new phase of managing, implementing evaluation of projects, and an associated shift in identity. This is a good example of how a study examined organisations, people, and the ways they work with and through their social identities. In parallel, a fundamental shift is the previously mentioned need to evidence, use theory, and evaluate rigorously in sport development. In a study of SDOs in 12 local authorities in two counties in the East Midlands (Mackintosh, 2012), it was established that for many, like the study by Bloyce et al. (2008), policy by government at national level had very critical implications on the most local or 'micro' experiences of this by SDOs. People who were interviewed expressed the challenges of not having the skills to deliver the policy requirements in practice.

Whilst the above studies offer insights into what would now be referred to as the paid sport development workforce, the very term 'workforce' in 2008 and 2012 was not yet coined. This emerged from government rhetoric and policy over the coming years (DCMS, 2015; Sport England 2016; Sport England 2017). As mentioned previously, the Sport England (2014) *Working in an Active Nation: The Professional Workforce Strategy for England* offered a specific vision for closer working links with CIMSPA and the state of England. At this point it is also worth acknowledging that this position is different in each of the four home nations. How they have approached, for example, the UK Coaching Certificate (UKCC) is a good indication of increasingly divergent and devolved policy approaches to core sport development issues and processes (Mackintosh and Carter, 2018). Likewise, how a national Sports Council responds subtly and differently to issues such as equality (Sport Scotland, 2015) will filter down to NGBs, schools, and organisations in general. Likewise, Wales and Northern Ireland opted out of the UKCC national review and, set alongside their strategies for sport development and coaching, it remains to be seen what coaching infrastructure emerges (Sport NI, 2009; Sport Wales, 2019). Furthermore, others may resist 'upwards' and perhaps not 'buy-in', and this could be volunteers, sports clubs, and individual coaches.

It is easy to say sport development is contested, complex, and nuanced because it is. But, as a new student to the subject, learners need some distinctions around their learning in the subject. It is sometimes not helpful to draw clear delineation between paid and unpaid work in sport development. The lines can very easily blur between the two, and relationships often cut across several organisations. For example, coaches can be paid but also volunteers; volunteers can also act as paid staff in other club roles. The voluntary sector is a sector that will be examined in more detail later. But, for now, it is a very useful context to examine the identities and organisational management of sport development. Voluntary sector clubs may have a member of staff that is paid (golf club secretary or pro), has some paid role (coach), or full voluntary formal roles (committee members/Directors) and then ad hoc volunteers that are 'episodic' (gardening, catering, and so on).

Whilst these are not seen by some as part of the contemporary modern landscape of sport development practice, the club and development of the clubs should be seen as core to the design, implementation, and evaluation of sport development initiatives. Nichols et al. (2019) in examining the voluntary sector talks of the collectivist motivations of those involved. Likewise, Cuskelly, Hoye, and Auld (2006) delineate between 'core' volunteers (chair, secretary, treasurer, and so on) and peripheral volunteers, or, helpers and informal episodic support for the club. For professionals from NGBs, Active Partnerships and governments in Wales, Scotland, England, and Northern Ireland, it is essential to understand this portfolio of organisations, motivations, and physical sporting settings. More of this sector will be considered later in the book.

Organisations and agencies in practice

Sport development has become one of the most diverse sectors in the last ten years in relation to the type and form of organisations that work through and with community and elite sport. This can be seen in the opening up of the sector through the DCMS (2015) strategy and respective countries' approaches in the home nations to delivery of their national strategies. Organisations are in one part brand (Sport England), one part legal status and entity (English Sport Council), and then, furthermore, a set of social meanings and cultural perceptions people have about them. So, for example, a sporting government quango may differ hugely from country to country based on perception, individual bias, policy role and perhaps levels of satisfaction with what they do. As researchers and future practitioners, it is critical that we understand this.

Equally, any of the many NGBs in the UK can differ considerably in terms of their organisational status with the clubs they support (Thompson, Bloyce, and Mackintosh, 2020). Swim England, Badminton England or Scottish Rugby Union are by definition a product of whether clubs and individuals buy in (literally) to their vision. How effectively they work in this sector is a complex mixture of unique patterns of behaviour in clubs, coaching session in a range of facilities and their own NGB (Collins, 2010). This will differ again from British Cycling, Archery GB, and small sports such as British Orienteering. Culture is critical to each of these examples. As a working sport development officer 'in the field' you will also find that a region may have a particularly good or bad reputation due to the last person that did your job. This makes the picture of what we mean by a neatly formed and discrete 'organisation' ever more subtly nuanced. The nuances of organisation in sport development cut across varied sectors that can include charities, voluntary sport clubs, local government, central government, leisure trusts, and NGBs. There is no definitive list. Furthermore, an increasing number of projects are delivered as a product of partnership working so the single organisation model blurs further again (Mackintosh, 2011; Baker, El Ansari, and Crone, 2016).

New organisations to the field are perhaps the greatest challenge as we don't have the 'organisational memory' (Jennex and Olfman, 2003) and tacit knowledge to draw upon. Tacit knowledge is often used in professions such as health around doctors and nurses. They behave instinctively and 'just do'. Footballers perhaps have a tacit understanding of a game, this is where they just act and think after all many processes are intuitive. In the case of organisational working in sport development, if we are working with prisons or young offender institutions to use football as a tool in crime prevention/youth rehabilitation, many sport organisations perhaps have just never done this (Erhart and Martin-Ros, 2016). This also has implications for the graduate going into a new job, specifically the form and processes of research and evaluation the sport development graduate will undertake in their role. New ways of working are needed. Other examples might be predominantly white NGBs working with faith centres that encompass different traditions to their own organisational 'norms'. Finally, for the sport development officer, where you work may be very different. Historically, it would have been highly likely 15 years ago you'd have been in an NGB or a local authority. Now the work of sport development may encompass working at Mind (the mental health charity), a National Trust centre using running as an activity for young mums and dads, or a professional sport organisation delivering faith-based interventions addressing crime and inclusion outcomes. This has also had implications for the working life and career pathway of a sport development officer. This is something we will consider in the concluding sections of the book.

Policy

Students start off with a clear idea of what policy is. It is a thing, a document, a set of pages, a core pamphlet, a webpage-based vision for a sport, or a PDF or Word document that can be downloaded. This is the first myth we need to dispel. From the perspective of this book, policy is made, constructed, and reconstructed in a cycle that essentially leads to it representing a set of meanings, attitudes, and beliefs (Bevir and Rhodes, 2016; Wagennar, 2011). For example, PE policy around sport development in England (e.g. the PE school premium) is a product not just of the national policy document on this. How teachers interpret and use such understanding (or do not) is critical. Likewise, a fundamental part of this policy sub-area in sport development is how private coaching companies and their owners and coaches rebuild and reinterpret the 'policy'. So, for example, seeing considerable numbers of private coaches delivering questionable standards of quality 'PE' as opposed to children's sport camp coaching is a complex interaction between many factors (Griggs, 2010; Griggs, 2012; Griggs, 2018). We will not be delving too deeply into the world of sport policy in this text. It is an introductory textbook for this very reason. But we are setting the scene for you to return to this introductory insight when you do look at policy elsewhere in your studies.

It is also worth noting that from the perspective of other academics, researchers, practitioners and local communities what we mean by sport development policy is philosophically potentially very different. Predominantly, this falls into two positions for you as a level 4 student to understand. First, there are positivists that view policy as a fairly fixed, measurable entity. The national curriculum for PE is the document and its impact on sport development and staff might be measured through a survey. The third category are seen as critical realists (Bhaskar, 1979) who see policy as part of an iceberg metaphor where what you 'see' and experience in terms of policy is the 'tip', and below the surface are a number of complex nuanced structural factors. Ultimately, wider discussion around sport policy can be embedded in even more narrow philosophical stances. But, for a student it is necessary that they understand at level 4 that academic work is written from a philosophical or academic position. Public sport policy is still a new subfield with the journal *International Journal of Sport Policy and Politics* (IJSPP) only being founded in 2009 and articles and books calling for further study beginning to emerge through the work of a small cluster of key academic authors (Bloyce and Smith, 2010; King, 2009; Houlihan, 1994; Houlihan, 2005; Houlihan and Lindsey, 2013)

Practice

When Hylton and Hartley (2012) talked of an emerging profession eight years ago, many questioned this insight and perspective. But, the reality of this is that unlike nursing, teaching, policing, and other domains of the public services, sport development and sport and recreation services seem to still lack the framework for being considered a clear profession. Indeed, the CIMSPA (2020) professional body for sport outline a framework, but the level of membership buy-in is still low in a field where thousands of individuals work in practice. The fact that we do not know the number of coaches, volunteers, and development officer staff across different sports is still an indicator of the further progress that is needed. Indeed, Pitchford and Collins (2010) argued ten years earlier that the likely scope for a distinct professional field in this area was a point of concern.

Practice is seen as the area of policy implementation, sport development delivery, and day-to-day 'work' of an SDO. As stated above, not only do we not know numbers working in this domain, but, also, research into this area is limited. There have been recent studies of modernisation of football develop-ment in England (Lusted and O'Gorman, 2010; O'Gorman et al., 2018), organ-isational change in national governing bodies of sport (Thompson, Bloyce and Mackintosh, 2020), professional practice of SDOs in East Midlands of England (Mackintosh, 2012), and changes in working realities of the SDO (Bloyce et al., 2008). This is in contrast to the parallel field of sport development policy anal-ysed from a political science perspective (Houlihan, 2005; Harris and Houlihan, 2016), which has seen considerable attention in the last 15 years. Perhaps an exception to some of this bias is in the sport-for-development research land-scape where numerous studies have attempted to look more closely at delivery, practice, and implementation (Sherry, Schulenkorf, and Phillips, 2016). These much wider debates are also beyond the scope of the book.

For me practice, is about the core aspects of what it means to be a deliverer. What practice means itself is a different debate in two different NGBs for example. But, this avoidance of a starting point is not helpful to a level 4 stu-dent. So, where to start? Here, the key is to acknowledge how the *policy* and *organisation* context is critical to what practice is being drawn upon. Sport development *practice* can be defined as the range of roles, functions, responsi-bilities, and activities that a SDO is employed to deliver. In considering this broad definition we can also consider values that represent an SDO:

1. SDOs should keep to the fore the rights, needs and overall benefits of sport and physical activity and the importance of promoting and main-taining the highest standards of provision and professionalism in sport development;
2. SDOs must respect all people equally without discriminating on the grounds of age, gender, race, ethnicity, religion, civil status, family status, sexual orientation, disability (physical, mental, or intellectual), or mem-bership of the Traveller community;
3. Core to SDO practice is a relationship between the SDO and the commu-nity or individual they work which is based on open communication, trust, kindness, understanding, and compassion. This could be elite or community sport participants or neighbourhoods they are working with;
4. Being an SDO is facilitated through an understanding of the social, emo-tional, cultural, spiritual, psychological, and physical experiences of indi-viduals, and is based upon the best available research and experiential evidence.

These are just a potential way of starting to understand and conceptualise your professional practice. Other factors to consider include how your back-ground (social and sporting), practice setting, and local and national policies and evidence may affect and influence your competence and training. Wales differs to England for many reasons. The socio-political and historical context of Northern Ireland is a highly unique for sport development practice. Scotland has a strong emerging new political identity and recent evidence has seen it forging ahead with increased expenditure on sport development

(Houlihan and Lindsey, 2013). As sport development moves increasingly towards more complex settings such as mental health (depression, anxiety, and so on), prison and young offender facilities, and 'complex' outreach programmes with challenging adults and young people, this will shape our very understanding of sport development practice.

CASE STUDY 4.1

The role and function of the sport development officer in practice

If we briefly return to sport development practice being defined as the range of roles, functions, responsibilities, and activities that a SDO is employed to deliver. Consider the case of one *organisation* in the *policy* context of sport development in and around Sport Wales. In this task what you now need to do is unpick the work that is sport development in a Welsh context. At this stage list each of the five aspects of the definition for one chosen organisation. Be prepared to evidence this from their policy documents, strategy, and website-based information.

- Roles
- Functions
- Responsibilities
- Activities
- Other research.

Seminar questions

1. Upon completing this activity, consider where possible how the nature of the organisation has affected and shaped, e.g. is it public, private, voluntary? What motivation does this drive?

2. As peers share your findings across organisations and consider how, whilst there is a national policy set by Sport Wales and linked work with DCMS (2015) you may have found different interpretations?

Further reading

Hylton, K. and Hartley, H (2012) Sport development: A profession in waiting?' in Harris, S., Bell, B., Adams, A., and Mackintosh, C. (eds) *Sport for Sport: Practical and Theoretical Insights into Sports Development*, Brighton: LSA.

References

Baker, C., El Ansari, W. and Crone, D. (2016) Partnership working in sport and physical activity promotion: An assessment of processes and outcomes in community sports networks, *Public Policy and Administration*, 32:2, 87–109.

Bevir, M. and Rhodes, R. (2016) *Routledge Handbook of Interpretive Political Science*, London: Routledge.

Bhaskar, R. (1979) *The Possibility of Naturalism*, London: Routledge.

Bloyce, D. and Smith, A. (2010) *Sport Policy and Development*, London: Routledge.

Bloyce, D., Smith, A. Mead, R. and Morris, J. (2008) 'Playing the game (plan)': A figurational analysis of organisational change in sports development in England, *European Sports Management Quarterly*, 8, 359–378.

Collins, M. (ed.) (2010) *Examining Sports Development*, London: Routledge.

Chartered Institute for the Management of Sport and Physical Activity (CIMSPA). (2020) *Occupations, job roles and specialism*. Available at: www.cimspa.co.uk/standards-home/occupations-job-roles-and-specialisms [accessed on 22/04/20].

Cuskelly, G., Hoye, R. and Auld, C. (2006) *Working with Volunteers in Sport: Theory and Practice*, London: Routledge.

Davies, H.T.O., Nutley, S., and Smith, P.C. (2007) *What Works? Evidence-based Policy and Practice in Public Services*, Bristol: Policy Press.

DCMS (2015) *Sporting Nation*, London: DCMS.

Erhart, N. and Martin-Ros, C. (2016) Knowledge management systems in sports: The role of organisational structure, tacit and explicit knowledge, *Journal of Information & Knowledge Management*, 15:2, 1–21.

Griggs, G. (2010) For sale – primary physical education. £20 per hour or nearest offer, *Education 3–13*, 38:1, 39–46.

Griggs, G. (2012) Standing on the touchline of chaos. Explaining the development of sports coaching in primary schools with the aid of complexity theory, *Education 3–13*, 40:3, 259–269.

Griggs, G. (2018) Investigating provision and impact of the primary Physical Education and Sport Premium: a West Midlands case study, *Education 3–13*, 46:5, 517–524.

Harris, S. and Houlihan, B. (2016) Implementing the community sport legacy: The limits of partnerships, contracts and performance management, *European Sports Management Quarterly*, 16:4, 433–458.

Houlihan, B. (1994) *Sport, Policy and Politics: A Comparative Analysis*, London: Routledge.

Houlihan, B. (2005) Public sector sport policy: Developing a framework for analysis, *International Review For the Sociology of Sport*, 40:2, 163–185.

Houlihan, B. and Lindsey, I. (2013) *Sport Policy in Britain*, London: Routledge.

Hylton, K. and Hartley, H (2012) Sport development: A profession in waiting? in Harris, S., Bell, B., Adams, A. and Mackintosh, C. (eds) *Sport for Sport: Practical and Theoretical Insights into Sports Development*, Brighton: LSA, 4–22.

Jennex, M. E. and Olfman, L. (2003) Organizational memory, in Holsapple, C. W. (ed.) *Handbook on Knowledge Management*, Berlin: Springer, 207–234.

King, N. (2009) *Sport Policy and Governance*, Oxford: Butterworth-Heinemann.

Lusted, J. and O'Gorman, J. (2010) The impact of New Labour's modernisation agenda on the English grass-roots football workforce, *Managing Leisure*, 15:1, 140–154.

Mackintosh, C. (2011) An analysis of county sports partnerships in England: The fragility, challenges and complexity of partnership working in sports development, *International Journal of Sport Policy*, 3:1, 45–64.

Mackintosh, C. (2012) The shifting dynamics of local government sports development officer practice in England: New identities and hazy professional boundaries, in Harris, S., Bell, B., Adams, A., and Mackintosh C. (eds) *Sport for Sport? Theoretical and Practical Insights into Sports Development*, Brighton: Leisure Studies Association, 113–130.

Mackintosh, C. (2018) UKSDN conference: Challenging the Status Quo, *Sport Management Magazine*, 3, 72–74.

Mackintosh, C. and Dempsey, C. (2017) The British Asian Muslim male sport participation puzzle: An exploration of implications for sport development policy and practice, *Journal of Youth Studies*, 20:8, 974–996.

Mackintosh, C. and Carter, J. (2018) *The Review of the United Kingdom Coaching Certificate (UKCC): A Shock to the Coaching System?*, Manchester: Manchester Metropolitan University.

Meeks, R. (2018) *A Sporting Chance: An Independent Review of Sport in Youth and Adult Prisons*, London: Ministry of Justice.

Morgan, H. and Batlle, C. I. (2019) 'It's borderline hypocrisy': Recruitment practices in youth sport-based interventions, *Journal of Sport for Development*, 7:13, 1–14.

Nichols, G., Hogg, E., Knight, C. and Storr, R. (2019) Selling volunteering or developing volunteers? Approaches to promoting sports volunteering, *Voluntary Sector Review*, 1–16.

O'Gorman, J., Fitzpatrick, D., Sibley, J., Hindmarsh, M., Saskova, Z. and Parnell, D. (2018) Contemporary issues in the management of grassroots football, in Chadwick, S., Parnell, D., Widdop, P. and Anagnostopoulos, C. (eds) *Routledge Handbook of Football Business and Management*, London: Routledge, 56–70.

Pitchford, A. and Collins, M. (2010) Sports development as a job, career and training, in Collins, M. (ed.) *Examining Sport Development*, London: Routledge, 259–288.

Sherry, E., Schulenkorf, N., and Phillips, P. (2016) *Managing Sport Development*, London: Routledge.

Sport England. (2014) *Working in an Active Nation: The Professional Workforce Strategy for England*, London: Sport England.

Sport England. (2016) *Towards an Active Nation*, London: Sport England.

Sport England. (2017) *Review of the Evidence of the Outcomes of Sport and Physical Activity: A Rapid Review*, London: Sport England.

Sport Northern Ireland (Sport NI) (2009) *The Northern Ireland Strategy for Sport and Physical Recreation, 2009 to 2019*, Belfast: Sport NI.

Sport Scotland. (2015) *Sport For Life: A Vision for Sport in Scotland*, Glasgow: Sport Scotland.

Sport Wales. (2019) *The Vision for Sport*, Cardiff, Wales.

Thompson, A., Bloyce, D. and Mackintosh, C. (2020) 'It is always going to change' – managing top-down policy changes by sport development officers working in national governing bodies of sport in England, *Managing Sport and Leisure: An International Journal*, iFirst, 1–20.

Wagennar, H. (2011) *Meaning in Action*, London: Routledge.

Wilson, R. and Platts, C. (eds.) (2017) *Managing and Developing Community Sport*, London: Routledge.

CHAPTER 5

Starting to understand, research, and read about sport development

Following on from the introductory chapter on paradigms of study, this chapter will explore the key ways sport development has been studied to date in the UK. It will act as a review of those authors that have studied the subject to date and offer different critical 'schools of thought' in the UK. By positioning these different ways of thinking academically about the field, students can begin to position themselves and navigate better the degree they are attending. Very few journal articles, and certainly no textbooks to date, have attempted to develop such a mapping exercise of the who's who of theorists in sport development. Most default to an overview of the Eady's (1993) pyramid of sport model and others related to the continuum (see Hylton, 2013). Theory has moved on considerably, and in multiple fields, in very different applications. This will provide a base from which students can systematically explore key authors, areas of study, approaches, and frameworks for theoretical analysis. Again, it will return to the 'why does this matter to a practitioner?' question to maintain engagement for the student audience. In essence, different schools of thought mean different worldviews, philosophy, and approaches to how we 'do', understand, and design sport development programmes. This will challenge the new student using applied examples to explore what is a complex area.

Starting to read, understand, and research sport development at university is about opening our minds to examining aspects of what we think we 'know' and begin questioning and looking at organisations, policy, and management of sport and physical activity more critically. Houlihan and Green (2013) argue that there are three broad areas of sport development in elite, community, and 'sport for social good'. However, we can see that there are no clear boundaries between these three areas; indeed, elite feeds community sport, and vice versa. Likewise, what is meant by sport development delivering social good has a multitude of complex, overlapping different meanings and ideas to different elements of the sport development policy and practice community. For this reason, it is perhaps most crucial that it is this layered, multi-faceted, and complex set of meanings around sport development that should be held most firm when we begin to explore professional management practice more deeply.

Sociology

The study of people, places, cultures and associated behaviours, norms, and attitudes is embraced by undertaking a theoretical sociological approach to sport development. This in recent years has been a particularly popular theoretical area of growth for the discipline (Bloyce et al., 2008; Malcolm, 2011; Bloyce and Smith, 2010). In itself, it does encompass a diverse and eclectic range of theories that can be used by students and practitioners to help examine and understand different aspects of society that sport development projects may focus on. For example, gender and equality has consistently been a forerunner to the 'modern' equity landscape of sport development in the UK. Underpinning studies that examine women and girls experiences, attitudes, and beliefs around sport are feminist theories and approaches. This is a particularly key area as it encompasses a major driver of much policy (DCMS, 2015; Sport Wales, 2019; Sport Scotland, 2019, Sport Northern Ireland, 2009) such as the gender imbalance in participation, visibility and operational management representativeness in sport development, and projects that specifically target females for various social policy goals (prisons, ageing, drug misuse, and so on). Typically, such theoretical work that you as a student will engage with will need you to start to engage with concepts such as patriarchy (male domination within and through society). Such sociological conceptual constructs allow us to explore the structures in sport development landscapes to empower society but particularly allow women to address the imbalances present. Even within a sociological feminist critical theorist position there will be divergences in how it can be used, and the type of concepts best used to explore sport.

Other sociological theoretical approaches include the seminal text underpinned by figurational sociology by Bloyce and Smith (2010). This analysis of social, historical, and political aspects of sport development evolution in the UK is specifically focused on the work of Norbert Elias and the exploration of sporting communities, structures, and organisations through the conceptual tool of figurations. There is not space here to give the whole book justice, but it is a rare example of a whole analysis underpinned by one theoretical standpoint. Many other studies in sport development are more likely to be a project level assessment that draws on a theory.

Much of the work in sport development relates directly to the landscape of volunteering, which some might argue has its own field of sociological or social theory (Harris, Nichols, and Taylor, 2017; Nichols, 2010). For others, it 'sits' in more of the domain of volunteer management and volunteer organisation (Cuskelly, Hoye, and Auld, 2006). The two are distinct; the sociological aspects locate the study and understanding in building knowledge of sport volunteers around why they volunteer, their position in society, and possible inequalities in who volunteers and why. Levels of volunteers also vary by gender and sport (Mackintosh and Mills, 2018) as well as 'race and ethnicity' (Hylton, 2015; Fletcher et al., 2014).

There is also a strong tradition of sport development academic theorists using social theory to explore issues of 'race' and ethnicity. Hylton (2015) himself, one of very few black academic professors, uses critical race theory (CRT) to examine sport systems, coaching, and patterns and norms in behaviour. This work is used to challenge the status quo in lower levels of representation in sport management position in NGBs, wider government, and society generally. Others have also looked in detail at specific sports such as cricket to unpick the subtle factors at play in why people do and don't participate (Fletcher et al., 2014). Such research is clearly critical as the theory and ideas emerging from it helps inform NGBs directly as to how they can improve professional practice and policy design.

Disability is a further area of sociological analysis and theorisation that sport development is entwined with as there has been a consistent level of inaction and engagement with addressing inequalities in this area (Fitzgerald, 2005; Fitzgerald, 2012; Ives et al., 2020). Theory in this area prioritises and amplifies the 'voices' of disabled participants, volunteers, coaches, and managers. It may also use the approach of considering the study from an *ableism* perspective and use the term (dis)ability (Ives et al., 2020). By doing so, researchers and students can challenge historic norms that participants or coaches cannot do activities or tasks. Instead, it offers the opportunity to show how social theory can be transformative and build new 'ways of seeing' (Berger and Luckmann, 1976). This link with sport development should not be underestimated for you as a student. We can too often forget that our own background is able-bodied, white, male, middle class. The latest government challenge to industry is to address this status quo (DCMS, 2015).

In considering gender, as we did earlier as an area of sport development practice, and how it overlaps with sociological theory, we did not consider the terms gender, sex, sexuality, and how for many students they are often used interchangeably. Gender is defined as a the socially constructed 'category' that has associated characteristics that come with history, culture, and societal layers of construction. Typically, we might hear sport professionals use words such as feminine or masculine. Why does this matter? Well, when it comes to traditional social categories we also have male and female. This 'fits' very neatly into what we might term binary social categories (Mackintosh and Dempsey, 2017). But as we now exist in an era of equity and equality, we must consider sport development within the context of the Lesbian, Gay, Bisexual, Transgender + (LGBT+) community (Robertson et al., 2019; Spaaij et al., 2018). This is a field that will be discussed further in the book, but at this stage it is worth being aware that its own area of specific theory has emerged named Queer Theory, which has been looked at to help explore oppression, resistance, and understanding of LGBTQ+ participation in sport (Johnson and Kivel, 2006). Other studies have looked at possibilities around exclusively gay men's rugby provision to consider the sport development potential of such approaches using other sociological theoretical lenses (Price and Parker, 2003).

Likewise, other authors (Long, Fletcher, and Watson, 2017; Medcalf and Mackintosh, 2019) have embraced intersectionality as a useful theoretical frame. This allows more complex nuanced social identities to be examined and the implications for this in sport development explored. At a local level this might be how an emerging transgender school athlete competes at regional level or how religion interacts and flows into and between sexuality, 'race', and gender for sport projects being planned in a deprived community.

Political theory

For some students, just the words political theory may switch them off from study. However, politics and policy around sport development is inherently interwoven with the landscape of sport. Look, for example, at devolution in the UK and how despite there being a DCMS strategy for sport and physical activity in the UK, each of the four home nation governments and their respective Sports Councils can now shape their own path, priorities, and ideology. Local sports clubs will be affected by changes in government at election time where changes can support them (e.g. tax relief) or hinder them (removal of support for PE, after-school sport or additional sport coaching). Broad ideological stance, meaning the underlying big ideas and philosophy of a government, will change with prime minister in the UK, but also how they wish to use sport as a vehicle for political gain or societal benefits.

But, in recent years, there has been an expansion of interest in politics of sport development (Grix, 2010; Harris and Houlihan, 2014; Houlihan, 1994; Houlihan and Green, 2013; Houlihan and White, 2002; Mackintosh, 2011; Mackintosh and Liddle, 2015; Philpotts, Quarmby, and Grix, 2011; Widdop et al., 2017). Sport development has a long history politically from its arguable origins in the Wolfenden Report (1960). It has a number of key political theorists that have tried to examine some of the main political motivations of government and government agencies in the central tasks of the sport development dual goals of winning more medals, and engaging the general population to get them playing sport more often. Theory in this paradigm differs from sociological approaches, but there are overlaps. A useful starting point is to identify Houlihan's (1994) text exploring the subject area across multiple countries. Between this text and others by Houlihan and Lindsey (2013) and King (2009), we see the emerging foundations for students to explore sport development using political ideas and concepts, although it remains a new substantive ('subject') area.

A useful starting point is to consider the 'unit of study'. For many, this has been the state (geographical jurisdiction), or government (political party, or parties) – these are 'macro' level issues to explore. We might here also explore national agencies such as Sport England and UK Sport (Houlihan and Green, 2009), although in this case a Foucauldian sociological theory was used as it involved how people (individuals) were exploring and using power and processes linked to modernisation. By this we mean they have used the ideas, concepts, and tools of analysis of Michel Foucault to explore specifically the work of government in sport policy and development. Others have also examined the politics of policy and why polices have or have not been enacted such as the removal of School Sport Partnerships (SSPs) by the then education minister (Mackintosh, 2014). Furthermore, there are certain 'meso level' (subregional) levels of government that have attracted political analysis such as local government (King, 2009; Mackintosh, 2012; Parnell, Spracklen, and Millward, 2017), sustainability in sport development delivery partnerships (Lindsey, 2008) and County Sport Partnerships (Baker, El Ansari, and Crone, 2016; Mackintosh; 2011).

Politics does not just occur at the macro and meso level. For many students when they first start to work, study, volunteer, or access internships it would be at the micro level where politics is experienced and understood. Examples of this in sport development are less well developed as theoretical approaches tend to focus on understanding policy, institutional power, and associated practices (Collins, 2014; Lindsey, 2009; Mackintosh, Darko, and May-Wilkins, 2016; Mackintosh and Dempsey, 2017). If politics seems a distant and hard to acknowledge phenomenon and system for many students, this localised impact can be helpful starting point. When we have a mega-sporting event with associated sport development programme, can we start to unpick the politics in this equation?

Business management theories

The work and associated emerging profession of sport development is increasingly overlapping with not just policy and development but also business management. In recent years, the UK has seen a growth in the language of what might be termed managerialism around the delivery of community, elite, and sport-for-development. In particular, this is significant to students if we look at the origins and core of what sport development was founded upon, and rooted in. Philosophically, there are obvious tensions here. For example, business often uses a language that differs considerably from many of the voluntary sector clubs that are the people, communities, and individuals that 'do policy' for government in partnership with various agencies. Theories of business management consider products, consumers, profit, loss, and markets for goods and services. Sport at an elite professional level in many quarters has moved into this domain (Waddington, Scott, and Malcolm, 2017). But, how this translates onto community sport, delivery of volunteer clubs run by what we term collectivist ideals, and shared social capital, bonds, and ideals is much more complex. Indeed, for some academics the movement to consider management as an appropriate lens to view sport development is a further neo-liberal step towards the commodification of sport and physical activity. If SDOs need to work with local communities, theories to support this working are varied and depend on the setting. If, as students of sport development, we are to study community sport settings and the delivery of social goals, we will draw upon theory and concepts that work well and offer further insight for us. Initial attempts to do this in the sphere of community sport coaching have proved fruitful in offering useful insights around the neo-liberal agendas impact on coaching in the community (Gale and Ives, 2019; Ives et al., 2019). Much remains in terms of exploring the scale and impact of professional modernisation in community sport development across the UK.

Marketing is a good area of a body of literature and theoretical work that sport development students can draw upon. In particular, it is important to understand how organisations in the field (NGBs, Active Partnerships, Sports Councils, charities, and so on) are trying to communicate, 'sell', and advertise their sport development programmes. Increasingly, across all four home nation areas what were projects are often now termed 'products'. A government may have a campaign, such as This Girl Can in England, that targets specific segments and hopes to address policy objectives through a social marketing lens-led approach. However, it is worth acknowledging that such a sport development programme of activity may be analysed by students sociologically, psychologically, politically, and through management and marketing theoretical lenses. This is a good point to introduce the idea of the participant, coach, and volunteer as customer, which for organisations like Sport England have become a mainstay of their organisational marketing narrative (Sport England, 2016; Sport England 2017). Herein lie some subtle differences across political boundaries in Wales, Scotland, and Northern Ireland. For example, it seems that both Scotland and Wales still endeavour to undertake more 'traditional' sport development with an increased focus on sport for sports sake. Degrees to which marketing ideas are employed across countries vary. Sport England has, for example, been using 'segmentation' from marketing to 'target' users and those with individual needs and motivations in sport for several years.

Organisational theory is less frequently taught in mainstream sport development early phases of your undergraduate degree. But, it essentially looks at elements such as organisational behaviour and culture. It can cross into organisational psychology whether this would be within the settings of sport development 'work' or activity, or how employees feel, are engaged by their work, and levels of satisfaction. Most recently, the clearest areas of policy overlap here are in the wellbeing in the workplace strategies of major employers through the deployment of sport, physical activity, and health as tools in both meeting government targets and addressing mental and physical wellbeing policy visions (DCMS, 2015). Organisational culture studies and theory associated with it can offer synergies with sociological theory mentioned earlier. Diverse studies have been undertaken examining elements of the UK sport development system like sport volunteer culture (Nichols, 2010), elite football academy culture around player welfare (Platts, 2014), and organisational partnership working in sport (Baker, El Ansari, and Crone, 2016; Houlihan and Lindsey, 2013; Mackintosh, 2010).

Many local authorities, NGBs, and other sport and physical activity agencies have strategies in place. Such strategies establish their three- to five-year vision alongside producing annual reports and plans that link into the day-to-day delivery and implementation of projects, programmes, and events. From the area of business management theory, this is an area that does sit comfortably with the study of sport development as examples of strategy and vision documents are extensive in the field. Theories of strategic management in this area are well developed and usually a matter of academic study at level 6. For an example of a useful entry text to sport strategic management that crosses over neatly with sport development, see Robson, Simpson, and Tucker (2013). What is worth acknowledging here is that, like other conceptual approaches to studying aspects of sport development phenomenon, there is a spectrum of different standpoints, models, and associated concepts that can be used. None are wrong or right; understanding theory and reading background literature on what the main concepts a theoretical framework uses is a good start. For students possibly new to theory, this is difficult. As peers who all may find this area difficult, it is about engaging with discussions in class, readings, and starting to explore your subject. It may be that certain areas 'appeal' – your world view, view of what makes sense in reality, and the best way to research topics will most likely be new questions for you.

CASE STUDY 5.1

Theory – thinking about sport development, the case of sporting after-school clubs

In this chapter we have considered sociological, political, and management theory as the three main areas of theory you will use and study whilst on your degree. Each degree is slightly different; there is no single disciplinary set of core texts. This is because sport development is often described as inter-disciplinary. By nature, it is defined as a subject at university that cuts across boundaries and uses theory where it needs it to help explain complex ideas and unpick understanding of a question or topic better. In this case study, we will look at the example of after-school sport in England, at first sight, a non-political, straightforward, and pleasant area of professional practice. We will then compare it to that in Scotland. What you need to do in this case study is consider how might (very broadly) each of the three different theoretical approaches be used to explore examining understanding after-school sport development processes and practice in England and Scotland.

- Sociology;
- Political theory;
- Management theory.

Sport development policy is different in England and Scotland in this area. In Scotland they use an approach called Active Schools and have themes that you can explore and examine in detail. In England it is principally based on the Primary PE and School Premium (PPESP) (at primary school) and at secondary school it is left up to individual schools to determine their approach. Much has been written on the PPESP (DfE, 2015, 2018; Griggs, 2012, 2016, 2018) and how it has been shaped politically, it has also got key management 'features' and the sociological impact is starting to be mapped out – on schools, teachers, children, and wider sport communities. In trying to first understand the two areas of policy, shape your understanding by reading the following two documents from 2019 and 2015 to look at how the two countries are now in different place with sport development provision in these areas.

1. Department for Education (2018) *Primary PE and School Premium Survey 2019*, London: DfE.

available at: https://assets.publishing.service.gov.uk/government/uploads/system/uploads/attachment_data/file/816676/Primary_PE_and_Sport_Premium_Survey_research_report.pdf

2. Sport Scotland/ODS (2015) *Active Schools Evaluation*, Scotland: ODS. available at https://sportscotland.org.uk/media/1739/active-schools-evaluation-report-final.pdf (last accessed 12/4/20).

As above, try and think about how theory, the theoretical approach, and the types of concepts you'd be using might allow you to explore the issues and different approaches. At this stage, do not worry about the specifics of a single theory, or a set of related concepts, for example feminist sociological theory, stakeholder theories, or institutionalist political theory. All this comes much later in your university time. For now, it is trying to find a starting point for theory, an anchor for new understanding. If you were a coach you would not ask new participants in a skill acquisition task to go straight into advanced motor skills or technical ability challenges/drills. For now, all you are being asked to think about in this task is to consider in three broad areas how theoretically sociology could help us, what it might move us towards studying, and what insights this might offer. Equally, exploring a political stance would give students a different lens. How could it shape our understanding of school sport development and how has it got to where it is now? How might these two historical documents offer us some ideas, too? Finally, if there was a business management approach to studying this, what kind of areas of theoretical study might appeal? Can sport development be managed differently and why might we need theory to help us explore this? Learning should be fun, and being overwhelmed is the worst start to life studying at university. Find your own pace and engage with learning, understand how you read best and start to use technology to aid you in your reading. For example, many articles can now be put on auto-read – you can use the dictation function in Word. These innovations will be key to helping you to manage learning in developing yourself as a theory competent sport development professional over the next three to six years dependent upon whether you progress to master's and PhD study.

Consolidation task

Take note, theory and concepts are difficult. But it doesn't go away when you study a subject at university; sport development is no different. You will be asked to learn specific theory that is beyond these three broad spheres as the subject changes. In recent times, crime prevention and sport development has moved the subject into realms such as criminology (Nichols, 2007), evaluation theory (Coalter; 2007; Harris, 2018), psycho-social behaviour change, and health (Rowe et al., 2013; Sport England, 2016) as well as digital technologies and sport development

(Thorpe, 2017). Perhaps most intriguingly, Thorpe (2017: 554) indicates that "new media technologies such as GoPro™, camera drones, and GPS tracking devices are changing action sport experiences and the relationship between 'human' and 'nonhuman' sporting bodies". Herein lies a challenge for the future of sport development where we need to look further afield for new theory to help us understand increasingly diverse sport and physical activity (and inactivity) norms that become central to policy and practice.

Part A

Stop for a minute now and take time for a reflective task:

What are your concerns about engaging with theory and conceptual reading?

- Why is this?
- How could you work with peers, tutors, and individually to address this early in your career?

Part B

How has your theoretical understanding improved from starting to engage with this task?

References

Department for Education (DfE) (2015) *The PE and Sport Premium: An Investigation in Primary Schools – Research Report*, London: DfE.

Department for Education (DfE) (2019) *Primary PE and Sport Premium Survey: Research Report*, London: DfE.

Griggs, G. (2012) Standing on the touchline of chaos. Explaining the development of sports coaching in primary schools with the aid of complexity theory, *Education 3–13*, 40:3, 259–269.

Griggs, G. (2016) Spending the Primary Physical Education and Sport Premium: A West Midlands case study, *Education 3–13*, 44:5, 547–555.

Griggs, G. (2018) Investigating provision and impact of the Primary Physical Education and Sport Premium: A West Midlands case study. *Education 3–13*, 46:5, 517–524.

Harris, K. (2018) Building sport development practitioners' capacity for monitoring and evaluation – reflections on a training programme for building capacity in realist evaluation, *International Journal of Sport Policy and Politics*, iFirst 1–20.

Nichols, G. (2007) *Sport and Crime Reduction: The Role of Sports in Tackling Youth Crime*, London: Routledge.

Rowe, K., Shilbury, D., Shilbury, S., and Hinckson (2013) Sport development and physical activity promotion: An integrated model to enhance collaboration and understanding, *Sport Management Review*, 16:3, 364–377.

Thorpe, H. (2017) Action sports, social media, and new technologies: Towards a research agenda, *Communication and Sport*, 5:5, 554–578.

Further directed reading (with annotated guide)

Palmer, C. (2013) Social theory, globalization and sports policy in a risk society, in Palmer, C. *Global Sports Policy*, London: Sage, 77–100.

A useful overview of major sociological and political policy theories used in sport development in student friendly language. This neat point of reference is a great entry to a new area that can be complex, but offers a useful student friendly overview of the main 'schools of thought' or types of theory.

Hoye, R. Smith, A.T.C., Nicholson, M., Stewart, B., and Westerbeck, H. (2012) Chapters 5–13 in *Sport Management: Principles and Applications*, Routledge, London.

These eight chapters provide a framework for introducing the broad business management theoretical frameworks that can be applied in sport development. See Wilson, R. and Platts, C. (2017) *Managing and Developing Community Sport* for further specific case studies detailing managing community sport development and associated management and social theories.

References

Baker, C., El Ansari, W., and Crone, D. (2016) Partnership working in sport and physical activity promotion: An assessment of processes and outcomes in community sports networks, *Public Policy and Administration*, 32:2, 87–109.

Berger, J. and Luckmann, T. (1976) *The Social Construction of Reality*, London: Penguin.

Bloyce, D. and Smith, A. (2010) *Sport Policy and Development*, London: Routledge.

Bloyce, D., Smith, A., Mead, R., and Morris, J. (2008) 'Playing the game (plan)': A figurational analysis of organisational change in sports development in England, *European Sports Management Quarterly*, 8, 359–378.

Collins, M. (2014) *Sport and Social Exclusion (2nd edition)*, London: Routledge.

DCMS (2015) *Sporting Nation*, London: DCMS.

Eady, J. (1993) *Practical Sport Development*, London: Longmann.

Fitzgerald, H. (2005) Still feeling like a spare piece of luggage? Embodied experiences of disability in physical education and school sport, *Physical Education and Sport Pedagogy*, 10:1, 41–59.

Fitzgerald, H. (2012) 'Drawing' on disabled students experiences of physical education and stakeholder responses, *Sport, Education and Society*, 17:4, 443–462.

Fletcher, T.E., Piggott, D., North, J. Hylton, K., Gilbert, S., and Norman, L. (2014) *Exploring the Barriers to South Asian Cricket Players' Entry and Progression in Coaching: Project Report*, Leeds: England and Wales Cricket Board/Leeds Beckett University.

Gale, L. and Ives, B. (2019). Emotional struggles and troubled relationships, in L.A. Gale and Ives, B. (eds) *Sports Coaching in the Community: Developing Knowledge and Insight*, Manchester: Manchester Metropolitan University.

Grix, J. (2010) The 'governance debate' and the study of sport policy, *International Journal of Sport Policy*, 2:2, 159–171.

Harris, S. and Houlihan, B. (2014) Delivery networks and community sport in England, *International Journal of Public Sector Management*, 27:2, 113–127.

Harris, S., Nichols, G., and Taylor, M. (2017) Bowling even more alone: Trends towards individual participation in sport, *European Sport Management Quarterly*, 17:3, 290–311.

Houlihan, B. (1994) *Sport, Policy and Politics: A Comparative Analysis*, London: Routledge.

Houlihan, B. and Green, M. (2009) Modernisation and sport: The reform of Sport England and UK Sport, *Public Administration*, 87:3, 678–698.

Houlihan, B. and Green, M. (2013) *Routledge Handbook of Sports Development*, London: Routledge.

Houlihan, B. and Lindsey, I. (2013) *Sport Policy in Britain*, London: Routledge.

Houlihan, B. and White, A. (2002) *The Politics of Sport Development*, London, Routledge.

Hylton, K. (ed) (2013) *Sport Development: Policy, Process and Practice*, London: Routledge.

Hylton, K. (2015) *Sport and Critical Race Theory*, London: Routledge.

Ives, B., Clayton, B., Brittain, I., and Mackintosh, C. (2020) 'I'll always find a perfectly justified reason for not doing it': Challenges for disability sport and physical activity in the United Kingdom, *Sport in Society*, iFirst 1–19.

Ives, B. A. Gale, L.A., Potrac, P. A., and Nelson, L. (2019) Uncertainty, shame and consumption: Negotiating occupational and non-work identities in community sports coaching, *Sport, Education and Society*, 1–17.

Johnson, C. W. and Kivel, B. D. (2006) Gender, sexuality and Queer Theory sport, in Carmichael-Aitchison, C. (ed.) *Sport and Gender Identities*, London: Routledge, 94–105.

King, N. (2009) *Sport Policy and Governance*, Oxford: Butterworth-Heinemann.

Lindsey, I. (2008) Conceptualising sustainability in sports development, *Leisure Studies*, 27:3, 279–294.

Lindsey, I. (2009) Collaboration in local sport services in England: Issues emerging from case studies of two local authority areas, *International Journal of Sport Policy*, 1:1, 71–88.

Long, J., Fletcher, T. and Watson, B. (2017) *Sport, Leisure and Social Justice*, London: Routledge.

Mackintosh, C. (2011) An analysis of County Sports Partnerships in England: The fragility, challenges and complexity of partnership working in sports development, *International Journal of Sport Policy and Politics*, 7:3, 45–64.

Mackintosh, C. (2012) The shifting dynamics of local government sport development in England: New identities and hazy professional boundaries, in Harris, S., Bell, B., Adams, A., and Mackintosh, C. (eds) *Sport for Sport? Practical Insights into Sports Development*, Brighton: LSA.

Mackintosh, C. (2014) Dismantling the school sport partnership infrastructure: Findings from a survey of physical education and school sport practitioners, *Education 3–13*, 42:4, 432–449.

Mackintosh, C. Darko, N., and May-Wilkins, H. (2016). Unintended outcomes of the London 2012 Olympic Games: Local voices of resistance and the challenge for sport participation leverage in England. *Leisure Studies*, 35:4, 454–469.

Mackintosh, C. and Dempsey, C. (2017) The British Asian Muslim male sport participation puzzle: An exploration of implications for sport development policy and practice, *Journal of Youth Studies*, 20:8, 974–996.

Mackintosh, C. and Liddle, J. (2015) Emerging school sport development policy, practice and governance in England: Big Society, autonomy and decentralisation, *Education 3–13*, 43:6, 603–620.

Mackintosh, C. and Mills, C. (2018) Girls who golf? What England Golf is doing to engage more women, *Sport Management*, 23:1, 70-73, available at: www.sportsmanagement.co.uk/pdf/SM_issue1_2019.pdf [accessed on 21 April 2020].

Malcolm, D. (2011) *Sport and Sociology*, London: Routledge.

Medcalf, R. and Mackintosh, C. (2019) *Researching Difference in Sport and Physical Activity*, London: Routledge.

Nichols, G. (2010) Social capital: Reaching out, reaching in, *Leisure Studies*, 29:1, 114–116.

Parnell, D. Spracklen, K., and Millward, P. (2017) Sport management issues in an era of austerity, *European Sport Management Quarterly*, 17:1, 67–74.

Philpotts, L., Grix, J. and Quarmby, T. (2011) Centralised grass roots policy and 'new governance': A case study of County Sport Partnerships in the UK – unpacking the paradox, *International Review for the Sport Sociology*, 46:3, 265–281.

Price, M. and Parker, A. (2003) Sport, sexuality, and the gender order: Amateur Rugby Union, gay men, and social exclusion, *Sociology of Sport Journal*, 20, 108–126.

Robertson, J., Storr, R., Bakos, A., and O'Brien, D. (2019) 'My ideal is where it is just Jane the Cricketer rather than Jane the Gay Cricketer': An institutional perspective on lesbian inclusion in Australian cricket, *Journal of Sport Management*, 33:5, 395–405.

Spaaij, R., Magee, J., Farquharson, K., Gorman, S., Jeanes, R., Lusher, D., and Storr, R. (2018) Diversity work in community sport organizations: Commitment, resistance and institutional change, *International Review for the Sociology of Sport*, 53:3, 278–295.

Sport NI (2009) *Sport Matters: The Northern Ireland Strategy for Sport and Physical Recreation 2009–2019*, Belfast: Sport NI.

Sport Scotland (2019) *Sport For Life: A Vision for Sport in Scotland*, Glasgow: Sport Scotland.

Sport Wales (2019) *The Vision for Sport*, Cardiff: Wales.

Waddington, I. Scott, A. Malcolm, D. (2017) The social management of medical ethics in sport: Confidentiality in English professional football, *International Review for the Sociology of Sport*, 54:6, 649-665

Widdop, P., King, N., Parnell, D., Cutts, D., and Millward, P. (2017) Austerity, policy and sport participation in England, *International Journal of Sport Policy and Politics*, 10:1, 7–24.

CHAPTER 6

Key concepts and theories in sport development

This chapter is very much a kind of scene setting for some of the key terms used in the academic and professional field. There is an established lexicon of what might be termed conceptual and technical language in sport development (*pathways*, *talent identification*, *bottom up/top down*, *implementation*, and so on). There is also an emerging new language of sport development in the UK (driven by modernisation, new technology, and professionalisation agendas) that needs exploring. It could be argued that this is a discourse, a discourse being a socially constructed language, set of beliefs, and behaviours that cut across society. By considering the more academic concepts and theoretical ideas around professionalisation and modernisation of sport development, this can offer a point of departure for examining new terms that whilst highly present in industry day-to-day practice are not currently reflected in existing undergraduate sport development texts. In this sense, there is an argument that industry needs to drive academia and this point will also allow staff and students to bring in the idea of research-informed professional practice for students (and staff) as is the case in other areas of public service in particular. A core assumption of this chapter is that students need support in their learning to engage with concepts through case studies, examples, and reference to past studies that have used theory and concepts in the sport development field. In a book from over ten years ago, Girginov (2008) talked of key *processes* in sport development. First, that of vision setting and the location of issues onto political agendas. Here arguing for bottom up processes from organisations and communities, *bottom up* here meaning embedding ideas, visions and goals from within and in partnership with local and regional communities as opposed to *top down* from national agendas. It seems this is a distant memory now, with the complexities in governance of organisations, agenda setting, devolution, Brexit, and funding. Second, he argued for the need for new sets of skills in management as collaboration and programme development extends. This seems ever more present, and is a constant theme within this text. Third, he suggested a focus would be the disadvantaged, under-represented in sport.

Certainly, in the four home nation strategic documents that emerged four to seven years after his book, these did materialise. This linked closely with his argument of a theme in the profession for the need to construct personal identity in specific settings. The final area is one that we turn to below, that of collaboration, co-creation, and partnership working across networks. It is interesting to reflect back on a vision of the pressing issues of sport development at a key time for graduates 12 years ago. I would argue, some areas have sped up, others have developed, and some have been radically reshaped.

Key concept 1: modernisation

Conceptually, the evolution of sport from amateur status and organisation is a core idea behind a historical understanding of sport development. From pre-formal government intervention in sport through to the codification of sport and into the emergence of NGBs and associated agencies such as Sports Councils and local government provision, it could be argued that there has been an ongoing process of modernisation. Modernisation is the ongoing development of sport development processes, approaches, and focus in society. Modernisation has received its critics (Houlihan and Green, 2009) as agencies have been seen to focus on targets, performance measures, and the delivery of targets sent to effectively 'discipline' and reward. A good example is the use of payment by results systems by UK Sport for elite sport and other agencies in Sport Scotland and Sport Wales. Indeed, in 2016 the RFU lost £1million for not meeting its Sport England participation targets. It could also be argued that modernisation plays out for the professional identities of sport development officers (SDOs) as they grapple with this new, modernising agenda that challenges long established values and practices (Mackintosh, 2012). A good example of a specific study around this is Bloyce et al.'s (2008) empirical examination of SDO identities, which found complex contrasts between those that were experiencing the transition from 'tracksuits to suits'. Likewise, Thompson, Bloyce, and Mackintosh (2020) have undertaken one of the few studies of organisational change in sport development. The study explores NGB change in a time of great policy undulations and agenda diversification using a figurational sociological lens. As new students of sport development, this new, latest era is perhaps all you have known. But, it is critical to understand the context of recent and longer-term history of your profession.

Key concept 2: governance

The movement away from 'big' government towards governance is an important conceptual and theoretical backdrop for sport development policy and practice in the UK. It is not a new one, as the role of networks is well established (Houlihan and Lindsey, 2008; Girginov, 2008; Hylton and Bramham, 2007). In essence, it was the position that 'large'-scale government invested in 'large' regional and local governments through high tax regimes. But, what has emerged is a 'hollowing out' (Skelcher, 2000) of the State where there is a far greater 'arm's length' role. In sport development terms, this concept is played out in the extensive governance networks that 'run' sport, from UK Sport to Sport Wales, professional sport clubs, charities, social enterprises, and the voluntary sector. Traditional notions of hierarchies are replaced by horizontal partnerships (see above) where organisations are part of *governance* systems not linear and traditional forms of *government*. Governance has also emerged as key policy point of reference in areas such as child protection, doping, ethics, accountability, and funding. From this there is now the UK Code of Governance (UK Sport, 2017). But, this specific policy document should not be confused with the wider theoretical and academic concept of governance. In sport development this is a key term for as students of this subject area, and potential graduates employed in this political environment, we need now more than ever to understand where we are positioned, who is governing, where power lies, and the shifting sands of authority as organisations and the public respond to agenda change.

Key concept 3: professionalisation

The concept of professionalisation is a vital one to command in relation to your position within the sport development landscape, but also your own professional identity in sub-sectors within the sport development profession. It is perhaps first pertinent to examine the very notion of whether sport development is a profession per se. Hylton and Hartley (2012) compared it to other professions such as law, social work and teaching and medicine and examined some of the differences and contrasts with these areas. They summarised that in 2012 it did not meet all the necessary criteria for a 'profession'. However, past estimates have seen sport development have an estimated workforce between 2500 and 5000 (Pitchford and Collins, 2010). As these three standpoints are all now dated, it is perhaps useful to revisit the notion of a professional in sport development in 2020. For most students looking forward to graduation, this means employment in three areas; 'sport-for-development', elite sport, and community sport for sports sake. In different countries in the UK there are slightly different focuses on these three areas, with associated scales of employment and markets for jobs. Many forget that no assessment has been made of the size of sport development graduate market; major employers in areas such as community sport coaching may employ hundreds of coaches. Charities such as Football in the Community at professional clubs and *Street Games* offer considerable paid work, linked to opportunities for progress in sport-for-development.

With a period of financial austerity (see explanation below) since 2008 in the UK and wider global economy, there has been a scaling back of local government sport employment (King, 2015; Widdop et al., 2017). As the major employer of professionals in sport, this no doubt has had an impact on the size of the market. But it could also be argued that professionalisation (Dowling, Edwards, and Washington, 2014; Taylor and Garratt, 2010) continues regardless and is a closely linked process to modernisation of sport development. A good example of this is who is working in what roles in the profession. It could be argued that NGBs are now predominantly run by a smaller core of professionals within their day-to-day staff. Many also have directors, boards, and chairpersons that lead the governance of 'the sport'. In addition, we now see sports reaching out to non-executive directors (NEDs), these external candidates are appointed specifically for their 'professional' expertise in non-sport areas such as finance, marketing, and Audit here being the ability to oversee processes of accountability and, often, financial regulation and monitoring of standards within an organisation. Dowling, Edwards, and Washington (2014) suggest that professionalisation is a multi-faceted concept but also one that can be defined in a range of ways dependent on philosophical and theoretical stance of the researcher.

Key concept 4: evidence-based practice (EBP)

The use of evidence to consider 'what works' (Cairney, 2016; Davies, Nutley, and Smith, 2000; Piggin, Jackson and Lewis, 2009) but also to embed research-informed thinking the development of public services is not new. Students of sport development need to be aware that concepts such as evidence-based practice (and policy) are now firmly at the forefront of funding allocation, grant provision, and the cyclical nature of allocation of money to sports, agencies, and government departments. Essentially, it focuses on the role of research, evaluation, theory, insight, information systems (as forms of evidence) in shaping provision, daily practices, and organisational processes. For some, EBP itself is a contested term and comes as part of the 'machinery' of government modernisation (Cairney, 2016; Houlihan and Green, 2009; Piggin, Jackson, and Lewis, 2009). But, as the industry moved long ago towards using research to inform policy and practice, it is what might be termed a contested conceptual argument. For students new to sport development, this is the use of theoretical different ideas and research to argue for and against the presence of, and existence of a phenomenon in society. It is perhaps neatly summed up by the former research officer from *Sport* Scotland John Best, who argued academic policy researchers never want to do the kind of research the sport development industry wants them to, and industry doesn't want to hear the research findings academia uncovers (Best, 2009). What is clear is that a veritable industry in 'insight' has emerged both in the public, private and charitable sectors (Table 6.1).

Key concept 5: partnership working

A constant within the world of sport development policy and practice has been the mantra and rhetoric of the importance of organisational partnerships to deliver policy goals (Baker, El Ansari, and Crone, 2016; O'Hanlon et al., 2020). If there is term that has now come to mean little, but is consistently used throughout industry, it is this concept. It can be argued that it is the areas of mutually beneficial working where two, or more organisations, or individuals

TABLE 6.1 Breakdown of the sport development research market by sector

Sector	Examples of research agencies involved in direct EBP
Public	Sports Council research and insight teams (Scotland, Wales, Northern Ireland, and England) English Institute of Sport Insight officer – NGB or non-specific roles across 300 NGBs in UK Insight officer – varied number across 43 Active Partnerships Local government research team (non-sport specific: 'policy units' or 'insight and evaluation teams')
Private	Sport Consultancy Practices, e.g. Substance, Strategic Leisure, KKP, PortaConsulting, S&L Consulting Mainstream consultants (sport element), e.g. KPMG, ECORYS, Deloitte Sports Business Group University-based research consultants and centres – theory and practice-led research
Charity	Street Games – knowledge manager (and in-house team) Football in the Community – researcher (in-house) Mainstream charities with externally commissioned sport research, e.g. MIND Charitable sector researchers

from within organisations collaborate in a multi-agency manner on a project delivery or initiative. For students new to the subject of sport development, it is worth being aware that it has been argued that the origins of this move to partner, collaborate, and work cross-agency to deliver could be seen as stemming from New Labour government's Third Way politics that emerged in the late 1990s (Houlihan and White, 2002; Houlihan and Lindsey, 2013; Mackintosh, 2011). The theoretical principles here are that organisations now need to work less in silos, perhaps akin to the 'old structures' of local government departments and work across teams, divisions, and departments. This is now, 20 years later, a critical and vital component of sport development practice. Few NGBs or major charities in sport development such as Street Games can deliver their organisational vision without getting others to work with or for them. Indeed, since the study of partnerships in public sector began to emerge, specific agencies branded as partnerships in the sector have been set up such as Active Partnerships in each region of England (formerly County Sport Partnerships). Studies in this conceptual area have considered the sustainability of this approach (Lindsey, 2008), power dynamics within the partnership (Baker El Ansari and Crone, 2016; Philpotts and Grix, 2010) and the fragility and complex reality of working through and within partnership (Philpotts and Grix, 2010; Mackintosh, 2011).

Key concept 6: civil society

The literature will often refer to civil society but for students new to sport development research and analysis as an academic study this will be a new concept for many. It tries to encapsulate the area of society that is located outside of formal structures and agencies of state and government. Often, it might be equated to the voluntary sector; again, by this we mean the volunteers, participants in the voluntary sector, and machinery of support and partnerships that are now at play here. But, it also includes churches, faith centres, and diverse other settings. For sport development, as the largest subsector sector in the volunteering community, this is a fundamental area for us to understand and engage with as professionals. It is also where much of our wider theorising, conceptual work sits and research leans towards. Consider an agency like the Rugby Football League (RFL) or British Orienteering, two NGBs that rely on their members, clubs, and participants to 'deliver' the goals and targets of government. Without a grasp of the civil society challenges at large, SDOs may make overly large expectations on volunteers. Research has shown the vital role that volunteers make in the delivery, or, indeed, non-delivery of sport development government policy (Harris, Mori, and Collins, 2009; Harris and Houlihan, 2016; Harris, Nichols, and Taylor, 2017). It is fundamentally important that we are therefore able to have an awareness of not only what civil society encompasses.

It is not just the voluntary sector in perhaps how the sport sector has seen itself. It also encompasses charities, social enterprises, not-for-profit agencies, religious-led projects and neighbourhood self-help-styled sport and physical and activity organisations. This has become a growth area for the sector that is hard to delineate and define but increasingly important (Marsden-Heathcote and Finney, 2018). It has been suggested, for example, that sport education-based social enterprises are the fastest area of growth within social enterprises in the UK (Marsden-Heathcote, 2017). Furthermore, with government policy in 2015 (DCMS, 2015) moving towards an increased focus on social policy outcomes (crime prevention, health, mental health, community development, individual development, and economic regeneration) traditional agencies such as NGBs, Active Partnerships, and perhaps local government were less flexible and less able to respond to this challenge. Civil society is a key concept and one that for all students in sport development remains a complex but important foundation of their subject knowledge, although this does overlap with the concepts of modernisation, austerity and professionalisation. Recent research has shown the sector of 30,967 social enterprise organisations is changing (Social Enterprise UK, 2019). In a study of 1068 social enterprises, there was a long-term trend away from organisations describing themselves as charities towards 33 per cent using the term social enterprise, 31 per cent community business and 26 per cent a cooperative. This could be seen as a shift away from civil society towards more of a 'business' community focus. Equally, this national study found that 33 per cent of organisations are under £50,000 turnover in scale and thus can be described as small or micro businesses.

Key concept 7: austerity

A consistent theme over the last ten years of sport development policy and practice has been the use of the term, concept, and political idea of austerity (King, 2014a, b; Mackintosh and Liddle, 2015; Widdop et al., 2017). The essence of the idea is the financial (or fiscal, as it is referred to in economist terms) tightening of budgets in the public sector with less expenditure to reduce government involvement in public services. It is suggested that it essentially arrived with the Conservative government in 2010 that argued it had inherited an 'overspending' Labour government from the 1997–2010 period of power. However, it is about more than balance sheets, income, expenditure, and gross domestic product (GDP). Sport development academics in this field such as King (2014a, b), through their surveys of local government, have shown how fundamental changes have occurred in the landscape of sport facilities, sport development, and hence neighbourhood of England. Whilst there are elements of devolution of power and decision making around sport, health, and other public services in the other home nations, central government does control central budgets in national agencies and hence there will be overall impacts on communities. Other authors have examined austerity from the what we might term the 'lived realities', or daily existences, feelings, and emotions of both sport workers (Gale et al., 2019; Ives et al., 2019) and local communities affected by austerity (Parnell, Millward, and Spracklen, 2016; Walker and Hayton, 2019). How austerity is influencing the situation in each of the four home nations should also be closely considered. For example, Jarvie and Birnbacher (2018) analyse sport, austerity, and economic choices in Scotland in an analysis of direct government expenditure on sport. This provides a useful backdrop to the context of sport development plans presented by Sport Scotland (2019). Indeed, other authors suggest that public expenditure between 1998 and 2010 had significantly increased since devolution (Houlihan and Lindsey, 2013). Finance remains a complex picture and one where bold generalisations should be avoided. Austerity remains a concept playing out at large for SDOs, the communities they work with, and the multiple agencies of the sector, whether it is SDOs finding it harder to recruit volunteers due to income pressures on families, or more macro issues of reduced funding for national agencies. All influence the landscapes of the profession. They also offer fertile grounds for undertaking undergraduate and postgraduate study as a researcher in sport development.

▌▌▌▌▌▌▌▌▌▌ **CASE STUDY 6.1** ▌▌▌▌▌▌▌▌▌▌

Putting theory into practice – examining sport coaching policy and practice

Development officers across the sport development workforce, whether in NGBs, active partnerships, Football in The Community set-ups, or in volunteer roles around *parkrun*, will all experience the above concepts in different ways. A good example to look at is that of community sport coaching and try to unpick some of the different challenges, understanding, and perspectives of each of these core issues to this textbook. Community sport coaching in the United Kingdom has for a number of years been overseen by SportsCoachUK, now known as UK Coaching (Burt and Morgan, 2014; Dowling, Edwards, and Washington, 2014). Since 2018, this has started to subtly shift across the home nations due to funding shifts and centralisation of support for UK Coaching from Sport England. Increasingly, Scotland, for example, are designing their own independent strategy, approach, and accreditation system. There are approximately 3 million coaches working at different levels of sport and physical activity in the UK. This case study is about trying to understand how they might be experiencing each of the different theoretical concepts but from an industry experience. Remember the previous chapter where we also introduced sociology, political theory, and business management (amongst other theories) as layering these onto the key concept, term, and idea will bring a slightly different view. If we lean towards sociology, we may be interested in people, communities, and individual norms and behaviours around, say, professionalisation or modernisation in coaching. If adopting a political theory stance, we may want to look at which policy coalitions or groups coalesce around a topic or theme linked to austerity or governance such as cuts to leisure centres. Finally, by engaging with theory on marketing in business we could look at how marketing segmentation is used to offer evidence for getting more people more active. At level 5, we then go on to start evaluating arguments around these debates.

So, we are now going to focus on one conceptual theme, that of professionalisation in community ('grass roots') sport coaching in the sport of Rugby Union in England. The UK has had an established coach development set of processes based around the United Kingdom Coaching Certificate (UKCC), in place for over 15 years in the four home countries. In 2018, the UKCC Review was undertaken (Mackintosh and Carter, 2018), which recommended changes for UKCoaching, Sport England and Scotland (Wales and Northern Ireland opted out of the review, but received the findings). It was a review undertaken with 1300 coaches submitting responses to an online survey and over 12 interviews with senior policy makers and 12 focus groups with universities, community coaches, and NGBs. The purpose of the review was to establish if the existing system was 'fit for purpose' for delivery of professionalisation and modernisation of the community through to elite sport coaching system. The report currently remains confidential.

Put yourself in the position of a potential level 1 rugby club coach who is considering volunteering at a local club and is told they need to do a Rugby Ready course and also a level 1 course (two days over a weekend) and a child protection course (a DBS check would be undertaken regardless by the club safeguarding officer). With this national review complete, CIMSPA are considering implication for national standard benchmarks in coaching and how this will work for each NGB.

Seminar questions

- What might a potential club coach feel?
- Why does this matter for the regional RFU development officer and their 'day job'?

- What should a national coach accreditation system include?
- What are the benefits and challenges of professionalising local grass roots community coaching through weekend 'badges' ?

Extension task

Although a more historical article, explore Burt and Morgan's (2014) study of RFU community coaches at levels 1 and 2. How does this article advance your understanding of the four questions above?

Suggested reflection task

Consider how your own understanding of your own sport coaching practice has been shaped by this task. Identify ways in which you would work differently as an RFU regional officer responsible for 30 clubs and their coaches as a result of this task.

References

Burt, E. and Morgan, P. (2014) Barriers to systematic reflective practice as perceived by UKCC level 1 and level 2 qualified Rugby Union coaches, *Reflective Practice*, 15:4, 468–480.

Dowling, M., Edwards, J., and Washington, M. (2014) Understanding the concept of professionalization in sport management research, *Sport Management Review*, 17:4, 520–529.

Mackintosh. C. and Carter, J. (2018) *The Review of the United Kingdom Coaching Certificate (UKCC): A Shock to the Coaching System?*, Manchester: Manchester Metropolitan University.

References

Baker, C., El Ansari, W., and Crone, D. (2016) Partnership working in sport and physical activity promotion: An assessment of processes and outcomes in community sports networks, *Public Policy and Administration*, 32:2, 87–109.

Best, J. (2009) What policy-makers want from research: What researchers want to tell them, *Journal of Policy Research in Tourism, Leisure and Events*, 1:2, 175–178.

Bloyce, D., Smith, A., Mead, R., and Morris, J. (2008) 'Playing the game (plan)': A figurational analysis of organisational change in sport development in England, *European Sport Management Quarterly*, 8:4, 359–378.

Cairney, P. (2016) *The Politics of Evidence-Based Policy Making*, London: Palgrave.

Davies, H.W.O., Nutley, S. and Smith, P.C. (2000) *What Works? Evidence-based Policy and Practice in Public Services*, Bristol: Policy Press.

Dowling, M., Edwards, J., and Washington, M. (2014) Understanding the concept of professionalization in sport management research, *Sport Management Review*, 17:4, 520–529.

Gale, L.A., Ives, B.A., Potrac, P.A., and Nelson, L.J. (2019) Trust and distrust in community sports work: Tales from the 'shop floor', *Sociology of Sport Journal*, 36:3, 244–253.

Girginov, V. (2008) *Management of Sports Development*, Oxford: Butterworth-Heinemann.

Harris, S. and Houlihan, B. (2016) Implementing the community sport legacy: The limits of partnerships, contracts and performance management, *European Sports Management Quarterly*, 16:4, 433–458.

Harris, S., Mori, K., and Collins, M. (2009) Great expectations: The role of voluntary sports clubs as policy implementers, *Voluntas International Journal*, 20:4, 405–423.

Harris, S., Nichols, G., and Taylor, M. (2017) Bowling even more alone: Trends towards individual participation in sport, *European Sports Management Quarterly*, 17:3, 290–311.

Houlihan, B. and Green, M. (2009) Modernisation and sport: The reform of Sport England and UK Sport, *Public Administration*, 87:3, 678–698.

Houlihan, B. and Lindsey, I. (2008) Networks and partnerships in sports development, in, Girginov, V. (ed.) *Management of Sports Development*, Oxford: Elsevier, 225–242.

Houlihan, B. and Lindsey, I. (2013) *Sport Policy in Britain*, London: Routledge.

Houlihan, B. and White, A. (2002) *The Politics of Sport Development*, London: Routledge.

Hylton, K. and Bramham, P. (2007) *Sport Development: Policy, Process and Practice (1st edition)*, London: Routledge.

Hylton, K. and Hartley, H. (2012) Sport development … a profession in waiting?, in Harris, S., Bell, B., Adams, and Mackintosh, C. (eds.) *Sport for Sport? Practical and Theoretical Insights in Sport Development*, Brighton: Leisure Studies Association, 4–22.

Ives, B. A., Gale, L.A., Potrac, P. A., and Nelson, L. J. (2019) Uncertainty, shame and consumption: negotiating occupational and non-work identities in community sports coaching, *Sport, Education and Society*, iFirst, 1–17.

Jarvie, G. and Birnbacher, D. (2018) Sport, austerity or choice in Scotland: An analysis of direct government expenditure on sport, *Scottish Affairs*, 27:2, 189–214.

King, N. (2014a) Local authority sport services under the UK Coalition government: Retention, revision or curtailment, *International Journal of Sport Policy and Politics*, 6:3, 349–369.

King, N. (2014b) Making the case for sport and recreation services: The utility of Social Return on Investment (SROI) analysis, *International Journal of Public Sector Management*, 27:2, 152–164.

Lindsey, I. (2008) Conceptualising sustainability in sports development, *Leisure Studies*, 27:3, 279–294.

Mackintosh, C. (2011) An analysis of County Sports Partnerships in England: The fragility, challenges and complexity of partnership working in sport development, *International Journal of Sport Policy and Politics*, 3:1, 45–64.

Mackintosh, C. (2012) The shifting dynamics of local government sport development officer practice in England: new identities and hazy professional boundaries, in Harris, S., Bell, B., Adams, A. and Mackintosh, C. (eds) *Sport for Sport? Theoretical and Practical Insights into Sport Development*, Eastbourne: Leisure Studies Association, 113–130.

Mackintosh, C. and Liddle, J. (2015) Emerging school sport development policy, practice and governance in England: Big Society, autonomy and decentralisation, *Education 3–13: International Journal of Primary, Elementary and Early Years*, 43:6, 603–620.

Marsden-Heathcote, J. and Finney, A. (2018) Enterprise and innovation in community sport, in Wilson, R. and Platts, C. (eds.) *Managing and Developing Community Sport*, London: Routledge, 196–212.

O'Hanlon, R., Mackintosh, C., Holmes, H-L., and Meek, R. (2020) Moving forces: Using sport and physical activity to support men and women in the military to civilian transition, *Managing Sport and Leisure: An International Journal*, iFirst, 1–22.

Parnell, D. Millward, P. and Spracklen, K. (2016) Special issue introduction: Sport management in times of austerity, *European Sports Management Quarterly*, 17:1, 67–74.

Philpotts, L. and Grix, J. (2010) Revisiting the 'governance narrative': 'Asymmetrical network governance' and the deviant case of the sports policy sector, *Public Policy and Administration*, 26:1, 3–19.

Pitchford, A. and Collins, M. (2010) Sports development as a job, a career and training, in Collins, M. (ed.) *Examining Sports Development*, London: Routledge, 259–288.

Piggin, J., Jackson, S., and Lewis, M. (2009) Knowledge, power and politics: Contesting 'evidence-based' national sport policy, *International Review for the Sociology of Sport*, 44:1, 87–101.

Skelcher, C. (2000) Changing images of the state: Overloaded, hollowed-out, congested, *Public Policy and Administration*, 15:3, 3–19.

Social Enterprise UK (2019) *Capitalism is Crisis: Transforming Our economy for People and Planet*, London: Social Enterprise UK.

Taylor, B. and Garratt, D. (2010) The professionalisation of sports coaching: Relations of power, resistance and compliance, *Sport, Education and Society*, 15:1, 121–139.

Thompson, A., Bloyce, D., and Mackintosh, C. (2020) 'It is always going to change' – managing top-down policy changes by sport development officers working in national governing bodies of sport in England, *Managing Sport and Leisure: An International Journal*, iFirst 1–20.

UK Sport (2017) *A Code for Sport Governance*, London: UK Sport.

Walker, C. M. and Hayton, J. W. (2019) An analysis of third sector sport organisations in an era of 'super-austerity', *International Journal of Sport Policy and Politics*, 10:1, 43–61.

Widdop, P., King, N., Parnell, D., Cutts, D., and Millward, P. (2017) Austerity, policy and sport participation in England, *International Journal of Sport Policy and Politics*, 10:1, 7–24.

PART II

Agencies and organisations in delivery, policy, and practice

This section of the book provides an overview of the agencies and organisation that are engaged in frontline, policy level, and the multiple other tiers of governance in sport development. The book is written from a theoretical standpoint that organisations are not marked merely by a single document or strategy they have produced. Neither are they represented solely by the 30–40 people that occupy an office, building, or virtual network of development staff. So, what is an organisation? How can we understand them differently, to give us a more critical insight? In the chapters that follow, organisations are seen as collections of ideas, meanings, memories, and beliefs that resonate around what we can refer to as constructs. When we say Sport Wales, this is understood differently in different policy spaces and across national divides and boundaries. If we evaluate Manchester United FC (Porter, 2008) and their counter organisation FC United (Porter, 2015), both are 'football clubs'. Both do 'work in the community'; both have sport development functions. They nearly share the same name, but have vastly opposing meanings, brands, and ideologies around what they do, how they do it and what their 'remit is'. Profit means something very different to both. The geography of where they are and the organisational setting is important to these meanings and the work they do. Both even have a place at the global table of sport development, but for hugely different reasons.

The landscape of sport development

Collins (2010) once described sport development as a 'convoluted bowl of spaghetti' (1995: 34, cited in Houlihan and White, 2002: 56). The policy of sport development is interwoven with organisations from different tiers of the 'system' and layered in complex and unplanned ways. Some have said that the landscape of sport development is fragmented, complex, and increasingly like a patchwork quilt (Mackintosh and Liddle, 2015). When analysing the existing landscape, historical analysis is an essential and powerful tool for the student. It offers insights into the pathways of policy and discourses that have led us to where we are now. Nothing exists in a vacuum, not policy, not practices or even ideas as to what we mean by this long-established area of public policy provision. In each of the home nations there is also a separate but related landscape. Since devolution and even before history, culture, and politics have fed into divergence and concentration of sport development policy ideas and organisations.

As a student new to the landscape, as someone that will hopefully enter the profession upon graduation, reading these next few chapters offers some building blocks in shaping your understanding and knowledge. It is, however, not possible to learn everything from a book. Much of what equips you with a sport development career are your soft skills and practical abilities that you will be learning through assessment at university and also volunteering and placement-led work. This said, it is possible to provide a UK-wide orientation that is without the assumption that you already know organisations, agencies, and what they represent and mean.

Managing and developing sport and physical activity

This book is positioned so that it sets a context for you to start your own independent learning through lectures and seminars and wider reading. This subject learning or substantive content has to start somewhere. It also builds on what may be your own 'tacit knowledge', or understanding you have acquired where it is fairly implicit who Sport Wales are, or what a local government sport development unit are. What is fundamental to this is that in recent years, and to be precise by this I mean the last ten years, there have been a number of cross-national and pan-organisational and policy debates that now sit at the heart of managing and developing sport development. In the next section, leading into the following chapters on specific organisational contexts and types I will set some context.

First, child protection has grown in importance. The rights and responsibilities of organisations around this theme are now core, as opposed to peripheral to day-to-day and strategy work they will be leading on. It was only in 1999 that Professor Celia Brackenridge wrote an article entitled 'Managing Myself' as a researcher in sport development in this field (Brackenridge, 1999). In this seminal piece, she identified NGBs such as gymnastics and swimming that had been refusing to engage with 'issues' and problems in their sports and how she received death threats for her pioneering research. Now in the work of Lang (2019), White and Lang (2018), Hartill and Lang (2018) and Lang et al. (2018) it is clear that child protection must be central to how an NGB, or any provider, manager, or agency engages in sport and physical activity. This legacy of academic work has been consolidated by the more recent Duty of Care in Sport Review by Baroness Tanni Grey-Thompson in 2018. This report identified seven key priority recommendations covering diverse areas including child protection, creating an ombudsman and training in NGB's and the wider industry. Indeed, as the book will explore, as we move into more diverse settings and alternative ways of delivery (online, digital, and virtual), we must take care to embed child protection. It is also not all about community spaces and practices; those of you that have been made aware of the long-standing historic child protection and abuse issues in football academies and coaching, alongside other sports, need to also see academies and elite sport as spaces to consider approaches to welfare (Platts and Smith, 2009; Hartill and Lang, 2018). Welfare and human rights of performers, participants, and coaches and those involved in our industry must also be a strand of what sport development officers do as standard not by chance. It will only become an ever more fundamental part of organisational practice and policy.

Second, thematic policy strands have emerged around the field of the social welfare or social policy function and the role of sport and physical activity (Bloyce and Smith, 2010; Houlihan and Lindsey, 2013; Widdop et al., 2017). This is not new. It is important to acknowledge that as students of the subject, this is not new. It is a policy tool that oscillates in currency and importance often based on the government of the time. A useful conceptual tool is what was first deemed *recreational welfare* (Coalter, Long, and Duffield, 1988). Although recreational welfare was introduced 27 years before the DCMS strategy (DCMS, 2015), it sets a vision for how sport can and should play a philosophical role in delivering welfare agendas for all. Not only did Coalter, Long, and Duffield (1988) suggest that sport should be 'for all', but that it should also be used as a tool for delivery of wider goals. Coalter (2007) later argued for the somewhat questionable clarity of the goals and outcomes of such policies in sport development where sport and physical actively were embedded as being capable of myopic (or 'blind delivery of') social policy goals including increased educational attainment, reduced crime, and improved social cohesion in highly fractured communities. Much of this was born out of the New Labour government of 1997–2010 but has been picked up and maintained under the conservative-liberal coalition (2010–2015) and present conservative lead (2015–2020 and onwards). Detailed analysis is provided in Houlihan and Lindsey (2013) and beyond the scope of this book. But, over-arching themes in this policy space are now firmly entrenched in UK policy. The specifics and degree to which they are part of individual countries policy in sport development varies. Scotland and Wales, for example, lean slightly more towards health and activity drivers as opposed to England, which does cover this but also touches on mental health, crime, youth, and community engagement and societal inclusion agendas.

Third, the presence of research, evaluation, and insight has become part of mainstream sport development (Smith and Leech, 2010; Wilson and Platts, 2018). It is evident that for the professionals of the future they will only know times when evidence-based practice (EBP) and use of research and insight to develop, design, and evaluate programmes and initiatives is the norm. More will be said of this later. Practical requirements of a book such as this are a gentle introduction to not just research methods as many degree courses have but the specific and bespoke traditions and discipline research boundaries present in sport development. Indeed, as mentioned earlier, a whole 'insight industry' has evolved in the last 15 years, arguably since Active People Survey (APS) was launched in 2005. Other surveys have also been in place before 2000, such as those measuring children's participation in Wales by Sport Wales and national quantitative evaluation reports led by Sport Scotland. However, a trend is the broadening of the scope of the 'reach' of evaluation expectation beyond central government and quango agencies into professional sport clubs, charities, local government, NGBs, and active partnerships. This research often is about putting in place a system for data collection to measure changes, develop insights, engage with theory, and see if projected impacts and outcomes have actually occurred. Take a sport and mental health project linked to a rugby club where the players go into local settings to raise awareness of the stigma around mental health. Research might be done initially into how we could conduct this and what the literature best practice and theory suggests design needs to focus on. Evaluation data collection may ask young people involved to either measure change in attitudes and beliefs or offer ideas for improvement. Findings may be presented in a video-based online YouTube story or documentary, a traditional report, or a further workshop with stakeholders (the people interested and engaged with the project). The key part to acknowledge here is the new and emerging set of professional skills that people in sport development need to possess. Indeed, as long ago as 2012, research with ten local authority sport development officers in five councils indicated concerns over their skill set in working in spheres such as crime prevention, social and community development, and mental health project evaluation (Mackintosh, 2012). More recently Thompson, Bloyce, and Mackintosh (2020) specifically identified the challenges and issues in NGBs going through change linked to national policy agenda shifts. Research expectations remained core to what NGB staff are expected to engage with. This said, recent books and discussions around EBP have divided processes around this evidence gathering into two strands. First, *rational* ways to support projects and programmes with literature reviews, empirical research, and secondary information (APS, Active Lives, Sport Wales national sport participation surveys) (Cairney, 2016). Second, *irrational* decision making using emotions, opinions, bias, and habits. This is particularly enlightening in sport development when we start to unpick why we work with who we do, how we work with them and the ways in which assumptions are held about organisational settings, deliverers and say volunteers. Gregory and Wilson (2018) offer a clear overview of the traditional sphere of sport development monitoring and evaluation theory, process, and practice. Here new theoretical standard practices have become part of the mainstream such as the development of 'logic models' and identification and testing of 'theories of change'. Whilst popular in areas of sport development research community, they are far from well understood. Furthermore, they are not the sole research processes that are appropriate or justified. Indeed, some of the more interesting research has been undertaken by Smith and Leech (2010) into how teachers and sport development staff have adapted to new M&E requirements where effectively they have altered data, changed focus, and not followed procedure. This study shows how we need a more nuanced understanding of M&E than the assumption that what we set out to do will simply deliver the final goals of the evaluation and neatly support a project.

Finally, sport development has always had a focus on exclusion, equity, and inclusion. This is no different when starting to explore this section of the book examining organisations and agencies. In particular, recent policy shifts have asked organisations to look far more closely at who they employ and their representativeness of their agencies (Sport England, 2016; Sport NI, 2009; Sport Scotland, 2019; Sport Wales, 2019). Over the last 20 years, considerable research has been undertaken in this space, identifying gaps in representation and opening debates for minority voices (Long, Fletcher, and Watson, 2018; Medcalf and Mackintosh, 2018). This can be around themes of (dis)ability (Fitzgerald, 2005; Ives et al., 2020), gender and sexuality (Caudwell, 1999; Norman, 2008), race and ethnicity (Meir and Fletcher, 2017; Mackintosh and Dempsey, 2017), and age (Hutchings, Jones and Fox, 2019, Pike, 2015). Sport development has at its heart a drive to address not just issues of participation inequality in such target groups but also for representation in coaching, volunteering, and administration. Sporting Equals have recently identified that only one Chief Executive Officer (CEO) is a Black, Asian, and Minority Ethnic (BAME) individual, and only 20 or so of all NGB board members also meet this social group classification (Sport Equals, 2020: online). Sport Equals (2020) identify that 14 per cent of the UK population is from a BAME background yet only 5 per cent of BAME board members are present within the whole sporting sector. In relation to the workforce in sport, only 3 per cent of coaches and only seven British Asians out of 630 athletes represented Team GB in 2016 Rio Olympics and Paralympics. Perhaps the starkest contrast is in local sport where it is suggested that "in 2018 that 40% of BAME communities had a negative customer experience in leisure centres compared to 14% of white British Communities" (Sport Equals, 2020: online). If we overlay other factors such as disability, this isolation from mechanisms of power and authority is even more pronounced (Ives et al., 2020) and this needs to change. In each of the chapters that follow it is perhaps considering the work each sub-sector of sport development industry is doing in each of these areas identified. If we are to address issues such as gendered attitudes and sexism in the Football Association as an issue (Hill, Roberts, and Andrews, 2017), we need to also transform education of sport development graduates. If we are to view disability less as a medical condition and instead as a socially constructed lens where we often fail to 'see' people's ability, then we need to actively consider ways to engage better with organisations, administrators, volunteers, participants, and coaches in the UK. This is perhaps the greatest opportunity that this book tries to open up conversations around. Each chapter in this section has a case study that is meant as a learning resource and space for debate, discussion, or individual study. In these organisational sector case studies, a varied style is taken – some are specific reflective tasks, others are based on 'live' scenarios, and some push you to read more to engage with additional peer-reviewed research. Most importantly, the chapters offer a point of reference for students at level 4, but through to level 6. If you are ever unclear what an organisation does, its background, or history then please return here. Hopefully, it is useful; it is based on consultation with your own academic community and practitioners.

References

Bloyce, D. and Smith, A. (2010) *Sport Policy and Development*, London: Routledge.

Brackenridge, C. (1999) Managing myself: Investigator survival in sensitive research, *International Review for the Sociology of Sport*, 34:4, 399–410.

Cairney, P. (2016) *The Politics of Evidence-Based Policy Making*, London: Palgrave.

Caudwell, J. (1999) Women's football in the United Kingdom: Theorizing gender and unpacking the butch lesbian image, *Journal of Sport and Social Issues*, 23:4, 390–402.

Coalter, F. (2007) *A Wider Social Role for Sport? Whose Keeping the Score*, London: Routledge.

Coalter, F. Long, J. A. Duffield, D. S. (1988) *Recreational Welfare: A Rationale for Public Leisure Policy*, Aldershot: Avebury.

Collins, M. (2010) *Examining Sport Development*, London: Routledge.

DCMS (2015) *Sporting Nation*, London: DCMS.

Fitzgerald, H. (2005) Still feeling like a spare piece of luggage? Embodied experiences of disability in physical education and school sport, *Physical Education and Sport Pedagogy*, 10:1, 41–59.

Gregory, M. and Wilson, J. (2018) Monitoring and evaluation, in Wilson, R. and Platts, C. (eds) *Managing and Developing Community Sport*, London: Routledge, 213–235.

Houlihan, B. and Lindsey, I. (2013) *Sport Policy in Britain*, London: Routledge.

Houlihan, B. and White, A. (2002) *The Politics of Sports Development*, London: Routledge.

Ives, B., Clayton, B., Brittain, I., and Mackintosh, C. (2020) 'I'll always find a perfectly justified reason for not doing it': Challenges for disability sport and physical activity in the United Kingdom, *Sport in Society*, iFirst, 1–19.

Lang, M. (2019) *Intergenerational Physical Contact (Touch) in Sport: A Review of the Evidence for UK Coaching*. Leeds: UK Coaching.

Lang, M., Mergaert, L., Arnaut, C., and Vertommen, T. (2018). Gender-based violence in EU sport policy: Overview and recommendations. *Journal of Gender-Based Violence*, 2:1, 109–118.

Long, J., Fletcher, T., and Watson, B. (2018) *Sport, Leisure and Social Justice*, London: Routledge.

Hartill, M. and Lang, M. (2018) Official reports of child protection and safeguarding concerns in sport and leisure settings: An analysis of English local authority data, *Leisure Studies*, 37:5, 479–499.

Hill, C. J., Roberts, S. J., and Andrews, H. (2017) 'Why am I putting myself through this?' Women football coaches' experiences of the Football Association's coach education process, *Sport, Education and Society*, 23:1, 28–39.

Hutchings, J., Jones, I., and Fox, D. (2019) Ethnography and autoethnography in researching a Masters swimming community, in Medcalf, R. and Mackintosh, C. (eds) *Researching Difference in Sport and Physical Activity*, London: Routledge, 71–84.

Mackintosh, C. (2012) The shifting dynamics of local government sports development officer practice in England: New identities and hazy professional boundaries, in Harris, S., Bell, B., Adams, A., and Mackintosh C. (eds) *Sport for Sport? Theoretical and Practical Insights into Sports Development*, Brighton: Leisure Studies Association, 113–130.

Mackintosh, C. and Dempsey, C. (2017) The Muslim male youth sport participation puzzle: An examination of the role of identity, religion and ethnicity in determining involvement in sport, *Journal of Youth Studies*, 20:8, 974–996.

Mackintosh, C. and Liddle, J. (2015) Emerging school sport development policy, practice and governance in England: Big Society, autonomy and decentralisation, *Education 3–13*, 43:6, 603–620.

Medcalf, R. and Mackintosh, C. (eds.) (2018) *Researching Difference and Otherness in Sport and Physical Activity*, London: Routledge.

Meir, D. and Fletcher, T. (2017) The transformative potential of using participatory community sport initiatives to promote social cohesion in divided community contexts, *International Review for the Sociology of Sport*, 54:2, 218–238.

Norman, L. (2008) The UK coaching system is failing women coaches, *International Journal of Sports Science and Coaching*, 3:4, 447–464.

Pike, E. (2015) Assessing the sociology of sport: On age and ability, *International Review for the Sociology of Sport*, 50:4–5, 570–574.

Platts, C. and Smith, A. (2009) The education, rights and welfare of young people in professional football in England: Some implications of the White Paper on Sport, *International Journal of Sport Policy and Politics*, 1:3, 323–339.

Porter, C. (2008) Manchester United, global capitalism and local resistance, *Belgeo*, 181–192.

Porter, C. (2015) Loyal to what? FC United's 'shaping walk' through football's 'muck of ages', *Sport in Society*, 18:4, 452-465.

Smith, A. and Leech, R. (2010) 'Evidence. What evidence?': Evidence based policy making and School Sport Partnerships in North West England, *International Journal of Sport Policy and Politics*, 2:3, 327–345.

Sport England (2016) *Towards an Active Nation*, London: Sport England.

Sport NI (2009) *Sport Matters: The Northern Ireland Strategy for Sport and Physical Recreation 2009–2019*, Belfast: Sport NI.

Sport Scotland (2019) *Sport For Life: A Vision for Sport in Scotland*, Glasgow: Sport Scotland.

Sport Wales (2019) *A Vision for Sport*, Cardiff: Sport Wales.

Sporting Equals (2020) *Leaderboard*, available at: www.sportingequals.org.uk/programmes/leaderboard.html [accessed on 27/4/2020].

Thompson, A., Bloyce, D., and Mackintosh, C. (2020) 'It is always going to change' –
managing top-down policy changes by sport development officers working in
national governing bodies of sport in England, *Managing Sport and Leisure: An
International Journal*, iFirst, 1–20.

White, A. and Lang, M. (2018) 'Removing the tackle from schools' rugby: A safeguarding perspective. *British Journal of Sports Medicine*', available at: http://blogs.bmj.
com/bjsm/2018/03/22/removing-the-tackle-from-schools-rugby-a-safeguarding-per-
spective/ [accessed 22/10/2020].

Widdop, P., King, N., Parnell, D., Cutts, D., and Millward, P. (2017) Austerity, policy
and sport participation in England, *International Journal of Sport Policy and Politics*,
10:1, 7–24.

Wilson, R. and Platts, C. (2018) *Managing and Developing Community Sport*, London:
Routledge.

CHAPTER 7

Central government and key national agencies

The chapter will start with a descriptive outline of how government and the state operate in the UK, specifically under devolution and in the context of Brexit. It is this contemporary political context that is unsurprisingly missing from the bulk of books published in 2002–2017. In particular, there is a gap in terms of an introductory book targeting teaching and learning perspective. The book will cover the role and function of the Department of Digital, Culture, Media and Sport (DCMS) and the new strategy (2015) and associated Sport England, Sport Scotland, Sport Wales and Sport Northern Ireland visions and strategy documents. This opens the text to be less Anglo-centric and better for the extensive Northern Irish, Welsh and Scottish students. At present, there are very few case studies and examples in competitor texts with non-England (UK) discussions and examples. Reference will also be made to other central government agencies (Dept. of Health, DEFRA, DCLG) and how they relate to sport development policy and practice. The next chapter will then move into a discussion of the role and function of what will be referred to as 'key national partner agencies'. These will include Sport and Recreation Alliance, CIMSPA, Youth Sport Trust, Active Partnership Network, Street Games, Sporting Equals and Activity Alliance (Disability inclusion sport). They provide national policy partnerships and leverage for deploying resources and strategy that students need to understand. Other agencies with national scope will be covered across other chapters. It is an important theme that 'traditional sport development' partners have already changed and new collaborations across sectors are now crucially located in funding and policy settings. Large private sector after-school sport coaching providers with hundreds of coaches, *parkrun* and Virgin are diverse examples.

Government policy has a central effect on the landscape of elite and community sport development (Houlihan, 1994; Houlihan and Lindsey, 2013; King, 2009). How a government chooses to use sport as a tool in its own politics, or how politics of the time is shaping communities, elite sport events, and aspirations is critical to how an SDO, whether working in local government, an NGB, or an elite sport research agency linked to the delivery of team GB success, is important to acknowledge. This chapter will establish the main national government approaches to sport development and some of the key agencies that operate at the highest level of policy. In recent years, a number of academic studies have focused on the critical analysis of sport development agencies under the 'modernisation' project of New Labour (King, 2009; Houlihan and Lindsey, 2013; Lindsey, 2006, 2008, 2009, 2010, 2013). In particular, they link around a strand of political policy analysis concerned with addressing the ongoing challenge of increasing mass participation through sport development practice. It has been argued that "over the past 20 years one of the constant themes in sport policy discussions has been the fragmentation, fractiousness and perceived ineffectiveness of organizations within the sport policy area" (Houlihan and Green, 2009: 678). More recently, the Coalition government has delivered considerable shifts in the School Sport Partnership (SSP) landscape that originally was set up to bridge PE, school sport, and community sport development in the lead up to the London 2012 Olympics. Most recently, a new policy strategic framework in the UK was set up in the publication of a new sport strategy (DCMS, 2015), new associated strategic frameworks in the home respective nations with their own priorities, and focus was given to the devolution agenda now in place.

Crucially, for the first time, this *Sporting Future: A New Strategy for an Active Nation* (DCMS, 2015) was produced as a cross-government department document. No single department had ownership of this. Whilst very pertinent to the Department of Digital, Culture, Media and Sport (DCMS), as it has the official United Kingdom remit for sport, it aims to make explicit the relevance of wider housing, health, education and environmental agenda. It touches upon business and economy by highlighting the relevance of the sport sector to the economy of mega-events and local/regional sport and physical activity to sub-regional economic systems. In theory, each department now has its role to play. This has considerable implications for SDOs who previous would have perhaps solely engaged in supporting, developing, and managing 'sport for sport sake' (Collins, 2010a; Collins, 2010b). The vision was a five-year plan for investment of over £250 million in targeting areas of need. Whilst the vision and strategy come from documents, decision making, and personnel in DCMS, it is important to be aware that given the inter-disciplinary and cross-cutting nature of SDOs, sport development, and particularly the new DCMS strategy content, many other departments of government are implicated. For example, much sport development work is conducted in school, around physical education (PE), after-school sport, and community use of sport facilities (Collins, 2010b; Mackintosh, 2014).

Now, to differing degrees between home nations, depending on their interpretation, uptake, and engagement with this UK strategy from HM Government, there will be further layers of policy fragmentation and diversification. There are some examples where policy does cut across the HM Government strategy and is implemented equally across Scotland, Wales, and Northern Ireland. First, the governance code for sports is applicable to all areas covered by UK sport and there are obviously some sports that as Olympic sports cover Great Britain's geographically focused governance sports (e.g. British Cycling). There are also some NGBs that are not English, Welsh, and Northern Ireland led so they relate back to the central vision and effectively fall into line with wider English sport.

A useful way to consider sport policy is in relation to 'retained powers' such as that of the military, foreign policy, and, in most cases, tax powers. Here, The United Kingdom government leads and has sovereignty in these areas, whereas sport 'fits' with devolved powers in the three other home nations in policy areas such as health, transport, and education. Obviously, what this means is that the picture of what both sport development implementation, policy, and agencies look like differs considerably across those four national landscapes.

England

Context

It seems fair to assume that most academic research has equated sport development in the United Kingdom to be what happens in England. This is a subtle but important mistake. Indeed, it is possible to consider the other three countries as 'small nations' in terms of their scale, scope, and position (Darko and Mackintosh, 2017; Sam and Jackson, 2016). Consideration of pre-devolution United Kingdom sport policy and development is well documented elsewhere (Houlihan and White, 2002; Harris and Houlihan, 2014). Engaging with and reading the new national strategy (DCMS, 2015) is the only way to understand the depth and reach of its recommended new framework and guidelines for moving sport and physical activity forward. England directly follows this and particularly of interest in this iteration of government sport development policy was a focus on five key strategic outcomes. These include (1) physical wellbeing; (2) mental wellbeing; (3) individual development; (4) social and community development, and (5) economic development. This is a fundamental step change for sport development as for the first time since *Game Plan* (HM Government, 2002) the focus is on softer social and economic policy outcomes of what sport can deliver. Arguably, this shifts the landscape for deliverers who have been working towards traditional or what industry calls 'core' aims, markets, and goals. Sport perhaps becomes less about just getting more people playing more often. Whilst important, how can sport in England use sports clubs and development pathway to achieve social aims? Also, the sport sector needs to be aware of how it looks after its athletes in terms of mental and physical health, an under considered question until now.

England has several major national agencies. The next part of this chapter will look at these in more detail. UK Sport and Home Nation Sports Councils (Sport Wales, Sport Northern Ireland and Sport England and Sport Scotland) are the two key national agencies for students to understand. But, for now, it is important we outline the national government positions that are devolved in relation to sport. Inevitably, these governmental stances, policy positions and resourcing of community and elite sport vary, but are indelibly linked with their home Sports Council who effectively act as the distributor of much of the money for grass roots sport and in many cases elite sport.

Scotland

Context

Scotland is an interesting example of a national devolved sport development policy within the UK. Sport Scotland, for example, are funded by the Scottish government and the National Lottery and report via Scottish ministers to the Scottish Parliament. There is insufficient space for an extensive analysis of sport development policy here. For this, see Houlihan and Lindsey (2013). The country does not need to follow DCMS and the Cabinet Office (HM Government) approaches to sport. You could argue that England has leaned towards a sport for social good agenda (Coalter, 2007) with elements of sport-for-development (Hayhurst, Kay, Chawansky, 2016). In contrast, Scotland has retained a traditional focus on 'sport for sport's sake' (Collins, 2010a) with a belief in the intrinsic value of sport. There is an acknowledgement of how sport is a valuable tool in society, communities, and for individuals. But, it is not a heavily justified economic argument that rationalises central government investment by measurable outcomes and changes in policy goals (mental health, physical health, wellbeing, and so on). For those working in NGBs, local government, charities, and other agencies of sport development in Scotland this is an important and fundamental shift from practice in England. This said, if you look at *Sport for Life: A Vision for Scotland* (Sport Scotland, 2020: online) there are specific themes around economy, physical activity, skills, and strengthening communities. Their specific vision is captured by:

> In an active Scotland we will all find ways to be physically active every day. Keeping moving at home and at work. Taking an active approach to getting around. Choosing to be active in our leisure time. More of us will take part in sport because we see it being relevant to our lives. Being involved in ways that suit us. Meeting fewer barriers. Feeling more included. We will all experience more of the benefits of sport. For some of us, by taking part. For others, through our communities.
>
> (Sport Scotland, 2020: online)

NGBs in Scotland would have a very core focus on delivery of targets around participation, performance, coach education and what some would describe as 'traditional sport development practice'. Systems of delivery are based around a number of policy ideas such as school sport hubs (Sport Scotland, 2015), also branded as Active Schools. These projects have had typically around £12 million investment each year. They stand in contrast to the removal of the school sport partnership system in England in 2010 and the introduction of the primary PE and school premium (PPESP) that has arguably begun building a parallel network of coaching and after school provision outside of state control. This has led to the removal of primary PE duties for many teacher and the opening of contractualisation arrangements with private coaching companies (Griggs, 2010; Griggs, 2012; Griggs, 2018). This is a very strong example how assuming policy is in unison across a national border is a dangerous oversight.

The Sport Scotland Business Plan 2019–2021 identifies the following spe-cific commitments beyond the broad aspirations, policy goals and outcomes framework it sets out:

"We will also support the delivery of specific commitments:

1. increasing the number of community sport hubs to 200 by 2020
2. increasing the participation, engagement, and promotion of women in sport
3. supporting the delivery of two hours of quality PE for children at school
4. supporting the Daily Mile beyond the school setting
5. promoting the benefits of sport and physical activity on mental health
6. helping to make sure major sporting events are successful."

(Sport Scotland, 2019)

These six policy initiatives are a useful point of departure for anyone study-ing sport development across the national boundaries and for students in Scotland to look towards the other three home nations for points of similarity and disagreement. As Cairney (2016) has suggested, not all evidence base for policy is 'rational'; some is based on habit, attitude, belief, and opinion. Good questions to start exploring are why a daily mile, and exactly a mile, why not more, or less? Why two hours of PE? What is meant by focusing on sport and mental health? Why a focus on women, but not on other minority groups?

In February 2019 Sport Scotland Launched the *Scottish Mental Health Charter – Sport Scotland Action Plan* (Sport Scotland, 2019a), which estab-lishes the key areas and priorities for sport development working across Scotland in this policy domain (Table 7.1).

Table 7.1 illustrates how Sport Scotland report on key policy directives and measure their progress over the last five years against these key performance indicators. It gives an indication of performance in sport development from a national policy perspective but should be viewed critically. How are these mea-sured? Do they offer a fair representation of the national population?

Scotland offers opportunities for 900,000 unique sports club memberships in 13,000 clubs coordinated in part through the efforts of 195,000 volunteers (Scottish Sport Association, 2014). This work is further positioned as part of the Scottish sport framework by the Scottish Sport Association (SSA), the rep-resentative body for Scottish Governing Bodies (SGBs) formed in 1982 after a requirement imposed on Sport Scotland after they were formed in 1972 under Royal Charter. The SSA currently represent 50 full members and 18 associate member SGBs (Scottish Sport Association, 2014). This provides the basic framework for sport alongside 697,989 pupils in 2476 schools (Scottish Government, 2019) and leisure centres in local government, sport development officers located in councils, charities, coaches, and professional sports clubs provide the workforce to deliver the vision of Sport Scotland. Finally, it is also worth being aware of the *Active Scotland Outcomes Framework* and partner-ship between multiple agencies in Scotland including Healthier Scotland Scottish Government, and Active Scotland (Scottish Government, 2020: online).

TABLE 7.1 Scottish sport development strategic policy priority areas (data sourced from Sport Scotland, 2019)

Policy theme	Annual reporting data 2015–2019
Participation	12% increase in Active Schools participants (309,000) 18% increase in playing members in clubs (556,000) 11% increase in playing memberships in Scottish Governing Bodies (SGBs) (787,000)
Places	145 sport facility awards £32.2 million invested directly, £155.4m enabled Usage by 16 SGBs
Equality	22% of Active Schools are now from 20% most deprived areas 48% female 5% LGBTQ identified 2% BAME background 8% of adult club members identified as disabled.

This has direct links to physical activity guidelines and the six key outcomes that form the basis for the framework.

Wales

Context

Sport Wales, or the Sports Council for Wales (SCW) as it was formerly known, is also an important home nation to consider as a slightly different entity as a 'small nation state' that has devolved powers in sport. Sport Wales' approach to achieve their Vision for Sport in Wales was set out in a number of strategic documents: *Elite Sport Strategy, Coaching and Volunteering Strategy, Child Poverty Strategy and the Community Sport Strategy* (Sport Wales, 2020: online). The *Community Sport Strategy* responded to the Government's expectations of public sector organisations on such areas as collaboration, delivery, and child poverty. A further key recommendation of the *Simpson Review – a Compact*, drawn up between Welsh Government and local government, provides a foundation for service reform and change at local levels as fundamental here.

The current local government structure was established in 1996, with a sustained debate around its effectiveness. The Welsh Government (2018) identified the initiation of

> a number of Commissions and reports over the last two decades, including the 'Beecham review' into public services, the 'Simpson review' on what services are best delivered where, and the 'Williams Commission'

on public service governance and delivery. Following the 'Williams Commission' recommendations in particular, the Welsh Government attempted to move the change agenda forward.

(The Welsh Assembly, 2018: 1)

For the period 2012–2020 Sport Wales set out how the sport sector could play a role in delivering wider government goals around child poverty and equality. It was also tied into aspirations for the most deprived communities in Wales. From these five strategic documents the country's focus on community sport development was led by the *Community Sport Strategy 2012–2020* (Sport Wales, 2012) focused on five key strategic priorities including sports clubs, local decisions, quality education, committed workforce, and appropriate facilities. Whilst traditional in the areas of policy and practice, it is the tying into national wider social and educational policy agendas that might draw parallels with Sport England as a sister quango. The fact there was a specific Child Poverty Strategy is in itself significant (Welsh Government, 2015).

More recently, the Welsh Government, Sport Wales, and Public Health Wales have established a £5.4m Healthy and Active Fund (HAF) with the specific aim of improving mental and physical health by enabling the adoption of healthy and active lifestyles. This is set up to run from April 2019 to March 2022 focused on strengthening community assets. Again, this is a similar focus to Sport England. It also shows how the day-to-day realities of an SDO moving forward for graduates in Wales will be developing mental health-led activities as opposed to assuming sport delivers some peripheral knock-on impacts. Design, evaluation, and implementation of such projects, understanding client groups, and communities come with nuanced and complex professional needs for the SDO. For example, awareness of how to work with those in diverse states of mental health distress and rehabilitation support in partnership with the NHS and other agencies is varied at best. Mental health is claimed to have considerable benefits from sport, but the processes, tools, and project design for doing so are still in their infancy.

Further projects are aimed to target deprived communities, older people, those around retirement age, and BAME women. Fundamentally, the income supporting the project is a cross-government income partnership. This also shows the 'partnership' concept in action and how individual teams and people are working to put funds in place to deal with complex issues that perhaps need multi-agency approach to address.

Additional change may be expected after a review of community sport development systems in Wales (Baker, 2017) where wider countries including New Zealand, Germany, and England were considered for partnership style delivery platforms at regional-local level. In this study Baker (2017: 1) argues for "A renewed focus on partnership working, targeted investment, user-led approaches and improvements in efficiency are likely to help create conditions for more effective delivery community sport development initiatives". In this he argues for regional sport agencies (RSAs) embedded in the coordination of community sport, possibly similar to what in England are now referred to as

Active Partnerships. This situation is ongoing, and the development of pilots is a potential route for testing the validity of the research. A total of 11 core recommendations were made; it may be worth exploring future policy outcomes in terms of how much uptake they offer. This key report will be explored in further detail in the case study. In parallel to these policy recommendations was *The Sport Wales Review: An Independent Report* on the scope and role of Sport Wales undertaken by independent panel members (Sport Wales, 2017). The scope of this review was to specifically examine:

- The current vision, aspirations, and strategic intent of Sport Wales in relation to achieving the government priorities and objectives;
- The current Sport Wales strengths, weaknesses, and opportunities in the delivery of these government priorities and objectives;
- How the delivery of these objectives can support the Wellbeing of Future Generations (Wales) Act 2015;
- The well-being outcome measures that Sport Wales could contribute to most effect;
- Learning and insight from other countries around creating a more active, healthy, and successful nation;
- The areas that Sport Wales should be targeting or influencing investment to have the greatest impact against the Welsh Government priorities;
- The appetite and capacity of Sport Wales to create innovative approaches to achieve in its objectives.

(Sport Wales, 2017: 5)

The current investment in Sport Wales by the Welsh Government at this time in 2017–2018 was £22.52m. This is a significantly smaller allotted investment budget than Sport England. But whilst income is one thing, coordination of policy is another. The independent review stated that

> Whichever document was regarded as the reference point for the strategic policy direction for sport in Wales, there was consensus that the strategy was about sport and its contribution to society, the economy, and the health of the nation as well as 'sport for sport's sake'. However, while the agenda was clear, there was a lack of clarity in terms of the connection between different parts of Welsh Government and the strategic alignment of policies, outcomes, investment priorities and measures.

(Sport Wales, 2017: 7)

This mirrored concerns by Baker (2017) in his study of community sport development delivery, partnership, and infrastructure options for the country of Wales. Again, detailed analysis of this policy period in Wales remains undone in academic terms. The implications of sport development's turbulent journey in the last decade alongside the devolution policy pathway leaves much still to be learned on the Welsh context for sport development.

Northern Ireland

Context

The starting point for the driver of policy is the central government agency responsible for sport in Northern Ireland known as Sport Northern Ireland (Sport NI). However, politics and the agency of sport development is never this simplistic. Variations across national devolved government boundaries, regional strategic agencies, and interactions with national governing bodies with different regional presences paints a fait more nuanced picture for the communities in this country. Here it is worth acknowledging a number of subtle nuances that may be new to some students. First, there is no sport department or agency that acts solely for sport in this country. Likewise, in the United Kingdom Whitehall government the department is the Department for Digital, Culture, Media and Sport (DCMS), which has undergone much reshaping since the 2010 change of government and is now working towards the delivery of its Towards an Active Nation Strategy (2015). This vision and strategic document for the UK is then something that agencies at national, regional, and local level position themselves with. It is the first new strategy since Game Plan in 2002 published by the Labour government of the time. Many of the existing textbooks on sport development cover the principles, history, and practices of the profession but do so without full reference to the period 2015–2020. Here is where this book considers itself important in giving students an insight into the contemporary sport development policy, practices, and processes that have begun to emerge from this critical new vision. In the case of Northern Ireland, the key agency is the quango and 'arms-length' agency *Sport NI*. Their strategy vision, *The Northern Ireland Strategy for Sport & Physical Recreation 2009–2019* (Sport Northern Ireland, 2013), established a view for how sport and physical activity could be delivered in the nation. In this country the sport development strategy had a three-pillared approach in sport development terms. First, mass participation and all this encompasses in relation to volunteers, sports clubs, and schools as well as adult target group populations. Second, performance and the elite pathways of sport development. Finally, 'places', the settings, and spaces to deliver sport and improvements in such facilities. In some ways, the Sport Northern Ireland vision looked more like the traditional sport development viewpoint with ideological and theoretical standpoints from a more distant time. The other three home nations seem to have moved towards a more social policy-led vision for sport and active recreation and not followed the 'sport for sports sake' policy rhetoric identified by some researchers (Collins, 2010a; Sport Wales, 2017). In many ways it also contains a good degree of continuation from the previous national policy, *The Strategy for the Development of Sport, 1997–2005* (Sport Northern Ireland, 1997).

Sport in Northern Ireland comes with its own complex nuances politically due to the historic layers of meanings, unrest, and violence that underpinned the evolution of the country. Local government, national governing bodies of sport, and cultural activities all have close political and cultural ties to parties on various sides of divides. Technically, with a devolved Parliament from London power rests with the parties, and power share of people and democracies in Northern Ireland. Likewise, decision making around sport and physical activity has also to be shared in such a way. Parliament and funding from Northern Ireland are driven through the national strategy. Balancing the binary policy priorities of mass participation and elite success remains a core focus of the strategy, although this is in contrast to the other home nations where this polarisation on two specific foci seems to have shifted (Sport England; Sport Scotland, 2019, 2019a; Sport Wales, 2020).

Specific core focuses for the government and sport development agencies in the country by 2019 were to be:

- Establish 'Active Schools Partnerships' linking health, education and community sport;
- Establish a network of multi skills clubs;
- To pursue a target for 2 hours physical education and sport per week;
- In consultation with children and young people, provide the opportunity for every child to access two hours extra-curricular sport and physical recreation per week through initiatives such as Extended Schools, Active Schools, and community sport programmes;
- Establish NI's facility needs and focus investment in line with identified priorities;
- Deliver a NI-wide network of accredited inclusive fitness facilities;
- Deliver a world class training programme and elite participant support offer.

(Sport Northern Ireland, 2013)

The above is intended as an indication of some of the policy drivers in Northern Ireland, and not meant as an exhaustive list. It is, however, useful to note that some of the more traditional areas of policy crossover with Scotland and some of the more welfare 'cross-cutting' social and health policy engines of sport development policy are not as present as in Wales and England. Furthermore, it is important to be aware that one change in minister or a variation in opinion on policy can move and shape existing alignments far beyond where they currently sit. This said, the above section is intended as an overview of the national policy context in each of the home nations.

▬▬▬▬ CASE STUDY 7.1 ▬▬▬▬

Mental health and wellbeing – what role for sport?

Many of the governments of the UK have considered a key role for sport and physical activity in addressing issues around poor mental health and community wellbeing. Sport Wales (Sport Wales, 2012), Sport Scotland (Sport Scotland, 2019a) and Sport England (Sport England, 2016, 2018, 2020) have outlined the role for sport to deliver in and through clubs, schools, programmes, and tailored projects specific to mental health. Projects such as the new £1.5million *Get, Set, Go* by Mind (Mind, 2020) are an example of where individuals are offered opportunities to play sport, but with a 'wrap-around' set of implementation features on a programme. Just running a project and saying it is a good for mental health does not show evidence of delivering such policy aims. Instead, features such as peer-support, counselling access, and a well training workforce in the specific challenges of the client group population are examples of how a local project may work well.

Other examples of this include *Everton Football in the Community Blues Project* (Everton FC, 2020), which has shown evidence of impact on local communities using the power and 'hook' of football to engage people but then with innovative design it has developed individuals that have attended to address challenges they face in mental health. Both these projects are examples of how a national policy theme, direction, or idea can filter down to the local (or what is known in sociology and politics as the 'micro' level). This is not to say that for all SDOs a new policy area linked to the DCMS (2015) vision will be helpful. Indeed, some NGBs may resist uptake of 'new areas', being more comfortable with their core business around sport clubs, pathways, and performance. The difficulty is that government as we discussed in the section on modernisation and professionalisation now 'pays by results' (Harris and Houlihan, 2016). So, power from above is inevitably felt by organisations if they rely, as many do on the money from home nation Sports Councils.

Seminar questions

1. Choosing one of the home nation countries – what is its national sport policy document?
2. What is its position on mental health and sport? (How does it express this?)
3. How might a NGB, local authority, and a charity interpret the main messages differently?
4. Why has mental health been linked to sport and physical activity and why is it important to central government?

Extension task

Locate and read the article below, which reviews the role of sport and physical in addressing, supporting, and intervening in mental health. Take notes on:

a. How was the piece of work carried out?
b. What were the main 'headline themes'?
c. What are the implications for sport development policy in the country you have chosen.

Further reading

Smith, A., Jones, J., Houghton, L., and Duffell, T. (2016) A political spectator sport or policy priority? A review of sport, physical activity and public mental health policy, *International Journal of Sport Policy and Politics*, 8:4 593–607.

References

Baker, C. (2017) *Coordination of Community Sport Development in Wales: An Investigation of Stakeholder Perspectives Concerning the Organisation and Structure of Community Sport in Wales*, Gloucester: University of Gloucester.

Cairney, P. (2016) *The Politics of Evidence-Based Policy Making*, London: Palgrave.

Coalter, F. (2007) *A Social Role for Sport: Whose Keeping the Score?*, London: Routledge.

Collins, M. (2010a) From 'sport for good' to 'sport for sport's sake' – not a good move for sports development in England?, *International Journal of Sport Policy and Politics*, 2:3, 367–379.

Collins, M. (2010b) *Examining Sports Development*, London; Routledge.

Darko, N. and Mackintosh, C. (2017) Challenges and constraints in developing and implementing sports policy and provision in Antigua and Barbuda: Which way now for a small island state?, *International Journal of Sport Policy and Politics*, 7:3, 365–390.

DCMS (2015) *Sporting Nation*, London: DCMS.

Everton Football Club (2020) *Everton FC in the community: Tackling the blues*, available at: www.evertonfc.com/community/health-and-wellbeing/the-projects/tackling-the-blues [accessed on 29 April 2020].

Griggs, G. (2010) For sale – primary physical education. £20 per hour or nearest offer, *Education 3–13*, 38:1, 39–46.

Griggs, G. (2012) Standing on the touchline of chaos. Explaining the development of sports coaching in primary schools with the aid of complexity theory, *Education 3–13 40*, 259–269.

Griggs, G. (2018) Investigating provision and impact of the primary physical education and sport premium: A West Midlands case study, *Education 3–13*, 46:5, 517–524.

Harris, S. and Houlihan, B. (2014) Delivery networks and community sport in England, *International Journal of Public Sector Management*, 27:2, 113–127.

Harris, S. and Houlihan, B. (2016) Implementing the community sport legacy: The limits of partnerships, contracts and performance management, *European Sports Management Quarterly*, 16:4, 433–458.

Hayhurst, L. M. C., Kay, T. and Chawansky, M. (eds) (2016) *Beyond Sport for Development and Peace: Transnational Perspectives on Theory, Policy and Practice*, London: Routledge.

HM Government (2002) *Game Plan*, London: Cabinet Office/DCMS.

Houlihan, B. (1994) *Sport Policy and Politics; A Comparative Agenda*, London: Routledge.

Houlihan, B. and Green, M. (2009) Modernisation and sport: The reform of Sport England and UK Sport, *Public Administration*, 87:3, 678–698.

Houlihan, B. and Lindsey, I. (2013) *Sport Policy in Britain*, London: Routledge.

Houlihan, B. and White, A. (2002) *The Politics of Sports Development*, London: Routledge.

King, N. (2009) *Sport Policy and Governance*, Oxford: Butterworth-Heinemann.

Lindsey, I. (2006) Local partnerships in the United Kingdom for the new opportunities for PE and sport programme: A policy network analysis, *European Sport Management Quarterly*, 6:2, 167–184.

Lindsey, I. (2008) Conceptualising sustainability in sports development, *Leisure Studies*, 27:3, 279–294.

Lindsey, I. (2009) Collaboration in local sport services in England: Issues emerging from case studies of two local authority areas, *International Journal of Sport Policy*, 1:1, 71–88.

Lindsey, I. (2010) Governance of lottery sport programmes: National direction of local partnerships in the new opportunities for PE and sport programme, *Managing Leisure: An International Journal* 15:3, 198–213.

Lindsey, I (2013) Prospects for local collaboration into an uncertain future: Learning from practice within Labour's partnership paradigm, *Local Government Studies*, 40:2, 312–330.

Mackintosh, C. (2014) Dismantling the school sport partnership infrastructure: Findings from a survey of physical education and school sport practitioners, *Education 3–13*, 42:4, 432–449.

Mind (2020) *Mind and Sport England extend Get Set to Go programme*, available at: www.mind.org.uk/news-campaigns/news/mind-and-sport-england-extend-get-set-to-go-programme/ [accessed on 27 April 2020]

Sam, M. and Jackson, S. (eds) (2016) *Sport Policy in Small States*, London: Routledge.

Scottish Government (2019) *Summary statistics for schools in Scotland: 10 December 2019*, Edinburgh: Scottish Government.

Scottish Government (2020) *Active Scotland Delivery Plan*, available at: www.gov.scot/publications/active-scotland-delivery-plan/ [accessed on 29 April 2020].

Scottish Sport Association (2014) '*Representing and Supporting Scottish Governing Bodies of Sport' Strategic Framework 2014–2020*, Edinburgh, Scotland.

Sport England (2016) *Towards an Active Nation*, London: Sport England.

Sport England (2018) *The Coaching Plan for England: Two years on*, London: Sport England.

Sport England (2020) *Shaping Our Future*, London: Sport England.

Sport NI (2013*) The Northern Ireland Strategy for Sport & Physical Recreation 2009–2019*, Belfast: Sport NI.

Sport Northern Ireland (1997) *The Strategy for the Development of Sport, 1997–2005*, Belfast, Sport NI.

Sport Scotland (2015) *Raising the Bar: Corporate Plan 2015–2019*, Glasgow, Sport Scotland.

Sport Scotland (2019) *The Sport Scotland Business Plan 2019–2021*, Glasgow: Sport Scotland.

Sport Scotland (2019a) *Scottish Mental Health Charter – Sport Scotland action plan*, Glasgow: Sport Scotland.

Sport Scotland (2020) *Sport for Life: a Vision for Scotland*, Glasgow: Sport Scotland.

Sport Wales (2012) *Community Sport Strategy 2012–2020*, Cardiff: Sport Wales.

Sport Wales (2017) *Sport Wales Review: Independent Report*, Cardiff: Sport Wales.

Sport Wales (2020) *Vision for Sport in Wales*, Cardiff: Sport Wales.

The Welsh Assembly (2018) *Public Service Reform in Post-devolution Wales: A Timeline of Local Government Developments – Research Briefing*, Cardiff: The Welsh Assembly.

Welsh Government (2015) *Child Poverty Strategy for Wales*, Cardiff: Welsh Government.

Welsh Government (2018) *Public Service Reform in Post-devolution Wales: A Timeline of Local Government Developments*, Cardiff: The Welsh Government.

CHAPTER 8

National agencies and key charities

Beyond the government departments and their associated respective arm's length quasi-non-governmental organisation (QUANGO) lies a diverse and complex array of agencies, organisations, and Third Sector institutions. Famously, one of the most dedicated researchers of the sport development sector described this area as a 'convoluted bowl of spaghetti' (Collins, 2010). A better, more simple, yet fitting quote it is hard to find. In mapping the sector and supporting your learning around who these agencies are, it is now increasingly necessary to consider each country in isolation as a picture of a unified and equitable United Kingdom system of sport development is not one that it is possible to paint.

England
Active Partnerships

A strong feature of the English system are the sub-regional system of partnerships and their networks now referred to as Active Partnerships. These 43 partnerships across the country emerged out of the embers of the dying original Active Partnerships Network in 2005 (see Mackintosh, 2011; Philpotts, Quarmby and Grix, 2010 for detailed historical accounts mapping their roots). These were multi-sport programmes at regional level targeted at the traditional realm of increasing sport participation. They were re-branded *County Sport Partnerships* and started off with 49 bodies hugely varied in staffing size, geographical scope, and organisational status (CSPN, 2015). Some were, and remain, charities, some were limited companies, and some were little more than a move of building for a County Council sport development unit. They have received various forms of research attention as a subject of research (Baker, El Ansari, and Crone, 2016; Philpotts et al., 2010: Mackintosh, 2008; Mackintosh, 2011). Some have argued that they constitute a fragile form of partnership with central Sport England funding a constant threat. Others considered how they offer a centralised vehicle for national sport policy at the local level (Philpotts et al., 2010).

Most recently, they have been overseen by the Active Partnerships Network (APN), formerly CSPN, that provides strategic network and support for all 43 partnerships. They are a key strategic agency and set the vision, framework, and targets for an area; whether Yorkshire or Greater Manchester, the different geographical contexts are crucial to shaping this vision. They are also now in some cases some of the largest individual employers in sport development, in some areas replacing the traditional bias towards large county council sport development and leisure units.

In England, they house many of the Sport England national pilots and as such are home to new ideas in how to deal with patterns of complex inactivity or barriers against inclusion. They can house sport development staff in diverse roles such as coaching, school sport, health and inactivity, and community development. Most have an insight team that undertakes data collection and research projects and they have backroom support in finance, marketing, and human resources. They are answerable to their boards, which are independent and act as 'check and challenge' figures to their work and ways of operating. All 43 receive core funding from Sport England, but also aim to draw down funding from an increasingly diverse range of wider funding sources to facilitate sustainability and advancement of their role.

Sport and Recreation Alliance

'The Alliance' or Sport and Recreation Alliance in their full organisational title are a form of trade association for the sport development and wider activity physical sector. They play a key role in policy advocacy and campaigning in the sector whether directly in the Houses of Parliament, select committees or All Party Parliamentary Groups (APPGs). For example, there is a DCMS select committee for sport, which they may be invited to present, discuss or be questioned on, around a policy issue or evidence. Furthermore, the APPGs include groups on areas such as golf where it may be the Sport and Recreation Alliance (SRA) seek experts and research evidence to support motions presented.

The Alliance operates where members join their association and for this they get membership benefits, supports, access to training and become part of a wider network. They perhaps best reflect an organisation that can help members get agendas onto the wider political agenda. This theme is one that Girginov (2008) predicted would become one that all national and local agencies in sport development would need to undertake more and more moving forward. An example of this is their work on *Reconomics* and the outdoor recreation sector, which provides an indication of how a local and regional topic was taken into debates in the House of Parliament (Mackintosh, Griggs, and Tate, 2019).

Street Games

Street Games are the largest national 'sport for good' charity in the UK. They draw their income from multiple sources and run on a partnership and network model where they have a central 'brand', training packages, and evaluation systems. They work across diverse geographical settings in England and in places that include sports hall, community centres, youth sport facilities, and open spaces. They have a central focus on disadvantaged communities and aiming to improve the lives of young people in these places through sport and physical activity. The organisation is made up of the Street Games Alliance, a collective of over 1000 agencies and institutions. Most of these are either a Community interest Company (CiC) or a local legally constituted club. Over 9000 learners have been through the activator learning project (Street Games, 2020). A major headline programme was the £20m *Door Step Sport* project targeting 100,000 young people in 1000 organisations across the Alliance (Street Games, 2018). They also encapsulate the partnership and network approach predicted by academics study sport development ten years earlier (Adams, 2008; Girginov, 2008; Lindsey, 2008; Mackintosh, 2008; Mackintosh, 2011). Furthermore, for example, in the summer of 2016, 32 projects were delivered by the *Coca-Cola ParkLives* programme in 37 parks, engaging 2230 participants against a target of 1480 participants. For some, whether major American Global organisations should be delivering events in UK community parks should be contested. For Street Games, they argue, however, for taking an Asset-based Community Activation (ABCA) approach, which is bottom up, not top down and hence this is an alternative area of sport development provision to others that 'receive' a product and deliver it ubiquitously in the same manner across the country. This also is a return to the 1970s and 1980s philosophy and approach of local SDO work in what is termed community development.

Active Communities Network

Another key agency in a similar sector as Street Games is the Active Communities Network (ACN). This agency is a network of partnerships with organisations and deprived communities that works at the intersection of sporting inclusion, sport-for-development, and with strong traditions in youth work. Founded in 2003, and now with around 65 directly employed staff, plus a wider volunteer and mentor network, ACN offers a clear example of the existence of sport development principles from another era. They prioritise outreach work and bottom up listening to the voices of young people in the UK's most deprived and complex areas such as Belfast, Hampshire, London, and Manchester. Projects are bespoke but draw heavily on the methodology and sport-for-development processes ACN has shaped over the last 16 years of its existence. SDOs are encouraged to 'know' their communities, engage with them, and consider the needs they have before dropping initiatives from upon high. This organic approach to sport development stands in stark contrast to the more modernised and 'professional' constructs of sport development we may read of or that which policy alludes to. Acknowledging the messiness, complexity, and fluidity of diverse and changing communities is at the heart of ACN's work and ethos. It is also arguably its strength. Recent evaluation reports they have undertaken with partners have shown positive approaches resulting in the establishment of outstanding relationships with the most complex young people around higher challenging issues (ACN, 2020).

Sporting Equals

This is a fundamentally important organisation to the sport development sector. They were first set up in 1998 as a body to address and consider inequalities in 'race' and ethnicity in the sector (Long, Robinson, and Spracklen, 2005), not long after the Race Equality Charter for Sport was brought in in 2000. The co-aims of these two policy developments are where sport development's original national remit in equality around race and equality lies. In particular, they identified inequalities by gender and social background for Black and Asian Ethnic Minority (BAME) groups in areas as diverse as coaching, officiating, administration, leadership, and participating. They have close links with anti-racism campaign organisations such as Lets Kick Out Racism (English FA – football) and NGB-driven equality projects such as England and Wales Cricket Board's *Breaking Boundaries* and Rugby Football League's *Rugby League Cares*. Much of their work is also informed by research and evidence, now evident from decades of longstanding and systematic and structural racism within England that act as very real barriers to progression. This is a key area of work for SDOs historically and now is largely covered under areas such as diversity and equity approaches and initiatives. For example, England Golf in their National Volunteer Plan (2018) aimed to address inequality and recruit more BAME volunteers in senior community club roles as well as address participation. This work relates to national advocacy and media work undertaken by Sporting Equals. This is a theme we will return to throughout the book.

Disability organisations

Equity and equality also relate to physical and mental impairments in the field of sport development. They also have close links to the roots of the sport development movement. The organisation previously known as the *English Federation of Disability Sport* (EFDS) was established to challenge the status quo around inequalities in access, participation, coaching, and opportunities in general. It is now branded as the *Activity Alliance* who run campaigns such as 'Says Who?', which sets out to challenge negative perceptions of disabled people around physical activity. In addition, there are eight National Disability Sport Organisations (NDSOs): British Blind Sport, Cerebral Palsy Sport, Dwarf Sports Association UK, LimbPower, Mencap, Special Olympics Great Britain, UK Deaf Sport, and WheelPower.

Local sports clubs often lack awareness of the most basic ways of making environments and sessions inclusive to all. Coaches had to move through a period where they had to embrace a social model of disability as opposed to a medicalised model where people are classified, objectified, and branded as disabled. In contrast, a more social model would begin to see disabled people for their multiple abilities, as opposed to disabilities that may limit them. It remains a complex area of policy but hence there is a lead agency in England in this area. Many local sub-regional bodies in England whether county council sport units or Active Partnerships may also have officers responsible for disability and equity. Furthermore, as organisations like Sport England and, historically, the EFDS invested and innovated in new areas and diversified where they worked and funded, so a wider network of organisations have emerged in this domain. Recent research has shown that austerity and financial impact of national policy have affected this provision (Walker and Hayton, 2017). But, also working in this area increasingly is also done so under the partnership proviso similar to Street Games in the deprivation area. Disability organisations working in sport find multiple challenges to engage with their potential audiences, which shows there is still a long way to go (Ives et al., 2020).

Youth Sport Trust

In England, a key policy advocate for the role of sport, PE, and physical activity in the school landscape has been the Youth Sport Trust (YST). Overseen in its leadership by Baroness Sue Campbell since its inception, it was established as part lobby and advocacy group, part training agency for teachers in practice. It had initial success over 20 years ago with the establishment of programmes such as TOP Play and TOP Sport national initiatives aimed at bringing kit, equipment, and training to schools in England and Wales. Many teachers have since benefitted from the resources of various formats they have developed. Indeed, they also have been integral to the development of the development of the School Sport Partnership system, which put in place support from primary link tutors (based in secondary schools) with their local network of primary school. They established a system of School Sport Coordinators (SSCs) as well and parallel in-service training for school staff. Monitoring of the effectiveness of the system has been questioned (Ives, 2014; Smith and Leech, 2010). But part of the embedded system was to develop a process and pathway for creating a sustainable participation legacy from the award of the Olympics to London in 2005.

Between 2005 and 2010, what cannot questioned was that a concerted effort was put in by the YST and the national network of schools to build improved quality levels of school sport, amounts of after school sport and physical activity and develop the School Games system in a mirror of the future London 2012 mega-event. The YST is critical to the history and current sport development landscape as in 2010 Michael Gove, the then education minister, decreed that the system be dismantled. This was met with public outcry and elite sport athletes that saw the importance of PE, sport, and physical activity in their school journey set about campaigning. This led to a very partial temporary turn-around. But, ultimately, the SSP system was dismantled two years before London 2012 leaving a fragmented, disjointed, and 'patchwork' level of provision (Mackintosh, 2014; Mackintosh and Liddle, 2015). It also repositioned the role of the YST for the next decade to more of a policy advocacy, advisory, and campaign group. See Houlihan and Lindsey (2013) for a more detailed analysis of this agency and its historical positioning in the UK.

Wales

The Welsh Sport Association was established to support NGBs in Wales. It works in the domain of supporting and developing governance arrangements of NGBs and national associations. It can offer training support for such NGBs and advisory and consultancy support in governance arrangements. More recently, it has also undertaken internal research exercises to assess its own impact. The Federation of Disability Sport for Wales as founded in 1985 and oversees a similar role to its English counterpart as a 'pan-disability' lobby, advocacy, and support group for participation and performance in this area.

Scotland

The Scottish Sport Association was formed in 1982 as a result of a condition of the royal charter foundation in 1972 of Sport Wales. It supports 50 SGBs and 18 associate member SGBs. It, like its Welsh counterpart, offers support specifically in governance, legal advice, policy advocacy, and oversight. It also has a research function capacity, although this is not a central avenue of the mainstay of its work.

Northern Ireland

The Northern Ireland Sport Forum (NISF) is the parallel agency in Northern Ireland acting as "the voice of voluntary sport in Northern Ireland" (NISF, 2020: online). They currently represent 71 NGBs, 24 associate members and 14 individual members, although these numbers can change if a newly approved activity becomes a designated sport with associated NGB for example. Or, if an agency decides it wishes to have their support and buy their services. It is also worth acknowledging that between England, Ireland, Scotland, and Northern Ireland there are some NGBs that sit in their natural home nation. Northern Ireland is a really good example of this, with some sport uniquely culturally represented across the country in activities such as Camogie. This is a (generally) a female-only sport that has a global participation population of over 100,000, and the NGB is the Ulster Camogie Council. Other NGBs that have a rather unique location in Norther Ireland culture and sport governance landscape include Ulster GAA, Ulster Ladies Gaelic and the two cricket NGBs for the region (NISF, 2020: online).

In 2017 NISF and the All Party Group on Sport and Recreation launched the New NISF Governance Code for Sport (NISF, 2017). This established the foundations of governance for sport development in the country going forward. It was designed in partnership with a wide-ranging group of individual organisations including Sport Northern Ireland, Disability Sport Northern Ireland, and Outdoor Recreation Northern Ireland alongside many NGBs. Between 2017 and 2020 a number of NGBs began reshaping their boards, operating processes, and governance approaches. Examples include Camogie, Canoe Northern Ireland, and Disability Sport Northern Ireland where the principles of best practice were used to redesign the sport development landscape of the country. These are interesting case studies to explore and also show useful comparators across the UK national boundaries.

▐ CASE STUDY 8.1 ▐

National agencies and the disability sport development context

Each of the four home nations has a unique political and historical background to its sport development system. It has layers of organisational complexity in a kind of public policy 'soup'. In aiming to untangle sport development agencies that co-exist alongside national government and national quangos such as Sports Councils, it can be one of the harder steps for students to take in their learning journey. Assuming we can visualise a national state agency (DCMS, Scottish government, Welsh Assembly, Northern Ireland Assembly), then we can see the home nation Sports Council that is funded and supported by that government (Sport England, Sport Scotland, Sport Wales, and Sport Northern Ireland).

But where things shift, is when 'layers' onto this model become nuanced, with different organisations and cultures across the countries. A really good example is comparing each of the four countries with the national approach to sub-regional agencies. This is not local government (e.g. Manchester City Council or Cardiff County Council). However, it is a tier of agencies that are established by national policy and have a national role in implementing public policy ideas. If we take the example of disability sport and trying to give communities, families, and individuals equal access to disability sport sessions, this has different agencies across countries and even regions. In England, for example, there are sub-regional agencies called Active Partnerships to help with strategic work in this area. In Wales there is consultation on whether to include similar structures (Baker, 2017). Scotland and Northern Ireland don't have such sub-regional features in their sport development landscape. All four home nations have a national agency for disability sport. But, the strata (meaning 'layers') of disability sport provision also encompass differential health and social care systems, allocation of funding for care, charity 'presence', transport support, and approaches by different home nation NGBs. So, for example, how the English and Scottish FA approach facilitation of activity for people that may have a disability is driven by financial and human resource but also cultural inclination and perceptions. This is sometimes referred to as the concept of 'ableism' where people can be socially defined as 'able to do' as opposed to perceived as disabled (Ives et al., 2020). If you begin to analyse the rich complexity of this field it can seem overwhelming, but it is why we are slowly unpicking this thread as opposed to assuming knowledge and understanding.

Seminar task

How many sport specific disability agencies can you find in one of the home nations? (Pick one you do not normally explore.)

a. How many of these are 'national' in their remit?

b. What is a difficulty in what you have found?

c. What might somebody or their family with a disability sport and physical activity experience?

Seminar question

Read Ives et al. (2020) and consider the key issues in disability sport provision emerging from this research with disability organisations:

- Key themes;
- Future recommendations;
- How has this helped your understanding of national agencies in sport development in disability sport?

References

Active Communities Network (ACN) (2020) *How we started*, available at: www.activecommunities.org.uk/ourstory [accessed on 29 April 2020].

Adams, A. (2008) Building organisational and management capacity for the delivery of sports development, in Girginov, V. (ed.) *Management of Sports Development*, Oxford: Butterworth-Heinemann, 203–224.

Baker, C. (2017) *Coordination of Community Sport Development in Wales: An Investigation of Stakeholder Perspectives Concerning the Organisation and Structure of Community Sport in Wales*, Gloucester: University of Gloucester.

Baker, C., El Ansari, W., and Crone, D. (2016) Partnership working in sport and physical activity promotion: An assessment of processes and outcomes in community sports networks, *Public Policy and Administration*, 32:2, 87–109.

Collins, M. (2010) *Examining Sport Development*, London: Routledge.

County Sport Partnership Network (CSPN) (2015) *'Good to Great' Mission Strategy Summary*, London: CSPN.

Girginov, V. (ed.) (2008) *Management of Sports Development*, Oxford: Butterworth Heinemann.

Lindsey, I. (2008) Conceptualising sustainability in sports development, *Leisure Studies*, 27:3, 279–294.

Houlihan, B. and Lindsey, I. (2013) *Sport Policy in Britain*, London, Routledge.

Ives, B., Clayton, B., Brittain, I. and Mackintosh, C. (2020) 'I'll always find a perfectly justified reason for not doing it': Challenges for disability sport and physical activity in the United Kingdom, *Sport in Society*, iFirst 1–19.

Ives, H. M. (2014) 'The social construction of physical education and school sport: Transmission, transformation and realization'. *PhD thesis*, University of Bedfordshire.

Long, J. Robinson, P., and Spracklen, K. (2005) Promoting racial equality within sport organisations, *Journal of Sport and Social Issues*, 29:1, 41–59.

Mackintosh, C. (2008) Bonding issues: Partnership working in sports development. *Recreation*, 20–21.

Mackintosh, C. (2011) An analysis of County Sports Partnerships in England: The fragility, challenges and complexity of partnership working in sport development, *International Journal of Sport Policy and Politics*, 3:1, 45–64.

Mackintosh, C. (2014) Dismantling the school sport partnership infrastructure: Findings from a survey of physical education and school sport practitioners, *Education 3–13: International Journal of Primary, Elementary and Early Years*, 42:4, 432–449.

Mackintosh, C., Griggs, G., and Tate, R. (2019) Understanding the growth in outdoor recreation: An opportunity for sport development in the United Kingdom, *Managing Sport and Leisure: An International Journal*, 23:4–6, 1–19.

Mackintosh, C. and Liddle, J. (2015) Emerging school sport development policy, practice and governance in England: Big Society, autonomy and decentralisation, *Education 3–13: International Journal of Primary, Elementary and Early Years*, 43:6, 603–620.

Northern Ireland Sport Forum (NISF) (2017) *NISF Governance Code for Sport*, Belfast: NISF.

Northern Ireland Sport Forum (NISF) (2020) *Northern Ireland Sport Forum: Background*, available at: www.nisf.net/about-us/background/ [accessed on 29 April 2020]

Philpotts, L., Grix, J., and Quarmby, T. (2010) Centralised grass roots policy and 'new governance': A case study of County Sport Partnerships in the UK – unpacking the paradox, *International Review for the Sociology of Sport*, 46:3, 265–281.

Smith, A. and Leech, R. (2010) 'Evidence. What evidence?': Evidence-based policy making and school sport partnerships in North West England, *International Journal of Sport Policy and Politics*, 2:3, 327–345.

Street Games (2018) *Park lives with Street Games 2018 Report*, Manchester: Street Games.

Street Games (2020) *What we do*, available at: www.streetgames.org/what-we-do [accessed on 29 April 2020].

Walker, C. M. and Hayton, J. W. (2017) Navigating austerity: Balancing 'desirability with viability' in a third sector disability sports organisation, *European Sports Management Quarterly*, 17:1, 98–116.

CHAPTER 9

Local authority sport development

Local government is still the largest provider of sport facilities in the UK. Sport development is, of course, not about facilities; it is more the domain of sport facility management. But, as sport development in the home nations is asked to do more with less in this time of austerity (Nichols et al., 2014; Widdop et al., 2017), it is ever more critical to consider and reposition the role of local government. This chapter will offer a conceptualisation of how this tier of government fits with central government, provide an overview of sport and leisure in local government nationally, and analyse how sport development operates in local government. It will also consider the changing role of local government post-2008 cuts in local funding and austerity measures. It will also consider the specific role of the local authority sport development officer as their role changed from 'tracksuits to suits' (Bloyce et al., 2008; Mackintosh, 2012) during modernisation processes. The chapter will reflect on how local government leisure provision is changing (movement towards charitable trusts, community interest charities (CICs), and outsourcing) and how these trends are affecting sport development practice but also are a reflection of central government policy and wider global trends. The chapter will draw specifically on landmark research with the Chief Leisure Officers Association (CLOA) by King (2014) to position a new way of understanding sport at local government level. The chapter will also make links with lottery funding, external new sources of funding approaches, and wider partnership working. The growing priority of health in local government and sport's role in delivering this agenda will also be considered.

Scale of local government

In the United Kingdom there are 408 principal (unitary, upper, and second tier) councils, 26 county councils, 192 district councils, and 190 unitary councils. The breakdown by country is most complex within England. England has 343 principal councils. Table 9.1 shows the breakdown of local authority by type of council (Table 9.1).

TABLE 9.1 Breakdown of local authorities by type in England, 2019–2020

Type of council	Number
County council (upper tier)	26
District (lower tier)	192
London borough (unitary)	32
Metropolitan borough (unitary)	36
Unitary authorities (unitary)	55
Sui generis authorities[a] (unitary)	2

a Relate to unique geographical or political cases in the UK
Source: Department for Communities, Local Government and the Regions, 2019

The picture is simpler in Wales, which has 22 unitary authorities, alongside Scotland with 32 unitary authorities and Northern Ireland that has 11 unitary authorities. Each council is run by elected councillors in local elections. They are supported by council officers who are paid permanent staff. In the case of sport and sport development, these officers encompass a range of roles, although a recent post-devolution policy debate has been running regarding the appropriate number and infrastructure in Wales (The Welsh Assembly, 2018).

Historically since the 1970s there would be department or sections run as sport and/or leisure. This came about with the emergence of large-scale leisure provision in leisure centres, sports halls, and Astroturf pitches alongside grass pitch provision. There are established historic case studies of sport development in four local authorities (Houlihan and White, 2002), and in specific localities such as in Belfast (e.g. Bairner and Shirlow, 2003), Leeds (Bramham, 1986), Liverpool (King, 2009), and Sheffield (Roche, 1992). The issue now is that these are now around 20 years out of date, and whilst useful as a cross-sectional point in time reference, there are considerable gaps in what we now know about local government in the UK.

Sport development services with local government across the United Kingdom emerged from the post-facility boom era (Collins, 2010; Robinson, 2007). The size, scope, and scale of these services varied hugely and understanding of the true scale of the market is still unknown due to the complexity of both defining service boundaries and gathering data on a reliable and systematic basis. King (2014: 356) in a landmark study of local government sport and recreation services (SRS) suggested

> Discretionary services such as SRS stand at a cross-roads in local government: either service areas become a minor and marginal outpost offering a few (largely unproven or ineffective) safety-net services to residents unable to access private and third sector provision, or service

leaders and local politicians with control of the leisure portfolio 'make the case' for sport and recreation provision and integrate discretionary services with components of statutory provision.

In the precursor to this academic paper King (2012) outlines for the Association for Public Service Excellence (APSE) a powerful vision for 'where next?' for local government SRS. In undertaking his research, he identified key thematic headline work for local government sport development (Figure 9.1):

Analysis of Figure 9.1 illustrates seven key themes to the work of sport development in 2012. In terms of core DCMS (2015) priorities, many of the broad priorities have stayed the same. The language may have change slightly but much of the targeted public policy 'speak' is similar.

Furthermore, in King's research examining the impact of post-2008 austerity on sport development, he found that central government cuts (suggested at between 25 and 40 per cent) to local government had unsurprising profound effects (King, 2015; Widdop et al., 2017). Walker and Hayton (2019) also located local sport development provision in downsizing, cost saving, and austerity landscapes. When asked about the provision across 12 local authorities in the East Midlands, Mackintosh (2012) found considerable pressures to change, survive on less resources, and manage an ever-changing set of policy agendas. The theme of change could be seen an ironic constant within this subsector of the sport development landscape.

King (2012) thematic priorities for local government sport and recreation services (SRS)

1. Facility-based delivery of services for the community and elite athletes
   Initiatives around place shaping that intended to re-image or showcase a locality through

2. Staging sport events and related to this, the pursuit of European and National 'City of Sport' status

3. Elite and performance-based sport-specific sports development

4. Investment in widening participation (within a community recreation remit) or Sport for All such as outreach work targeted 'hard to reach' groups

5. Sport and physical activity programmes as components of social policy where sport is an instrument to improve health, for example, within a 'social inclusion' agenda

6. Sport and physical activity in schools, where the local authority is a partner, e.g. dual-use site management

7. Support for grass-roots sport and recreational opportunities delivered through the voluntary or 'Third' sector, including grant-aid

Source: King/ APSE (2012; 13)

FIGURE 9.1 A thematic analysis of the policy priorities for local government SRS in 2012

Some local authorities have lost considerable aspects of sport development officer provision (Mackintosh, 2012; King, 2014). But equally, in looking across the four home nations where provision is present, the roles and remits will vary dependent upon national policy and strategy and then local and regional agendas. For example, if a particular unitary authority has a strongly deprived population and focus on health and wellbeing, with this geographical 'unit' of work SDOs are likely to work in partnership from their bases in town halls to deliver towards these goals. Increasingly, more are also asked to generate their own income, funding, and external resource packages to make projects more sustainable. Some of these sources may even 'pay' for SDOs own ongoing salary costs. It does show the new horizon of careers in this area. Interestingly, progression through to the very highest levels of unitary government offer some of the highest paid roles in the sector. Another good example of why work varies is the nature of the communities resources available, so, for example, inner city and suburban compared to rural communities leave the likely position of an SDO and their team as highly variable. A project linked to local government cycling and walking on the west coast of Scotland or coastal path region of west Wales will need and require very different sport development and activity planning skills to that of an inner-city skateboard project for youth crime diversion. Herein lies part of the essential appeal of the subject we study, research, and develop our skill sets in.

Typically, as recently as 2008 many of the skills of the SDO were those that existed for the previous 20 years (Bloyce et al., 2008; Collins, 2010; Mackintosh, 2008; Mackintosh 2012). However, debates coalesce around whether there is a specific profession for SDOs (Hylton and Hartley, 2012) and the skills that once dominated come to be acknowledged as reflecting changes in government approach and the emerging organisation and culture of sport development. Part of what this book is aiming to do is to encourage you as students to take control of your own learning alongside your degree to embrace technological change, social media, and new ways of working. For the profession to remain relevant, SDOs of the future workforce need to understand the core principles, and structures (such as local government) but also how we can work with such structures in new and innovative ways. For example, crowdfunding technologies and software used to support income generation for clubs, projects and ideas in sport development did not exist in 2008.

There is not space to engage with a full empirical analysis of the time line of change in local government sport and leisure in the UK. Suffice to say that this can be located in Houlihan and White's (2002) and Houlihan and Lindsey's rich historical texts that act as a benchmark of detailed information on this matter. Furthermore, King (2009) provides an understanding of how Liverpool has a regional public sector unit of analysis for change in local government, and also how national policies affected changed on this specific area of sport development practice. Where it is useful to turn to next is the emergence of new forms of regional and sub-regional organisations and agencies that now work in the field of sport development. In part, it could be argued these organisations step into the gaps in provision left by restructure and austerity (Walker and Hayton, 2019; Widdop et al., 2017). They do, however, have close links to local government, and are important for students of sport development to be aware of.

Local government and the third sector and not-for-profit organisations

The not-for-profit sector encompasses voluntary, civil society, and social enterprise styled organisations that work in sport development. In some cases, there is a historic close link to a specific local government authority where a section of officers work with a specific remit is put out to tender and people can bit for this. Some view this as privatisation of public sector provision. Others, on the other end of political ideology, consider it making efficiencies to save money, time, and make innovation more likely. Examples of this might be the selling off of a sport development unit (King/APSE, 2012; King, 2014) into a social enterprise that then works not-for-profit doing very similar work to perhaps what they did before. They can operate slightly more freely and also still apply for many of the grants available. They do so from outside the operational realms of the council officers. A second example might be using volunteers to deliver what previously had been done by paid staff; this has happened in many areas of the public sector (police, fire service, gardening, libraries) (Nichols et al., 2014). In other cases, social enterprises can be defined slightly differently to charities and clubs. Here, Marsden-Heathcote and Finney (2018: 200) suggest,

> it is about having a purpose, trade to generate impact and profit. Every social enterprise should have a clear social and environmental purpose at the heart of what they do and have their mission statement articulate this.

Here, there is a spectrum of social enterprise designs from traditional charity at one end of the spectrum, through to social enterprise and moving through to more traditional business with a more core focus on financial value as opposed to social value and impact (Reid, 2003; Simmons, 2004). Sport development has started to thrive in this domain. Again, where 20 years ago there would barely have been any presence in this landscape (charities excluded), now we see a stronger but also at times more free market environment in this sector (Hodgkinson and Hughes, 2012). By free market, we mean unregulated, so operating in a local government jurisdiction, perhaps using their facilities and even staff, but not 'owned' by the state and local council. Indeed, whilst some have painted a picture of such organisations offering a straightforward solution to many of the ills of community sport, others have suggested such a 'fairy tale' is not the case (Reid, 2017; 1). In Reid's (2017) study he explores the social enterprise arm of a Scottish football club; it is important to acknowledge here the mix of outcomes, balancing positives of recruiting youth workers, developing more 'authentic' partnerships with the mythical 'win-win' scenarios, and the challenge of juggling financial goals with social outcomes and impacts.

Broadly speaking, social enterprises may set themselves up as an approach for schools perhaps to deliver community sport coaching or to run projects around mental health, crime prevention, or other more nuanced aspects of the new government policy. There are now some coaching consortiums of this nature with as many as 700 employees. They have far greater scope than a sport development unit of, say, 10–15 staff for a mid-sized unitary authority with a real commitment to sport and physical activity. This is the landscape pointed out by King (2009, 2012, 2014) in his multiple studies of this sector, whilst still potentially working around many of the themes in Figure 9.1 identified earlier. However, the historical organisational case studies of Belfast, Leeds, and Sheffield now stand as testament to how sport development has been repositioned. Even the thematic issues that a local government sport development team is aiming to address have shifted, in part due to evolving sport policy from central government. In a study of Rochdale sport development, such a theme was 'community empowerment' and 'community involvement' (Partington and Totten, 2012). In this research with communities, local residents associations and the local authority skills emerged in the need for capacity building and developing more innovative resident and community-focused monitoring processes. A further study by Snape and Binks (2008) looked at the need for local government to rethink how it works with British South Asian Communities in Blackburn using more community development-led approaches of consultation and how well local government orientated its services to its users. They argue that such factors "were integrally related to Muslim religious-cultural identity of the neighbourhood" (Snape and Binks, 2008: 28). Both this project and Partington and Totten's (2012) study acknowledge cultural and community safety as central themes for local authorities to deal with in partnership with their communities. As Cleland (2014) has identified with ethnic minority population growing by 53 per cent between 1991 and 2001, local authorities must work more closely with their ethnic minority populations and wider sport organisations such as clubs, coaching organisations, trusts and charities.

For students studying this domain, it remains a paradox. If we want to identify the natural sporting resources available to 'the public' such as athletics tracks, hockey pitches (3G, 4G, and older astro turf) alongside grass playing pitches, open spaces, and parks, these are still largely the domain of local government. A major shift is that 'ownership' may be local government but the contract for running the service in sport and recreation may be through a leisure provider or leisure trust. Trusts are a rapidly evolving entity across the UK and show how the contractualisation, modernisation, and neo-liberal new ownerships models are well embedded. Sport development was always a non-essential, optional service in local government (Houlihan and Lindsey, 2013; Houlihan and White, 2002). The provision of state-run sport development services has declined in nearly all regions of the UK. In some areas where there is a contractualisation of the relationship between local government facilities and sport development delivery, it was clear that leisure centres and facilities will win. Less profit-driven, softer sport development delivering social policy-led outcomes and community-facing development opportunities for under-presented groups proved harder to build into a profit-led contract.

Charitable trusts are an example of an organisation that increasingly runs sport alongside local government. They are also not-for-profit, but at the more formalised charity end of the social enterprise spectrum. They will need to be recognised as a charity and have appropriate tax, legal, and governance approaches and paperwork in place. In some cases, there may be a regional 'presence' of a national sporting charity. Examples of this will 'deliver', implement, and often evaluate national policy priorities at regions and localised hubs of activity. Examples of this include Active Communities Network (CAN), Comic Relief and Street Games. All work in the sport-for-development area addressing social policy goals through sport in various guises. However, it is perhaps worth acknowledging that historically this might have been work in the 1970s and 1980s that local government would have done. This is a good example of why history, understanding history, and seeing where today's sport development has come from gives us a stronger understanding of the landscape we may be working in.

Community Interest Charities (CIC) tend to be smaller organisations but they still do often have links to local government. It might be, for example, that a voluntary sector club has an opportunity to take over a pavilion and run it instead of the local authority. In addition, they bid to become a CIC and run specific sessions targeted at BAME girls in participation and coaching. Across all the above areas of provision in sport development, it is clear that there is a broad movement away from direct 'large state' provision towards the state acting as an enabler of sport and leisure development. In other words, it can be argued that "those who advocate a minimalist state have sought to downsize, privatize, re-engineer or re-invent government" (Jackson, 2016: 27). In considering this sector and how it may 'fit' with future sport development practices, it seems that we have an increasingly challenging context. For example, Bovaird and Loeffler (2016: 396) identify a number of key models that may play out for public sector sport development management. Table 9.2 draws on their typology of changes and applies it to sport development.

It seems clear that more so than many other sectors, agencies, and organisations the local government council is one that has experienced some of the more fundamental shifts since early studies in the field were undertaken (Houlihan and White, 2002). Indeed, 25 years ago MacDonald predicted the death of sport development (MacDonald, 1995) and whilst this predication has not come true, it is apparent that a host of public sector challenges have emerged (Bovaird and Loeffler, 2016). It now remains far less clear as to the distinctions between local–regional–national government, and patterns of public–private expenditure. We can refer to this as binary dualisms where definitions act as polar points of reference as opposed to more of sliding scale or spectrum of contexts or philosophical positions. For example, local public

TABLE 9.2 Analysis of the implications of changes to 'big government' in the UK for local authority sport development funding, policy, and practice between 2012 and 2020

Changes in big government	Cuts and privatisation of sport development in local government
Public sector provision undertaken by private and third sector organisations.	After-school clubs in primary school delivered by private coaching companies. Sport development units in government replaced by social enterprises.
Users and communities co-produce public value and outcomes that are publicly desired – this complements the traditional public sector.	Community Interest Companies (CiCs) offer options for local government to not run sport facilities, development opportunities, and coaching.
Public sector are subject to stronger audit, inspection, and regulation – this also applies to private markets.	Primary and secondary school PE are subject to OFSTED inspection with associated implication and 'quality' testing. Private coaching companies must regulate around coach qualifications and Disability and Barring Service (DBS) for child protection.
Corporate social responsibility is a key strategic theme to successful companies encompassing their impact on local community.	Professional sport clubs can 'offer' a far reaching sport development provision, far beyond their specific sport as part of CSR. Major corporate entities such as banks, fast food outlets, and insurance companies can support major event-led legacy and community participation.
Third sector agencies offer increasing importance in terms of commissioning and delivery of public services.	Voluntary sector agencies with a wide reach can compete and successfully deliver commissioned sport for development programmes where local government did before.

provision may be part of a national leisure provider part of national contract awarded by multiple local authorities. Similarly, national policy in sport development may be entirely ignored or totally re-interpreted at the local public service level in a youth or community centre so policy outcomes look very different to those planned.

This said, for students new to this domain of study, I consider it fundamental to their grasp of sport development that they must understand this tier of ever-changing government and governance. For, if governance is to be deemed a critically important lens through which we may study communities, sport development, and the organisations that shape experiences and policy implementation, we need to understand the local council. Navigating the space and geographical communities of our major towns and rural villages will continue to be critical for many. Much professional practice will embrace these recreational spaces. It is just that it will no longer be delineated as the role of a single sport development unit as perhaps was a trend 15–20 years ago. Now the nuanced governance relationships, patterns of delivery and partnerships is the driver.

CASE STUDY 9.1

Local government SDO identity and change

The challenge of doing more with less at local government level and micro delivery scale will be considered in this case study and there will be a discussion of the potential issues around competing programmes of delivery in different sectors that operate in local government spaces. The specific example of mental health will be addressed using the example of Mind organisation's 'Get Set Go' project and *parkrun* national volunteer-led scheme that operates in many local authority parks for free that doesn't explicitly target mental health, but does focus on community wellbeing.

Public parks and open space land are predominantly owned in the main by local government. If we take the example of Manchester City Council, they own, run, and service a number of parks. But the days of them having an extensive sport development unit are long gone. If we consider the governance of sporting activities that are delivering goals for DCMS (2015) and Sport England (2016) as well as supporting the sub-regional sport and physical activity of Greater Sport (Greater Sport, 2017: online) *parkrun* offers an interesting learning case study. Many of you may have run in a *parkrun*, some of you will have volunteered as a 'back marker', starter, timer volunteer, or various other roles. *Parkrun* started as an individual English one-off event. It is now a global phenomenon and shows how sport development no longer remains tied to the council chambers of local government. Considering 'who', what, where, why, and how *parkrun* operates offers five critical questions and provides a vast insight into change in the professional domain over the last 20 years. Many *parkruns* are founded, led, and run by volunteers that emerge from communities to run 'their' event. It is a 5 km run that is social, fun, and principally not an overtly competitive event. Most are run in council-owned parks and as for why – well this is what you need to consider. They are also heavily underpinned by technological innovation, social media and web-led organisation

Seminar question

Consider why *parkrun* has been such a success. However, also take the example of a few isolated councils that have shown interest in and an inclination to ban the event unless they can charge people for it. Why might this be?

Seminar questions (with guided reading)

Hindley, D. (2018) 'More than just a run in the park': An exploration of parkrun as a shared leisure space. *Leisure Sciences*, 42:1, 85–105.

1. The article above provides further insights into why *parkrun* is what it is. Explore the evidence in the paper and unpick either individually or in a group why *parkrun* seems to have a magic sport development formula?

2. Why might Sport England or an Active Partnership be interested in *parkrun*? (justify)

3. How might we learn lessons from the research and the *parkrun* model in other areas of sport development officer professional practice?

References

Bairner, A. and Shirlow, P. 2003. When leisure turns to fear: Fear, mobility and ethnosectarianism in Belfast. *Leisure Studies*, 22(3): 203–221

Bloyce, D., Smith, A., Mead, R., and Morris, J. (2008) 'Playing the Game (Plan)': A figurational analysis of organisational change in sport development in England, *European Sport Management Quarterly*, 8:4, 359–378.

Bovaird, T. and Loeffler, E. (2016) Public management and governance: The future?, in Bovaird, T. and Loeffler, E. (eds) *Public Management and Governance*, London: Routledge, 26–38.

Bramham, P. (1986) Leisure, the local state and social order, *Leisure Studies*, 5:2,189–209.

Collins, M. (2010) *Examining Sport Development*, London: Routledge.

Cleland, J. (2014) Working together through sport? Local authority provision for ethnic minorities in the UK, *Sport in Society*, 17:1, 38–51.

DCMS (2015) *Sporting Nation*, London: DCMS.

Greater Sport (2017) *Changing Our Lives Together*, available at: www.greatersport. co.uk/about-us/our-strategy-and-action-plan [accessed on 30 April 2020].

Hodgkinson, I. R. and Hughes, P. (2012) A level playing field: Social inclusion in public leisure, *International Journal of Public Sector Management*, 25:1, 48–63.

Houlihan, B. and Lindsey, I. (2013) *Sport Policy in Britain*, London: Routledge.

Houlihan, B. and White, A. (2002) *The Politics of Sport Development*, London, Routledge.

Hylton, K. and Hartley, H. J. (2012) Sport development ... a profession in waiting?, in Harris, S., Bell, B., Adams, A., and Mackintosh, C. (eds.) *Sport for Sport? Practical and Theoretical Insights in Sport Development*, Brighton: LSA Publication 117\ Leisure Studies Association, 4–22.

Jackson, P. M. (2016) The changing shape of the public sector, in Bovaird, T. and Loeffler, E. (eds) *Public Management and Governance*, London: Routledge, 26–38.

King, N. (2009) *Sport Policy and Governance: Local Perspectives*, London, Routledge.

King, N. (2012) *Report Local authority Sport and Recreation Services in England: Where Next?*, Oxford: APSE.

King, N. (2014) Local authority sport services under the UK Coalition government: Retention, revision or curtailment, *International Journal of Sport Policy and Politics*, 6:3, 349–369.

King, N. (2015) Making the case for sport and recreation services: The utility of social return on investment (SROI) analysis, *International Journal of Public Sector Management*, 27:2, 152–164.

MacDonald, I. (1995) *Sport for All-'RIP'. A Political Critique of the Relationship between National Sport Policy and Local Authority Sports Development in London*, Brighton: Leisure Studies Association Series edition 55, 71–94.

Mackintosh, C. (2008) Bonding issues: Partnership working in sports development, *Recreation*, 20–21.

Mackintosh, C. (2012) The shifting dynamics of local government sport development officer practice in England: New identities and hazy professional boundaries, in Harris, S., Bell, B., Adams, A., and Mackintosh, C. (eds) *Sport for Sport? Theoretical and Practical Insights into Sport Development*, Eastbourne: Leisure Studies Association, 113–130.

Marsden-Heathcote, J. and Finney, A. (2018) Enterprise and innovation in community sport, in Wilson, R. and Platts, C. (eds) *Managing and Developing Community Sport*, London: Routledge, 196–212.

Ministry of Housing, Communities and Local Government (2019) *Guidance: Local government structure and elections*, available at: www.gov.uk/guidance/local-government-structure-and-elections [accessed on 30 April 2020].

Nichols, G., Taylor, P., Barrett, D., and Jeanes, R. (2014) Youth sport volunteers in England: A paradox reducing the state and promoting a Big Society, *Sport Management Review*, 17, 337–346.

Partington, J. and Totten, M. (2012) Community sports projects and effective community empowerment: A case study in Rochdale, *Managing Leisure*, 17:1, 29–46.

Reid, G. (2003) Charitable trusts: Municipal leisure's 'third way'?, *Managing Leisure*, 8, 171–183.

Reid, G. (2017) A fairytale narrative for community sport? Exploring the politics of sport social enterprise, *International Journal of Sport Policy and Politics*, 9:4, 597–611,

Robinson, L. (2007) *Managing Public Sport and Leisure Services*, London: Routledge.

Roche (1992) Mega-events and micro-modernisation: On the sociology of the new urban tourism, *British Journal of Sociology*, 43:3, 563–600.

Simmons, R. (2004) A trend to trust? The rise of new leisure trusts in the UK, *Managing Leisure*, 9, 159–177.

Snape, R. and Binks, P. (2008) Re-thinking sport: Physical activity and healthy living in British South Asian Muslim communities, *Managing Leisure*, 13, 23–35.

Sport England (2016) *Towards an Active Nation*, London: Sport England.

The Welsh Assembly (2018) *Public Service Reform in Post-devolution Wales: A Timeline of Local Government Developments – Research Briefing*, Cardiff: The Welsh Assembly.

Walker, C. M. and Hayton, J. W. (2019) An analysis of third sector sport organisations in an era of 'super-austerity', *International Journal of Sport Policy and Politics*, 10:1, 43–61.

Widdop, P., King, N., Parnell, D., Cutts, D., and Millward, P. (2017) Austerity, policy and sport participation in England, *International Journal of Sport Policy and Politics*, 10:1, 7–24.

CHAPTER 10

National governing bodies of sport

The NGB organisational setting is a hybrid and complex space with the field of sport development practice. The origins of the NGB lie in varied historical and cultural spaces across diverse timelines (Thompson, Bloyce, and Mackintosh, 2020). Some NGBs are extremely new and have emerged from recent sport and physical activity, and arguably global cultural movements. For example, Tchoukball UK, Korfball, and Parkour are all examples of emerging modern landscape of smaller NGBs that stand in contrast to major long-standing sports such as rugby, football, cricket, golf, and cycling that deliver and compete in multi-million-pound global mega events as well as support considerable national UK community club infrastructures. The histories of each NGB will not be discussed here. The aim of this chapter is to provide an accessible introduction to what NGBs do, are positioned to deliver and what relationships they cultivate with clubs, government, and participants. Typically, the NGB has moved from 'kitchen table top' organisation administering memberships, clubs, volunteers, and coaches towards more professional NGBs that even in the smaller cases of under 15–20 core staff deliver modern professional 'backroom' infrastructure in areas of what is now referred to as strategic and operational governance (Taylor and O'Sullivan, 2009; Thompson, Bloyce, and Mackintosh, 2020). Typical areas of coverage for this work include child safeguarding systems, coach education, membership and affiliation, and club support. Obviously, the scope of this varies dependent upon the income of the NGB and the level of financial support from home nation Sports Councils. Where an NGB has say 95 per cent reliance on Sport England or Sport Scotland support, it is very closely tied to their work vision and goals, and failure to deliver their targets can be perilous. In larger NGB cases they may derive considerable funds from sources such as top-tier competitions, advertising, or global hosting of events. This can open greater flexibility as to their strategic direction.

The landscape of NGBs in the UK has transformed considerably since the 1996 Atlanta Olympics in elite delivery of medals (Green, 2004; Houlihan and Lindsey, 2013; Mackintosh, 2013). When Team GB delivered its worst ever medal haul, the government the National Lottery and NGBs were asked to deliver to a new aspirational set of targets. Furthermore, community sport administration, funding, and governance of sport in the UK has also shifted considerably under four rounds of Whole Sport Plans since 2004. This chapter will provide a unique insight introducing the historical origins of NGBs through to the modern-day role of staff, structures, and organisations. In particular, it will outline patterns of overall investment, changes in eras of different governmental involvement, and how the work of the NGB officer is changed and has changed since earlier delivery and community coaching-focused work. It is also important to provide context on alternative NGBs that are not English such as the GAA. The chapter will consider the specific cases of 'high-performing' NGBs and recent examples of those that have been disciplined and suffered financial sanctions due to reliance on new public management regimes in the UK. The chapter will also introduce how NGBs relate to other sector partners such as Active Partnerships, the voluntary sector, and local government. Devolution and how this has impacted on NGB work in each of the home nations can also be considered so that the book remains relevant to those in Scotland, Wales, and Northern Ireland. In particular, the chapter will then go on to look at how NGBs need to further prioritise and address inequality in sport across 'race', gender, religion, disability, and sexuality.

Governing bodies from across the UK all play key roles that are relatively similar to each other in the administration, governance, and development of their sports. In the UK there are now 113 recognised sports across the different home nation governments and whilst they differ in scope and size many of them are pragmatically aligned to fulfil very similar functions. Indeed, DCMS (2002) recognised over 300 NGBs across 113 sports (Taylor and O'Sullivan, 2009) showing a broad growth in the types of sports now recognised by government and quangos. Many see themselves as the guardians of the grass roots of their sport. Some are UK in remit (e.g. UK Athletics) whilst others are sport specific in a geographical national state context (e.g. Ulster Camogie, Welsh Canoe Union, and Scottish Rugby). They are closely linked to voluntary sector sport clubs that are part of civil society in sport-specific clusters in each country and below that across regions and localities. More will be said later in terms of the sport development and community development aspects of clubs. The size of NGB varies from larger NGBs in England like the FA, RFU, LTA, Amateur Swimming Association, England Golf, through to medium-sized sports like Badminton, Rugby Football League, down to smaller micro NGBs such as British Orienteering, Basketball, and GB Waterpolo. Staff can have a mix of volunteer officers and paid, permanent officers located centrally at their headquarters or in regional offices around the UK. Rugby Football Union (RFU), for example, had 350 development officers and centrally managed community rugby coaching staff in 2019. But, it also has other departments such as elite coaching, schools, further/higher education and events and marketing. England Golf, as a top-five sporting NGB has around 100 staff in total. This will vary dependent on funding cycles.

In a study of UK NGBs, Tacon and Walters (2016) surveyed all 300 NGBs in the UK, from which they received responses from 75 NGBs (accounting for

25 per cent of all UK NGBs). Whilst not a complete picture, it gives a good impression of the varied scope and remit they may have. They suggested respondent NGBs varied in size, with the smallest having no full-time employees and the largest having 300, with an average number of full-time employees of 26 and a median of only four. Their study explores the tensions of what they deem accountability 'technologies' surfacing around performance management, modernisation, and professionalisation of NGBs in the current era of target-driven funds and commercialisation (Tacon and Walters, 2016).

Most NGBs also have staff that sit above the paid officers and an office running the sport that is a governance board made up of a mix of key staff acting as a check and challenge to the sport's vision, ideas, and accountability processes. The last ten years has seen an explosion in non-executive directors (NEDs) that support this process in NGBs and bring new skills of professionalisation and market-orientated marketing and accountancy to interrogate what previously were highly amateur organisations (Malcolm, Sheard, and White, 2000). The long-standing debate around the movement away from amateurism to professionalism (Dowling, Edwards, and Washington, 2017, 2014; Taylor and Garrett, 2010; Williams, 2008) still runs in NGB contexts. For some, it is a binary discussion between good and bad, the old and the new, and the inefficient and efficient, whereas in reality there must be a case for considering a case-by-case assessment for sports that may not be financially viable in the current austere climate. Equally, aspects of change in modernisation are often underpinned by an interest in performance management and accountability in relation to use of public funds (Houlihan and Green, 2009). When the government evaluates its funding increases or decreases for certain sports, it is in part using this framework in assessing NGBs as to those that are capable of delivering mass change in policy objectives. Cyclical funding patterns of around four to five years are common and given NGBs, for example, know they may be far off targets by, say, year 3, this generates considerable instability for the delivery and planning regime in sport.

NGB history

The origins of NGBs working in sport development was arguably when they started appointing SDOs in the early 1970s targeting coaching in elite squads (Connolly, 2016; Houlihan and White, 2002). As Thompson, Bloyce, and Mackintosh state, "this was broadened from the late 1980s onwards to involve working with athletes, coaches, club officials and volunteers from their affiliated VSCs, on organizing a range of activities for participants to enter and progress within their respective sports" (2020: 231). This was an important step change for NGBs in their evolution (Coghlan and Webb, 1990; Harris and Houlihan, 2014; Harris and Houlihan, 2016; Houlihan, 2011; Houlihan & White, 2002; Nesti, 2001; Winand et al., 2010). Typically, NGBs appointed a national SDO post with parallel regional SDO posts (Harris and Houlihan, 2016; Houlihan and Green, 2009; Houlihan & White, 2002). As there became increased levels of funding from the later 1980s to mid-1990s, this facilitated stronger government intervention (Bloyce & Smith, 2010), which allowed NGBs to develop a wide-ranging collective partnership of SDOs involving regional and county level posts. Some suggest that NGBs had a focus on elite sport goals as opposed to addressing wider welfare state ideologies such as improving health and reducing crime (Bloyce et al., 2008).

In 2008, both DCMS and Sport England strategies and policy documents built a refocused commitment to sport for its own sake by placing NGBs at the centre of their plans. This was built around a four-year funding cycle that was now fully embedded within Sport England and use of the voluntary club sector to help support the delivery of policy goals (Harris, Mori, and Collins, 2009). Such four-year plans required eligible NGBs to submit a whole sport plan (WSP) outlining development of their sport (Sport England, 2008). In 2008, Sport England awarded 46 NGBs funding to implement these plans to increase participation in sport, which, in 2013, was increased to 46 NGBs receiving £493m of funding.

This process forced NGBs into performance management frameworks and a more 'results-oriented approach' (Green and Houlihan 2006; Grix and Carmichael, 2012; Harris and Houlihan, 2016). Resultant changes in policy then began to reposition the previous 'sport-for-sport's sake' focus of sport development work in NGBs towards the inactive and other target groups that are excluded from sport and physical activity (Harris and Houlihan, 2016). As Thompson, Bloyce, and Mackintosh (2020) argue, the view that the traditional club may not be the right, and the most popular place for managing and developing participation with the inactive populations began to alter relationships between NGBs and the voluntary sector. Sport England and DCMS also began encouraging NGBs to engage and partner with wider organisations that perhaps draw on a less competitive and more casual vision for delivery. For a detailed analysis of the historical evolution of this policy area in NGBs and their key partners, see Thompson, Bloyce, and Mackintosh (2020).

From a Sport England perspective at a community level, and UK Sport at elite tiers of competition and sport development, modernisation of NGBs has brought a disciplining and punishment set of processes (Houlihan and Green, 2009). Targets are set for NGBs to deliver in various areas of 'performance' and measurement is undertaken centrally by nationally agencies. If such NGBs do not deliver, then they will receive either financial gain or loss. This has knock-on effects on their delivery systems, staffing, human resource processes and coaching at the local club or elite level. Badminton is a good example of this where it experienced high levels of fiscal punishment after the London 2012 Games. Arguably, such tight accountability has left it still recovering now, 12 years later. In terms of their remit and scope, Badminton England are involved in wide-ranging sport development activities. NGBs are typically independent, self-appointed organisations that govern their sports through the common consent of their sport. Below is a list of activities that Badminton England (2020a) outline:

- Control and regulate the environment of its sport;
- Administer the practice and participation of its sport;
- Prepare and implement a vision and strategic plan for its sport and determine how it will be implemented nationally, regionally, and locally;
- Promote its sport;
- Manage the rules and regulations of its sport, including anti-doping, child protection and equality;
- Implement a governance framework for its sport;
- Administer officials of its sport;
- Establish and maintain links with the UK/Ireland and the international governing body/federation;
- Encourage and grow participation;
- Develop coaches, athletes, officials, and participants;
- Organise and host competitions.

(Source: Badminton England, 2020a)

The organisational chart in Figure 10.1 shows a typical NGB development department. This sits alongside other functions such as governance, legal, marketing, human resources, and elite talent development and support (Figure 10.1).

Badminton is just outside the top-five sports in the UK NGBs in terms of size, so it is a useful sport to analyse in terms of the scope and remit it delivers. Ultimately, they have 28 development officers including two specialists in child protection. As Figure 10.1 illustrates, they also encompass other roles and development staff that are more variable in positions such as Disability, Insight and Open data. It, therefore, is critical to locate the NGB development team within the overall NGB structure. Again, no two NGBs in any of the four home nations are the same. This should provide you with a starting point for exploring the specific NGB that interests you (Figure 10.2).

Programmes are the lifeblood of NGB sport development. They are essentially national rollout projects with specific aims devised and designed by the

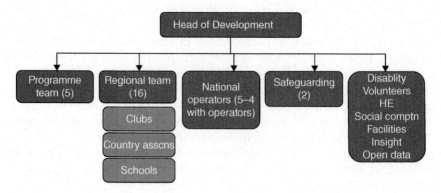

FIGURE 10.1 Overview of the staffing of Badminton England development team (2020a)

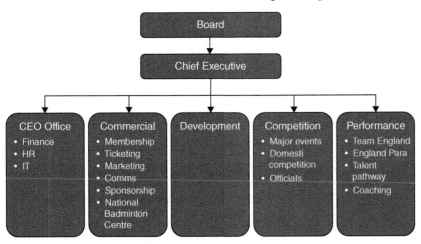

FIGURE 10.2 Overview of the organisational governance structure of Badminton England (2020a)

NGB to deliver goals and policy visions that align with supporting (usually) the home nation Sports Council and/or central government strategic priorities. In the case of Badminton England as an NGB, they have a number of headline programmes, which include Rat Pack targeting 5000 English primary schools and 62,000 U-11s playing the sport to deliver 1100 new U-11 club members (Badminton England, 2020b). This shows that, although sport development has changed immeasurably, there are also elements of the landscape that remain very similar to some of the initial programmes and policy ideas from the 1980s. What has changed is the degree to which performance against such targets is managed by central government and its arms-length agencies (Harris and Houlihan, 2016). A knock-on effect is that whilst some of the broadest principles remain, levels of professionalisation in such programmes and in the wider sector are ever present (Dowling, Edwards, and Washington, 2014). The Rugby Football Union (RFU) in England representing men's rugby and Rugby Football League (RFL) representing the parallel code of the game both lost £1m due to failed attempts to meet targets they were set for community sport participation based on what then was the Active People Survey (APS). Some have suggested this is more of a tool for control of NGBs and indirectly voluntary sport clubs than a vision of modernisation for sport in the UK (Houlihan and Green, 2009; Rowe, 2009). As we have shown, the last decade or two has been a period of real change for the NGBs of the UK. A detailed analysis is beyond the scope of this book and worthy of an outright text in itself. But, as we stop to reflect on the professional practice of NGB sport development individuals and organisations, it appears clear that new ways of working and spaces for collaboration are emerging. Accountability, target setting, and professionalisation are here to stay (Dowling, Edwards, and Washington, 2014). However, how sports governance is used and implemented across each of the four home nations is varied. How community sport experiences support from SDOs also varies as policy is understood and interpreted slightly differently. However, NGBs and their relationship with the three million sport coaches and over one million volunteers, alongside the clubs and participants they are directly aligned with, remains a core vehicle for sport development policy implementation success or failure (Harris and Houlihan, 2016; Thompson, Bloyce, and Mackintosh, 2020).

▌ CASE STUDY 10.1 ▐

The changing face of the governance and development of golf

Sport policy in golf in England is a complex set of interwoven organisational decisions, meanings, and politics positions. As of yet, it remains very minimally researched (Philpotts and Grix, 2012). It is also worth acknowledging how golf was positioned and positioned itself in relation to school sport. A core partner here is the Golf Foundation, which was established in 1953 (Golf Foundation, 2020) with 108 registered schools instructors and 3500 young people involved. It has been suggested that "golf's relationship with schools began in the 1950s as a response to a decline in levels of participation in the game generally and a significant reduction in membership of golf clubs" (Philpotts and Grix, 2012: 36). Crucially, with the emergence of the National Curriculum for Physical Education (NCPE) in 1989 golf was an excluded sport. It was the further exclusion from the PE and school sport and club links (PESSCL) strategy in 2003 that further cemented the need for policy and strategy reform in the NGB and wider sport. It was suggested by civil servants at the time that golf was not 'fit for purpose' and England Golf itself admitted that the traditional club was under threat and experiencing a shortage of members (England Golf, 2004).

In 2004, England Golf, the national governing body (NGB) for the sport of golf in England, published a vision for becoming a 'Leading Golf Nation by 2020' (England Golf, 2004). This Whole Sport Plan covered the period 2005–2009. The NGB expressed in this document the need to become "golf centred, not an organisation centred approach to the sports development" (England Golf, 2004: 2). At this time, the sport was organisationally structured around the England Golf Partnership (EGP), a collaborative structure including the England Golf Union (EGU), English Ladies' Golf Association (ELGA) and the Professional Golf Association (PGA). The Partnership was underpinned by financial support from The Golf Foundation and Sport England. It is also worth acknowledging that at this cross section in time the game had 1915 courses and 400 driving ranges but, more crucially, in excess of 60 'development-led' initiatives. In parallel, the 2004 vision drew comparisons with policy in the *Swedish Golf Federation Strategy* (2004) and *American Golf 20/20 Vision Strategy* (2000) and suggested that there was minimal overarching strategy with limited policies for golf in England (England Golf, 2004). The EGP was then formally established in April 2005, followed by modernisation reviews of core partners EGU, ELGA, and Golf Foundation. Sport England gave an award through their whole sport plan (WSP) of £9m for the period 2005–2009, plus an additional £1.2m through the community development fund. As part of the next few year cycles of WSP funding, England Golf 2010–2016 and 2017–2021 emerged as a major top-five NGB with influence across its 2000 sports clubs, 400 driving ranges and 44,000 core volunteers. A range of new programmes emerged aligned with the DCMS (2015) and Sport England (2016) strategy visions such as Girls Golf Rocks with a more appealing, participation friendly and social media-led development approach. Use of Instagram, Facebook and Twitter in this arena shows how far an NGB has had to come to meet its core market and delivery innovation so that it obtains a share of the highly competitive youth girls sport, physical activity, and leisure domain. In an article examining this and wider women and girls trends in the sport, Mills and Mackintosh (2019) suggest that golf is challenging the status quo in a sport where long-held assumptions, biases, and misunderstandings are rife in the sport policy field.

Seminar questions

1. Based on the above background context and what you know (and perceive) of golf consider why golf development has had to undergo a considerable change in approach between 2003 and present day.

2. Why do Sport England want England Golf to challenge golf clubs to work differently with their volunteers? (see video resource and article)

Additional three-minute video resource

Mackintosh, C. (2018) Value your customers, available at: www.youtube.com/watch?v=zHvWhO3t5x4&feature=emb_logo [accessed on 30/4/2020]

Further reading

Mackintosh, C. and Mills, C. (2019) Girls who golf, *Sport Management*, 23:1, 70–73, available at: www.sportsmanagement.co.uk/pdf/SM_issue1_2019.pdf [accessed on 30/4/20].

References

Badminton England (2020a) *Discover badminton 2017–2023*, available at: http://online.anyflip.com/kvun/dzip/mobile/index.html#p=1 [accessed on 30 April 2020].

Badminton England (2020b) Who are Badminton England and what is their role?, presentation at Manchester Metropolitan University, Manchester on 24 February 2020.

Bloyce, D. and Smith, A. (2010) *Sport Policy and Development*, London: Routledge.

Bloyce, D., Smith, A., Mead, R., and Morris, J. (2008) 'Playing the game (plan)': A figurational analysis of organisational change in sport development in England, *European Sport Management Quarterly*, 8:4, 359–378.

Coghlan, J. and Webb, I. M. (1990) *Sport and British Politics Since 1960*, London: Falmer Press.

Connolly, J. (2016) Elias and habitus: Explaining bureaucratisation processes in the Gaelic Athletic Association, *Culture and Organizations*, 22:5, 452–475.

DCMS (2002) *Game Plan*, London: DCMS/Cabinet Office.

Dowling, M., Edwards, J., and Washington, M. (2014) Understanding the concept of professionalisation in sport management research, *Sport Management Review*, 17:4, 520–529.

England Golf (2004) *Whole Sport Plan 2005–2009: A New Plan, New Partnership and New Investment*, Woodhall Spa: England Golf.

Golf Foundation (2020) *History*, available at: www.golf-foundation.org/about-us/history/ [accessed on 30 April 2020].

Green, M. (2004) Changing policy priorities for sport in England: The emergence of elite sport development as a key policy concern, *Leisure Studies*, 23:4, 365–385.

Green, M. and Houlihan, B. (2006) Governmentality, modernisation and the 'disciplining' of national sporting organisations: Athletics in Australia and the United Kingdom, *Sociology of Sport Journal*, 23:1, 47–71.

Grix, J. and Carmichael, F. (2012) Why do governments invest in elite sport? A polemic, *International Journal of Sport Policy and Politics*, 4:1, 73–90.

Harris, S. and Houlihan, B. (2014) Delivery networks and community sport in England, *International Journal of Public Sector Management*, 27:2, 113–128.

Harris, S and Houlihan, B (2016) Competition or coalition? Evaluating the attitudes of national governing bodies of sport and county sport partnerships towards school sport partnerships, *International Journal of Sport Policy and Politics*, 8:1, 151–171.

Harris, S., Mori, K., and Collins, M. (2009) Great expectations: The role of voluntary sports clubs as policy implementers, *Voluntas International Journal*, 20:4, 405–423.

Houlihan, B. and Green, M. (2009) Modernization and sport: The reform of Sport England and UK Sport, *Public Administration*, 87:3, 678–698.

Houlihan, B. (2011) Introduction: Government and civil society involvement in sport development, in Houlihan, B. and Green, M. (eds) *An International Handbook of Sport Development*, London: Routledge, 51–54.

Houlihan, B. and Lindsey, I. (2013) *Sport Policy in Britain*, London: Routledge.

Houlihan, B. and White, A. (2002) *The Politics of Sport Development*, London: Routledge.

Mackintosh, C. (2013) An evaluation of outdoor table tennis imitative pilot programme in London: 'Ping pong in the fresh air how does that work?', *Managing Leisure*, 18:3, 226–238.

Malcolm, D., Sheard, K. and White, A. (2000) The changing structure and culture of English rugby union football, *Culture, Sport, Society*, 3:3, 63–87.

Nesti, M. (2001) Working in sports development, in Hylton, K., Bramham, P., Jackson, D., and Nesti, M. (eds) *Sports Development: Policy, Process and Practice*, London: Routledge, 195–213.

Philpotts, L. and Grix, J. (2012) The increasing politicisation of physical education and youth sport policy: A case study of school-club links, in Harris, S., Bell, B., Adams, A. and Mackintosh, C. (eds) *Sport for Sport: Theoretical and Practical Insights into Sports Development*, Brighton: Leisure Studies Association, 23–46.

Rowe, N. (2009) The active people survey: A catalyst for transforming evidence-based sport policy in England, *International Journal of Sport Policy and Politics*, 1:1, 89–98.

Taylor, B. and Garrett, D. (2010) The professionalisation of sports coaching: Relations of power, resistance and compliance, *Sport, Education and Society*, 15:1, 121–139.

Tacon, R. and Walters, G. (2016) Governing bodies of sport: How modernisation influences the way board members perceive and enact their roles, *International Journal of Sport Policy and Politics*, 8:3, 363–381.

Taylor, M. and O'Sullivan, S. (2009) How should national governing bodies of sport be governed in the UK? An exploratory study of board structure, *Corporate Governance: An International Review*, 17:6, 681–693.

Thompson, A., Bloyce, D., and Mackintosh, C. (2020) 'It is always going to change' – managing top-down policy changes by sport development officers working in national governing bodies of sport in England, *Managing Sport and Leisure: An International Journal*, iFirst 1–20.

Winand, M., Zintz, T., Bayle, E., and Robinson, L. (2010) Organizational performance of Olympic sport, *Managing Leisure*, 15:4, 279–307.

Williams, P. J. (2008) Cycle of conflict: A decade of strife in English professional rugby, *The International Journal of the History of Sport*, 25:4, 65–81.

CHAPTER 11

Sub-regional agencies
The Active Partnerships in a UK context

In considering the governance and management of sport development in the UK, there is a need to consider the agencies that sit at what could be termed the sub-regional level. In the case of England, this is principally referring to the Active Partnership, formerly known until 2019 as County Sport Partnerships (CSP). These are a sub-regional agency unique to England, although they have been considered in Wales as a policy option for community sport development infrastructure (Baker, 2017; Sport Wales, 2019). This is an important policy and practice dimension to understand how the UK sport development system differs between home nations. The chapter will provide students with an understanding of the emergence of the Active Partnership as a strategic regional agency, current research on how effective they have been and outline the recommendations from the National Reed Review undertaken in 2016 (Reed, 2016). In this review it was stated that "CSPs have evolved over a number of years in their roles and responsibilities and given that the government strategy points to a very different set of outcomes it is important that CSPs are refreshed to meet this new challenge" (Reed, 2016: 1). These agencies are not strictly a delivery agency, but equally the 43 of them that exist in England are now playing an increasingly fragmented and diverse role. They offer a key vehicle for policy interpretation in each region, but also operate very closely with regional arms of NGBs and local government provision. Their remit is also increasingly widening into other non-sport sectors and this will be discussed to illustrate the evolving position of the Active Partnership.

In Scotland, Northern Ireland and Wales, consideration will be given to the sub-regional level as this differs to England since devolution in 1998. But, despite a review of community sport development sub-regional governance structures in Wales (Baker, 2017), they remain only a feature of England. However, given the strategic role they play, that adds to the uniqueness of the English sport development landscape and they must be analysed in detail. How each home nation Sports Council has evolved will be given attention to set a contrasting context for students to be aware that national (UK) sport development driven by the latest DCMS (2015) strategy did not determine other home nations' strategic direction. How this is played out at regional and sub-regional level in the other three countries is currently not discussed in any mainstream sport development text. This is a feature of the book that has immense value to avoid an Anglo-centric view of UK-wide sport development. For each of the other three home nations, there are attempts by the Sports Council to strategically deliver and implement policy in sport development through the creation of parallel agencies. It is worth acknowledging that all three have a version of Active Partnerships but they differ slightly in scale and scope, in part due to funding and population differences.

In Northern Ireland, they are delivering Active School Partnerships, which link health, community, and education in school sport and physical activity (Northern Ireland Sport, 2009). This also fits alongside the development of ten School-Club Partnerships and 100 multi-sport club hubs. Whilst not strategic agencies that oversee decision making in sub-regions, they are important to recognise for understanding and examining the context of sport development in this devolved national context from the UK. In their vision from 2009 to 2019, the focus on sport participation for social good and talent development are clear, and it seems these varied strategic investments are crucial to delivery of their ambitious targets. They also argue for the need to, "review, strengthen and modernise existing delivery networks including the voluntary, community and statutory sectors. Establish systems and structures that enable improved dialogue between key stakeholders delivering the Strategy at a local level" (Sport Northern Ireland, 2009: 20).

This potentially presupposes an agency or network of agencies broadly similar to Active Partnerships in England. However, the full nature of this is yet to be analysed in any research detail.

Wales as a further devolved agency in the UK system also needs clarity around how sub-regional agencies are beginning to emerge in sport development. It is a similar context to Northern Ireland in the sense of a small population in comparison to England, with a heavily bureaucratic concentration of 22 local authorities given the scale and size of the country and no direct comparison to Active Partnerships. However, in recent times Sport Wales and the government of Wales, the Welsh Assembly, has agreed to develop regional sport agencies referred to as Community Sport Active Partnerships (CSAPs) where a number of local authority geographical areas are combined into sub-regional areas in the North and South and so on (Sport Wales, 2019). This emerged in part from the Baker Review (2017) of community sport delivery systems in Wales. These CSAPs each have an independent lead agency such as a university or private agency. They are currently evolving and the scope of their function is yet to be fully tested, whether they will be form-led as opposed to scoped in terms of functional remit remains to be seen.

Sport Wales (2017) in a recent independent government review of its role has argued "the traditional sports development officer has all but disappeared or at least the responsibilities of the role have changed so much that they are more about developing healthy and active people than traditional sport". As a consequence, the use of sub-regional partnerships that cut across the previous silos of traditional delivery and implementation systems is crucial. These CSAPs have a critical role to play in focusing on the 'big issues' of the current landscape in communities. Activity, health, mental health, and community regeneration are now the focus not just sport pathways and talent identification. It is again too early to identify what full role the CSAPs will play. The context for this in terms of legislation is now firmly embedded with the *The Wellbeing of Future Generations (Wales) Act 2015*. Interestingly, the *Sport Wales Review: An Independent Report* (2017) identified several concerns about establishing such sub-regional partnerships and even the concept caused them to highlight several implications for the implementing the concept. These included level of consultation, implications, potential other models, costs, prescriptive nature of outcomes, layers of bureaucracy, and reduction of investment reaching the 'coalface'.

Finally, Scotland also has no direct comparison with an Active Partnership. They do have Community Sports Hubs (CSHs), which bring a networked approach together within communities. The number of such CSHs increased from 59 to 179 between 2014 and 2019 (Sport Scotland, 2019a). It is acknowledged that,

> they bring together sport clubs and key local partners who want to develop and grow the sporting offering in the community. They focus on sustainable, community-led approaches that get clubs working together to develop welcoming, safe and fun environments for sport.
>
> (Sport Scotland, 2019a: online)

Arguably, they are not sub-regional in reach across local government boundaries and county boundaries. However, they do offer a useful case study of an alternative approach to the delivery and shaping of community provision to deliver the Sport Scotland strategy vision (Sport Scotland, 2019b) and wider government vision for the Active Scotland (2019) Outcomes Framework *A More Active Scotland: Scotland's Physical Activity Delivery Plan*. Interestingly, it was a direct response to delivering a participation and community sports club legacy from Glasgow Commonwealth Games 2014. It has an annual expenditure of £1.5 million.

Sub regional sport development governance: the structure, scope, and role of English Active Partnerships

The origins of sub-regional governance of sport are a much longer debate than there is space to accommodate here. Indeed, there was a period when regional sports boards existed across wide expanses of England with various reaches of power and links to what was then The English Sports Council (Houlihan and White, 2002). Furthermore, sport was also located within economic and social development agencies such as the Regional Development Agencies, for example. These various historic agencies had what can be described as devolved powers from central Parliament to set agendas, build strategic frameworks, and, in some areas, distribute finance. This detailed historic story is not the focus of this chapter, but it is worth being aware of this as a precursor to and background context to the CSPs and most recently Active Partnerships that now dominate this scale of the sport development landscape.

With the arrival of the Coalition government of 2010 and the much vaunted 'bonfire of the quangos' (O'Leary, 2015), many areas of policy experienced the loss of sub-regional structures and agencies. But, sport survived this cull of non-departmental public agencies (NDPAs). CSPs technically emerged from the regional Active Sport Partnership delivery networks across England in key sports. In 2009, there were 49 CSPs across Sport England's former nine regions. This picture is complicated by the varied form, structure, and legal entity of these CSPs. For example, research undertaken by Mackintosh (2011), some of the first on CSPs, identified a fragmented system across the East Midlands. In his study, one CSP was a wholesale movement of a local government sport development department (20 staff), another was a limited company with ten staff and a number of part time delivery staff, and a third CSP was a charity, with two based in a university building as a partnership arrangement. Philpotts, Quarmby, and Grix (2011) likewise argued for how CSPs played a key role in delivering centralised government policy at grass roots level.

However, this is far removed from the largest challenge of the CSP, and now Active Partnerships, which is explaining to partners, the sport sector, and communities what they do and represent. Arguably, the Active Partnership Network (APN) (2020) defines an Active Partnerships as

> locally based strategic organisations that recognise that activity levels are affected by a complex system of influences and no single organisation or programme create sustainable change at scale. By adopting a collaborative whole system approach, Active Partnerships seek to make active lifestyles the social norm for everyone and address the worrying levels of inactivity in society.
>
> (APN, 2020: online)

This illustrates a complex and fluid identity for a key strategic sport and physical activity agency in a region. Active Partnerships partly reflect the varied geography, economies, and social and cultural contexts they encompass. A rural Active Partnership that covers the domain of farming communities with high social class will engage differently with its populations, NGB regional officers, and local governments. Likewise, Greater Sport, which covers a population of around 3 million people in Greater Manchester's ten local authorities, will have a very different radical challenge with some of the most inactive, deprived, and unhealthy communities in the UK in the backdrop of the 'Northern Powerhouse'. In some electoral wards, such partnerships will have to work with complex multi-faceted social issues which the latest government strategy has outlined (DCMS, 2015). This will see them position officers and staff at the front line of delivering social impacts through sport in areas such as mental health and community regeneration and development. In other areas they will draw down monies from sources to facilitate and strategically enable delivery with minimal paid internal delivery teams. Active Partnerships are funded centrally by Sport England, but they can also apply for other core funding for projects to target certain population groups. They also play a fundamental role now in marketing, messaging, and campaigning around key thematic projects they are delivering. It is here that evolving roles in sport development are emerging in professional social media management whether linking to national campaigns like #ThisGirlCan or devising and generating local content that builds interest in traditional gyms or outdoor wellbeing projects such as *parkrun*.

Strategic sport development: what do we mean by this?

Arguably, the key role for the CSP that has evolved into Active Partnership, and may yet develop in Wales and other nations, is to play the role of strategic agency for a region. This is particularly pertinent in the latest iteration of Sport England's strategy with its focus on people (think local communities, diversity, and workforce), place (where people live and the range of communities they represent), and sport specific challenges and developments where NGBs cross over with Active Partnerships for a regional approach. At level 4, it is arguably too soon to explore the theoretical management literature around strategy and sport management. However, it is important to be aware of the notion of sport development officers being strategic as opposed to operational. Operational work is the day-to-day existence of a workforce, the partners they collaborate with and places and spaces of sport and physical activity they use in delivery. Strategy could be defined as the establishing of medium- to long-term goals and putting in places strategy, action plans, and vision documents to make sure an organisation and its stakeholder communities deliver the goals, aims, and objectives. This applies for a region aligned to Active Partnerships and their orientation to national Sport England goals, DCMS strategy, and even wider goals such as health and obesity plans.

In introducing sport development policy, practice, and theory, this chapter consider the agencies that play this role at what is referred to as 'sub-regional' organisational level, which is often how Active Partnerships are described. Key skills that would be implicated in such work include:

- Advocacy – sharing knowledge and arguing for and against policy changes in a region.
- Research, evidence, and insight – building strong region evidence and what is increasingly referred to as 'market intelligence' on user groups, statistics for the region, progress again region key performance indicators (KPIs).
- Marketing – use of social media and digital to develop online 'presence' for campaigns, regional issues, events, and mass participation programmes.
- Programme delivery – implementation of project delivery (e.g. coaching, mental health and sport, interventions with youth 'at risk'; pilot projects).
- Accountability – offer a voice for the region internally and externally with funders who provide public money to support general services and specific projects.
- Funding – act as a vehicle for collaboration with external strategic partners to draw down high level macro funds at a sub-regional level.
- Advisory and expertise on strategic matters – work with partners such as NHS, local government sport services, mental health, youth services and education, social and health care and politics on matters relating to sport and physical activity.

All Active Partnerships also operate through a board that sits 'above' the main organisation. This board has to operate independent of the organisation and 'check and challenge' the daily operational work and strategic plans of the organisation. Most Active Partnerships operate in a variety of forms from limited company through to charity. They also are located in a range of physical locations from university buildings, business parks, to sport-specific settings. Size of Active Partnerships varies and at present no research is available on the 43 strategic agencies in terms of employees and balance of sport development professionals by age, gender, ethnicity, and sexuality. Given other areas of imbalance in board membership and Chief Executive Officers (CEOs) such as NGBs (Long, Robinson, Spracklen, 2005; Sporting Equals, 2020), it would be interesting to explore this national picture.

What is clear is that such shifts towards partnership-based delivery models for sport development are not unique to the UK. In other research sport development, academics have explored the mechanisms of how effective they are in Canada (Misener, Harman and Doherty, 2013; Parent and Harvey, 2009) and partnerships and the development of capacity building in stakeholders in Australia (Casey, Payne, and Eime, 2009). Partnership is not a UK, or English phenomenon for organisation delivery. It is arguably part of a global trend in the delivery of sport and physical activity (MacDonald, 2005; Parent and Harvey, 2009; Philpotts, Quarmby, and Grix, 2011). Likewise, whilst often viewed as a 'panacea', or ultimate solution for delivery challenges, others have expressed long-standing concerns over the centralisation control it gives government over sport development (Philpotts, Quarmby, and Grix, 2011). Mackintosh (2011) in his analysis of four CSPs (pre-conversion to Active Partnerships) recognised that the very nature of these partnerships is often fragmented, complex, and fluid. Indeed, 15 years ago, MacDonald (2005: 597) in a national study of CSPs identified,

> enlarging managerial power in this model clearly sits at odds with devolving power to local communities. However, in this vein, the strategic partnership approach may not be so useful in satisfying the government's goal of dramatically increasing levels of physical activity within the population.

In this quote, we see early concerns over the controlling and centralising potential of large-scale management partnerships in regions. If we assume, conservatively, there are now an average of 20 staff in Active Partnerships, this moves the workforce towards around 800 employees driven by a central policy agenda from DCMS (2015) and Sport England (2016). There is a parallel agenda that is emerging, which is the need to ground partnerships in local, community-led projects that are 'bottom-up' not 'top down'. It remains to be seen if Wales did proceed with their regional tier of decision making and policy implementation on top of existing local government (Baker, 2017; Sport Wales, 2017) or whether like England there would be a relative stagnation in sport participation patterns (Widdop et al., 2017). It is clear that Active Partnerships have a growing presence nationally and regionally in terms of their workforce scope and scale. Whether the sport development and community development approaches taken in all areas are working remains to be seen. Perhaps the most significant people to ask are the communities they service. As MacDonald (2005: 597) identified in relation to CSPs before they became rebranded Active Partnerships "merely because governments or other agencies declare an arrangement as a partnership, it does not follow *ipso facto* that *it is* a partnership". A slightly more critical lens through students of sport development will allow you to consider which agencies are working better, which strategies are effective and question whether approaches are employing evidence-based policy or policy-led evidence (Cairney, 2016). A total of 43 Active Partnerships, then mapped over 113 sports with over 300 NGBs, gives considerable room for varied cultures, organisational leadership, and positioning of 'community' in community sport development. This doesn't even take into account the multiple local authorities at various tiers and over 150,000 voluntary sports clubs and their body of sports participants and volunteers and coaches. Weaving a neat partnership 'whole system' approach that ACN (2020) talk of may be aspirational at best but brings back the metaphor of Collins (1995) of how the sport development system in the UK resembles a complex bowl of spaghetti. Here he drew the analogy of how organisational and command and control structures often failed to align correctly and more likely became entwined and challenging to understand. Navigating and understanding the system is the first step for the student of sport development. Making decisions about the most effective routes to deliver project and programme outcomes becomes the next step for us to consider. Strategic visions and structures are in place. It is for you as critical scholars of a professional subject to evaluate their policies, programmes, and processes.

▰▰▰▰▰▰▰ CASE STUDY 11.1 ▰▰▰▰

Regional sport strategy policy 'drift' and devolution in Wales

Wales is a useful comparison case in sport development policy terms with England. England has 43 sub-regional agencies, previously 49, in what seems an ever-decreasing concentrated number of strategic bodies responsible for the implementation of national sport policy at a more local sub-regional level. The English partnerships have been in place since their original formation as Active Sports delivery network partnerships in key sports in each region. Over 15 years they have evolved into strategic agencies that play a key role in shaping agencies and individual communities regionally to be able to support the national vision of Sport England to embed the DCMS (2015) policies. If we take the example of Greater Manchester, an area with 3 million population encompassing very diverse communities in ten local authorities, the Greater Sport vision for addressing inactivity is a highly complex sub-regional social-welfare 'wicked issue'. It is not a simple top-down approach that is done from the Active Partnership 'to' its recipients in individual homes and communities. Likewise, sport development officers responsible for market insight and data across this area now use data sets that can cover entire other nations. Thus, these platforms need to be thought of as complex partnerships (Baker, 2017; Mackintosh, 2011).

This case study uses the context of England to relate to the potential use of sub-regional agencies in wales. The Baker Review (2017) of community sport development and Sport Wales (2017) proposals establish various recommendations. These embrace what are a mix of principles and ideas from research evidence. If we already have NGBs and local government, schools, private providers, and higher education alongside large numbers of volunteer-led sports clubs, why have another tier of sub-regional platforms for sport development? It could be argued that there are other options for delivery, planning and advocacy (campaigning and policy work) for sport development in Wales.

Read the review by Baker (2017) – this is a typical review of many that surface in the realm of sport development. They have research, recommendations, methodologies, and an outline for what next. In reading this report evaluate the following:

Seminar questions

- The scope and aims (why has it been designed? What does it want to establish?)
- Methodology (what are the strengths and weaknesses?)
- Findings from data and literature (what is the key information here?).

Seminar role play questions

Following the Baker Review (2017) what would you have recommended?

- New sub-regional structure or not?
- If yes/no – why? (try and justify)
- What can we learn from the evolution and implementation of Active Partnerships in England?

Key resource:

Baker, C. (2017) *Coordination of Community Sport Development in Wales: An Investigation of Stakeholder Perspectives Concerning the Organisation and Structure of Community Sport in Wales*, Gloucester: University of Gloucester, available at: http://eprints.glos.ac.uk/4322/3/Coordination%20of%20 Community%20Sport%20Development%20in%20Wales%20-%20Final%20 Report.pdf [accessed at 1/5/2020].

Historical context of Active Partnerships (were County Sport Partnerships until 2019)

See Mackintosh, C. (2011) An analysis of County Sports Partnerships in England: The fragility, challenges and complexity of partnership working in sports development, *International Journal of Sport Policy and Politics*, 7:3, 45–64.

References

Active Partnerships Network (APN) (2020) *What are Active Partnerships?*, available at: www.activepartnerships.org/?gclid=EAIaIQobChMI5dXdrZ2S6QIV27tCh2T_ AABEAAYASAAEgJfy_D_BwE [accessed on 1 May 2020].

Active Scotland (2019) *A More Active Scotland: Scotland's Physical Activity Delivery Plan*, Glasgow: Active Scotland.

Baker, C. (2017) *Coordination of Community Sport Development in Wales: An Investigation of Stakeholder Perspectives Concerning the Organisation and Structure of Community Sport in Wales*, Gloucester: University of Gloucester.

Cairney, P. (2016) *The Politics of Evidence-Based Policy Making*, London: Palgrave.

Casey, M. W., Payne, W. R., and Eime, R. M. (2009) Partnership and capacity building strategies in community sports and recreation programs, *Managing Leisure*, 14:3, 167–176.

Collins, M. (1995) *Sports Development Locally and Regionally*, Reading: Institute of Leisure and Amenity Management (ILAM).

DCMS (2015) *Sporting Nation*, London: DCMS.

Houlihan, B. and White, A. (2002) *The Politics of Sports Development*, London: Routledge.

O'Leary, C. (2015) Agency termination in the UK: What explains the 'Bonfire of the Quangos'?, *West European Politics*, 38: 6, 1327–1344.

Long, J. Robinson, P., and Spracklen, K. (2005) Promoting racial equality within sport organisations, *Journal of Sport and Social Issues*, 29:1, 41–59.

MacDonald, I. (2005) Theorising partnerships: Governance, communicative action and sport policy, *Journal of Social Policy*, 34:4, 579-600.

Mackintosh, C. (2011) An analysis of County Sports Partnerships in England: The fragility, challenges and complexity of partnership working in sports development, *International Journal of Sport Policy and Politics*, 7:3, 45–64.

Misener, K., Harman, A. and Doherty, A. (2013) Understanding the local sports council as a mechanism for community sport development, *Managing Leisure*, 18:4, 300–315.

Parent, M. M. and Harvey, J. (2009) Towards a management model for sport and physical activity community-based partnerships, *European Sport Management Quarterly*, 9:1, 23–45.

Philpotts, L., Grix, J. and Quarmby, T. (2011) Centralised grass roots policy and 'new governance': A case study of County Sport Partnerships in the UK – unpacking the paradox, *International Review for the Sport Sociology*, 46:3, 265–281.

Reed, A. (2016) *Appraisal of the Future Role of CSPs*, Loughborough: Sageimpact.

Sport England (2016) *Towards an Active Nation*, London: Sport England.

Sporting Equals (2020) *Leaderboard*, available at: www.sportingequals.org.uk/programmes/leaderboard.html [accessed on 27 April 2020]

Sport NI (2009) *Sport Matters: The Northern Ireland Strategy for Sport and Physical Recreation 2009–2019*, Belfast: Sport NI.

Sport Scotland (2019a) *Sport for life*, available at: www.sportforlife.org.uk/ [accessed on 1 May 2020].

Sport Scotland (2019b) *Sport for Life: A Vision for Sport in Scotland*, Glasgow: Sport Scotland.

Sport Wales (2017) *Sport Wales Review: An Independent Report* (2017), Cardiff: Sport Wales.

Sport Wales (2019) *A Vision for Sport in Wales*, Cardiff: Sport Wales.

The Welsh Assembly (2015) *The Wellbeing of Future Generations (Wales) Act 2015*, Cardiff: The Welsh Assembly.

Widdop, P., King, N., Parnell, D., Cutts, D., and Millward, P. (2017) Austerity, policy and sport participation in England, *International Journal of Sport Policy and Politics*, 10:1, 7–24.

CHAPTER 12

Voluntary and third sector sport development

This chapter will provide an update on the voluntary sector in the UK and its differential scale across the home nations where possible. It will also give you as students an outline of the significance of the sector to both the economy, delivery of policy, and role in achieving social and political outcomes in sport development. Volunteering will also cover more nuanced concepts that have become more common in recent iterations of England's Volunteer Strategy (Sport England, 2017) such as recruitment, retention, and also the multiple pathways into becoming a volunteer. The chapter will also challenge conventional approaches to volunteering in sport development by locating them within wider policy debate around relationships with NGBs and new organisations such as *parkrun*. It will consider the differences between episodic (one-off) and core volunteers and the approaches of traditional NGBs to core funding work from home nation Sports Councils to how they work with these groups. Volunteers are the focus of policy, co-designers and deliverers of public policy and this issue will be examined through the interplay of sport clubs, government and other partners that seek the resources of the volunteer to implement sport development policy. For the sport development professional this opens discussions around what their role is now, as collaborations and partnerships become increasingly diverse, at times pressured and fragmented.

Size of volunteer market

In 2013, Sport and Recreation Alliance (SRA, 2013) research indicated that there are approximately 151,000 voluntary sports clubs in the UK with an average of around 24 volunteers in each of those clubs. Further research has identified that the average club has 204 members and thus a volunteer ratio of 1:8.5 (Join In, 2015). In England, 75 per cent of volunteers are located in sports clubs, the remaining 25 per cent work outside this formal volunteer setting. From 2017 to 2021 Sport England set out in its Sport Volunteer Strategy key commitments for sport development. These were to be used to support the DCMS (2015) vision for a more active nation from 2015. These included:

* £26m investment into volunteering between 2017 and 2021;

- £3m investment into the Opportunity Fund targeting people from disadvantaged areas;
- Up to £3 million investment into the Potentials Fund for those aged 10–20 years of age;
- £3m set aside for club support in 2016/17.

(Sport England, 2017)

In more recent research (Sport England, 2019), it was estimated that 6.2m people volunteered in sport, around 14 per cent of adults. Typical areas include providing transport (40%), coaching (38%), fulfilling committee or administrative roles (35%) and refereeing, umpiring, or officiating (22%).

Men are more likely to volunteer with 58 per cent of the population volunteering compared to 41 per cent of women. Furthermore, lower socio-economic class groups (NS-SEC 6-8) are under-represented with only 11 per cent volunteering compared to making up 31 per cent of the total population. This lower social class includes (NS SEC 6-8): semi-routine (e.g. postman, shop assistant, bus driver) and routine occupations; long-term unemployed or never worked. In other areas, such as age, there are clear clusters of popularity in the 16–24-year-old age category (19%) and the 45–54-years-olds (20%). Disabled individuals represent only 13 per cent of volunteers despite accounting for 21 per cent of the population. The research did, however, identify that the volunteer profile is generally reflective of the ethnicity profile of the country (Sport England, 2019).

Defining volunteers in sport

Defining a volunteer might seem an easy task. In sport development terms, it is the person that coaches for free, supports junior cricket sessions on a rainy evening by 'just helping out'. or collects tickets for entry to an event. However, as we start to explore volunteering in sport development, it will become clear that we need to unpick such terms carefully and with attention to the subtle conceptual and theoretical differences and similarities between individuals and communities of volunteers. The national context of each of the four countries is important also in starting to examine the landscape of what we might term 'sport development voluntarism'. Place is also important as this is also a shifting concept for us to understand in terms of who, where, and how people are volunteering in sport development. Here, new spaces are emerging where people effectively volunteer in online and virtual capacities. Furthermore, the roles undertaken by the voluntary sector in sport development are expanding into policy campaigning and advocacy, bid writing, funding applications, strategy consultation, business planning, and employee and volunteer management.

In definitional terms, this chapter works towards the voluntary sector encompassing organisations that are formal, not-for-profit, and constitutionally independent from state and are self-governing. Such organisations can, and do, engage with, and employ paid staff such as coaches and clubhouse bar staff; the assumption is that they do so for public rather than stakeholder benefit (Milligan and Conradson, 2011). A sports club in Scotland that employs six coaches, four bar staff; and a club secretary still remains voluntary membership in its focus and outlook. This is especially the case if it has an underpinning club constitution and code of conduct and governance. Where a club moves into profit orientation, commercialisation, and investment for the purposes of future income generation for those beyond the club (e.g. board members, club owners or share and stakeholders), it loses its voluntary status. Sport development officers have a long history of working with such clubs as their 'core business' whether they are in an NGB, charity, or local government agency.

When scoping what we mean by a volunteer, a number of books consider this issue in far more detail (see Cuskelly, Hoye, and Auld, 2006a; Cuskelly et al., 2006b). In this book, the essence of this most fluid of terms is worth exploring specifically from a sport development perspective. First, it is useful to use the context of Anheir (2005) who makes the distinction between *formal* and *informal* volunteering. Here, if a sport coach conducts voluntary work outside the boundaries of any formal organisation (friends, family, neighbours) this is an *informal voluntary role*. If, in contrast, a sports club or church is the base for a voluntary sport helper this, according to Anheir (2005), is a *formal volunteering* capacity. Kendall and Knapp (1995) famously state that any attempt to neatly define the role of the volunteer is at best something that resembles a 'loose and baggy monster'. Indeed, Hoye et al. (2008) argue that the challenge of even considering the role and position of volunteers in sport development is the shifting historical scope of this policy area over time.

To help students begin to unpick this complex area of a most important of areas with sport development, it is worth focusing on a model presented by Cnaan et al. (1996). This allows for researchers in this area to explore this framework and consider where on this spectrum of categories and dimensions volunteering in sport development an individual or activity may 'sit'. For example, if a Welsh hockey club has links with a university to recruit volunteers that are unpaid, but part of a compulsory unit they have to complete, we can begin to unpick this activity as that which has an obligation aspect, perhaps provides reimbursement for expenses, is formal, and offers a number of intended benefits to different people (club, participants, and the university student). This moves the debate on from perhaps volunteering just being deemed formal or informal (Anheir, 2005).

There is considerable literature that asserts the importance of the voluntary sector (Nichols et al., 2019; SRA, 2020; online; Findlay-King et al., 2018; Hayton, 2016). Indeed, in the UK the sport and physical activity sector is the largest sector in terms of volunteering. Thus, given the crossover between the role of those working in sport development and the infrastructure of the volunteers, clubs, activities, and delivery of government policy through voluntarism, it is clear how significant this sector is. As already stated in this book, and elsewhere, sport development in the UK is diverse and has an intertwined history with government ideology (Collins, 2010; Cuskelly et al., 2006a; Wilson and Platts, 2018). When government has, for example, seen an increased role for volunteers over those members of the public sector pay role, this can be described as 'rolling back of the state' (Nichols et al., 2019; Widdop et al., 2017). Some have suggested the percentage involvement of the public sector is at its lowest ever level in decades at 20 per cent of the total sport and leisure stock (Wilson and Platts, 2018). Here, alongside the concept of austerity, we see volunteers being asked to step into providing sport, and even aspects of sport development provision previously provided by the state and other public sector funded bodies. This is perhaps also part of an increased focus for some volunteer clubs and voluntary associations on commercialisation, profession-alisation, and modernisation. As they move further away from their amateur origins and custodians of the game, they originally sought to volunteer around a gap is emerging that researchers are beginning to question (Harris, Mori, and Collins, 2009; Harris, Nichols, and Taylor, 2017).

The sport volunteer has become more central to the delivery of government targets and visions, and insight from research suggest that other public, private, and third sectors are facing ever greater challenges in sport development (Mori, Harris, and Collins, 2009; Harris and Houlihan, 2016). Consequently, for the sport development student working in collaboration and partnership with community sport, volunteer clubs across each of the home nations is now an imperative. First, students must understand the political and policy context of the volunteer setting, and how this is playing out for clubs, coaches, and participants. Second, the specific geographical context needs to be considered, in particular, the spatial and physical infrastructure that make up the 'place' aspects of sport development. For example, are there quality limitations around the infrastructure of playing fields, parks, built facilities or pools that constrain access and uptake? Furthermore, what perception barriers exist for populations that are under-active, non-engaged or not buying into a project. Here, it could be issues around gender, BAME misrepresentation, social class stereotypes, or sexuality representations. Finally, there are questions around the volunteer capacity to deliver the various visions, which incorporates numbers of coaches, volunteers, and the skill set (training, background, and knowledge) (Figure 12.1).

Volunteer sport development context

Figure 12.1 illustrates the very fluid and changing nature of the volunteer management context for sport development officers. Whether working as a regional officer in an NGB in Scotland or a Welsh local school that has attempted to develop links with a local triathlon club, this model attempts to illustrate how there will always be a considerable range of interacting factors. What is crucial is that you begin to understand that managing volunteers is core to any role in sport development. It may be that to achieve a critical local and national goal of using sport to challenge mental health a network of clubs is needed to implement a project in a city. For this to work we need to understand our volunteers, what motivates them and how they work. This is a vast area of academic research and fundamental foundational area of your sport development knowledge and skill set.

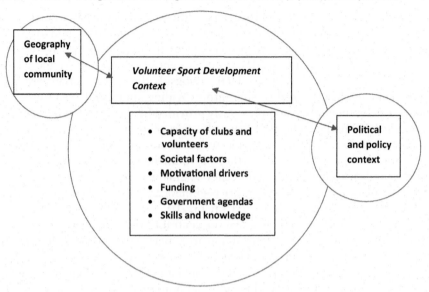

FIGURE 12.1 Dimensions of defining volunteering in sport communities

CASE STUDY 12.1

Mass participation in voluntary sport clubs

This professional issue will consider the NGB-volunteer interaction within the sport of amateur golf. It will outline the changing landscape of golf between 1980 and 2020 and how the NGB has had to change its approach to working with clubs, how golf as an industry is changing and the challenges with the voluntary sector in England. The issue will provide context for students to explore how the key sector of volunteer sport provision is experiencing a changing relationship with NGBs in an era of business relationships, the participant as consumer and clubs and participants as customers. The NGB for the sport of golf, England Golf, has long argued for the need to change (England Golf, 2004; England Golf 2008; Mills and Mackintosh, 2021 forthcoming). However, as others have argued more broadly to do with the voluntary sector as a vehicle and implementation tool for government sport policy, uptake and interest from the volunteers and their clubs can vary hugely. In this case study we look at the example of golf clubs particularly in relation to changing attitudes, bringing about organisational change, and building a fresh exciting new vision for a sport that has been viewed as sexist with heavily gender practices both inside and outside the clubhouse (Perkins, 2010; Vamplew, 2016).

England Golf is an NGB with around 100 paid staff that are located partially as working from home mobile staff across the regions and at central HQ at Woodhall

Spa in Lincolnshire. To put this in perspective, there are around 1900 golf clubs and an estimated 44,000 volunteers across the country that support playing members, ad hoc participants, and those that turn up to 'pay and play' (Mills and Mackintosh, 2021; forthcoming). A recent survey by England Golf (2018) indicated that there is an average membership of 484 members – considerably higher than Sport England estimates of 204 as the average membership and volunteer base of 23 people (Sport England, 2017). But, perhaps more crucially, this study showed that there was an average of 70 women and 6 junior girls. Thus, if we want to even gender imbalance nationally in sport policy terms some sports have more to do than others. They also have a more well-established set of gendered practices, by which we mean sexist behaviours, norms, and opinions within the clubhouse, committee spaces, and fairways and greens of the participation spaces.

The Equality Act 2010 offered a starting point for challenging practices that differentiated by gender and sex. No longer can club houses offer 'areas' for women, or memberships that are differentiated and give different 'access' or options. This would be deemed discriminatory. So, is golf starting to change? In 2018 the Royal and Ancient (R&A) the global body for the rules and coordination of golf outside of the USA (think FIFA for football, or the ICC for cricket) launched the Women and Girls Golf Charter (Royal & Ancient, 2020). This global policy and framework is meant as a line in the sand for moving forward the global game. It is also worth thinking back to earlier chapters about global factors that can shape local sport development. The Professional Golfers Association (PGA) has also launched "We Love Golf", an initiative meant to target women and girls participants. This launched in March 2017 and has around 85 clubs running it. An initial survey of clubs identified had attracted around 1000 junior participants in its first six months (PGA, 2018). Approximately 40 per cent of these were female. This form of programme could well be the lifeblood of future female volunteering. It has also been noted that,

> In July 2018, England Golf led the promotion of Women and Girls Golf Week, an industry wide social media campaign to raise awareness of women in golf and to challenge perceptions of the sport among women. The campaign, which was also supported by Scottish Golf, Wales Golf, the Irish Ladies Golf Union, and The R&A, encouraged female golfers to share their golfing stories on social media using the hashtag #WHYIGOLF. The response far exceeded England Golf's expectations. The campaign reached more than 2.5m people on Twitter and generated over 12million impressions.
>
> (Mackintosh and Mills, 2019)

Between these two programmes, it seems there is hope for golf to shape volunteer programmes in the future as more members move through into volunteer positions, formal and informal. Age and gender need to be considered as less of a factor and, if anything, a positive feature of a committee 'characteristic' to give diversity and diverse thinking as opposed to predominantly male perspectives on club, volunteer and participant governance and marketing.

Seminar questions

1. As a female regional development officer for England Golf, identify the potential challenges of approaching a heavily male biased golf club about the issue of gender equality.

2. You have a #WHYIGOLF social media campaign that you want to get a set of ten golf clubs (in a county) to use as part of the next Women and Girls Golf Week. What would be your approach and why? (What might be the challenges around working with volunteers?)

3. How could you sell the "We Love Golf" initiative by the PGA to these ten clubs? What volunteer skill set may be missing from the rollout and what might you do as SDO for golf in this county?

4. From the case study above, and your own wider reading, who are the key stakeholders for female volunteers in golf clubs in their attempts to seek better representation amongst the 44,000 national population of golf volunteers.

Further reading

Mackintosh and Mills (2019) Girls Who Golf: How England Golf is working to engage more women, *Sports Management*, 23:1, 70–73.

Mills, C. and Mackintosh, C. (2021 forthcoming) Sports club volunteering: The case of English golf clubs, *Sport in Society*, iFirst 1–20 forthcoming.

Harris, S., Mori, K. and Collins, S. (2009) Great expectations: Voluntary sports clubs and their role in delivering national policy for English sport, *Voluntas International Journal*, 20:4, 405–423.

References

Anheir, H. (2005) *Nonprofit Organizations: Theory, Management, Policy*, London: Routledge.

Collins, M. (2010) From 'sport for good' to 'sport for sport's sake' – not a good move for sports development in England?, *International Journal of Sport Policy and Politics*, 2:3, 367–379.

Cuskelly, G., Hoye, R. and Auld, C. (2006a) *Working with Volunteers in Sport: Theory and Practice*, London: Routledge.

Cuskelly, G., Taylor, T., Hoye, R., and Darcy, S. (2006b) Volunteer management practices and volunteer retention: A human resource management approach, *Sport Management Review*, 9:2, 141–163.

Cnaan, R., Handy, F., and Wadsworth, M. (1996) Defining who is a volunteer: Conceptual and empirical considerations, *Nonprofit and Voluntary Sector Quarterly*, 25:3, 364–383.

DCMS (2015) *Sporting Nation*, London: DCMS.

England Golf (2004) *Whole Sport Plan 2005–2009: A New Plan, New Partnership and New Investment*, Woodhall Spa: England Golf.

England Golf (2008) *Whole Sport Plan for Golf Development in England 2009–2013*, Woodhall Spa: England Golf.

England Golf (2018) *Club Membership Questionnaire: Key Findings 2018*, Woodhall Spa: England Golf.

Findlay-King, L., Nichols, G., Forbes, D., and Macfadyen, G. (2018) Localism and the Big Society: The asset transfer of leisure centres and libraries–fighting closures or empowering communities?, *Leisure Studies*, 37:2, 158–170.

Harris, S. and Houlihan, B. (2016) Implementing the community sport legacy: The limits of partnerships, contracts and performance management, *European Sports Management Quarterly*, 16:4, 433–458.

Harris, S., Mori, K., and Collins, M. (2009) Great expectations: The role of voluntary sports clubs as policy implementers, *Voluntas International Journal*, 20:4, 405–423.

Harris, S., Nichols, G. S. and Taylor, M. (2017) Bowling even more alone: trends towards individual participation in sport, *European Sport Management Quarterly*, 17:3, 290–311.

Hayton, J. (2016) Plotting the motivation of student volunteers in sports-based outreach work in North East England, *Sport Management Review*, 19:5, 563–577.

Hoye, R., Cuskelly, G., Taylor, T., and Darcy, S. (2008) Volunteer motives and retention in community sport: A study of Australian rugby clubs. *Australian Journal on Volunteering*, 13, 40–48.

Kendall, J. and Knapp, M. (1995). A loose and baggy monster: boundaries, Definitions and typologies, in Davis-Smith, J., Rochester, C. and Hedley, R. (eds), *An Introduction to the Voluntary Sector*, London: Routledge, 65–94.

Mackintosh, C. and Mills, C. (2019) Girls Who Golf: How England Golf is working to engage more women, *Sports Management*, 23:1, 70–73.

Milligan, C. and Conradson, D. (eds.) (2011) *Landscapes of Voluntarism: New Spaces of Health, Welfare and Governance*, Bristol: Policy Press.

Mills, C. and Mackintosh, C. (2021 forthcoming) Categorising sports club volunteering by goal focus and activity: The case of English golf clubs, *Sport in Society*, iFirst, 1–20 forthcoming.

Nichols, G., Hogg, E., Knight, C., and Storr, R. (2019) Selling volunteering or developing volunteers? Approaches to promoting sports volunteering, *Voluntary Sector Review*, iFirst, 1–16.

Perkins, C. (2010) The performance of golf: Landscape, place, and practice in north west England. *Journal of Sport & Social Issues*, 34:3, 312–338.

Professional Golfers Association (PGA) (2018) The PGA launches We Love Golf, 22 May 2018, available at: Cwww.pga.info/news/the-pga-launches-we-love-golf/ [accessed on 01 June 2020]

Royal and Ancient (2020) *Women in Golf Charter: A commitment to a More Inclusive Culture within Golf*, S Andrews: R&A.

Sport England (2017) *Sport Volunteer Strategy*, London: Sport England.

Sport England (2019) *Sports Club Volunteering 2018: Summary Report*, London: Sport England.

SRA (Sport and Recreation Alliance) (2013) *Sports Club Survey 2013: A Review of Clubs including Membership, Facility Access, Finances, Challenges and Opportunities*, London: SRA.

SRA (2020) *Hidden diamonds: Uncovering the true value of sport volunteers*, available at: www.sportandrecreation.org.uk/pages/volunteering-research [accessed on 01 June 2020].

Widdop, P., King, N., Parnell, D., Cutts, D., and Millward, P. (2017) Austerity, policy and sport participation in England, *International Journal of Sport Policy and Politics*, 10:1, 7–24.

Wilson, R. and Platts, C. (2018) *Managing and Developing Community Sport*, London: Routledge.

Vamplew, W. (2016) Empiricism, theoretical concepts and the development of the British golf club before 1914, *Sport in Society*, 19:3, 425–454.

CHAPTER 13

Coaching, coaches, and sport development

Sport development and sport coaching have always been closely linked spheres of professional practice as well as policy intervention by government. The chapter will set the scene for considering coaching policy and practice in the UK. In particular, it will look at the emergence of the UK Coaching Framework, associated levels 1–4 UKCC awards that have been explicitly tied to the governance, funding, and development of coaches in the community and at elite levels for the last two decades. It will consider the recent *Review of the UKCC* (2018) by DCMS and Sport England (Mackintosh and Carter, 2018) and, how this will affect community clubs, coaches, and the volunteer sector as countries such as England launch the *Coaching Plan for England* (Sport England, 2017). The chapter will not focus on the sport coaching process extensively, and wider conceptualising of coaching and the coach per se. A considerable number of books already do this (see Cassidy, Jones, and Potrac, 2009 for a starting point). However, it will revisit the place of coaching and the coach within sport development policy and provision. In 2017, UK Coaching, the strategic professional development agency for sports coaching in the UK, undertook a survey of 50,000 members of the public to ascertain coaching attitudes, behaviours, and qualification background. The survey was repeated again in 2019. Of those interviewed, 58 per cent had no qualification at all, 19 per cent had level 1 or 2 (or equivalent) badges and 8 per cent had level 3 or 4 (or equivalent). The UK Coaching research team estimated that there are approximately 3 million sports coaches in the UK from this research (UK Coaching, 2019). It will again consider the traditional tensions present within coach development work of local sport development officers and the evolving landscape of coaches that operate as volunteers in very diverse settings beyond traditional boundaries of sport for sports sake. As sport policy shifts, and sport development process, practice, and assumptions within organisations and the profession, so does the role of coaching. A good example of this has been the policy assumption that sport can play a social welfare role in deprived communities, tackling myriad policy goals such as mental health, literacy, and crime prevention. With this pivot of policy comes a complex dynamic for sports coaching and the agencies involved. Ultimately, how and whether they can deliver such promises could remain a panacea or reveal lucrative windows for charities, NGBs, and others to access central government funds acting as the delivery arm of sport development policy.

Coaching and sport development policy context

UK Coaching is the national agency responsible for coach education and professional development in the UK. Formerly known as Sports Coach UK, it has a long history that dates back to the Coaching Task Force work around 2000 and the development of national plans for coaching. Emerging from such centralised policy work came the United Kingdom Coaching Certificate (UKCC), the framework for accreditation of coaching 'levels of awards' across a number of NGBs in the four home nations. This system provides the quality assurance benchmarking process against which NGBs apply to have an award at a particular level, go through accreditation and then get approved to 'run' the award. Although, since the 2017–2018 review of the UKCC, arguably the centralised control of UK Coaching has been reduced. It was originally founded around a similar time as what might be deemed the heyday of 'coaching development work' where many NGBs had a heavy focus on volunteers and paid staff moving through a pathway of development.

In 2017, a review of the UKCC was commissioned by Sport England and Sport Scotland, undertaken by the Sport and Recreation Alliance and Manchester Metropolitan University. The research review component of this was undertaken to establish if the system was 'fit for purpose' in its current form, within the current context of policy and framed against its original historical policy goals and objectives (Mackintosh and Carter, 2018). This research involved interviews with 12 key national agencies as stakeholders in sport coaching policy, and 12 focus groups encompassing coaches from minority groups, higher education coaching course providers, and covering around 40 NGBs across the two countries. In addition, an online survey with around 1300 coaches was undertaken to establish feedback on the UKCC system from their perspective, Specifically how meaningful, useful, and flexible UKCC courses are across over 46 core funded NGBs. Sport Northern Ireland and Sport Wales opted out of the research, although they did receive the findings process. At this stage, the report and its findings remain confidential due to the implications of the recommendations.

However, what is clear is that a new platform for sport development, and in particular community sport coaching education, is emerging. It seems that The Chartered Institute for the Management of Sport and Physical Activity (CIMSPA) has now developed 26 different professional skill and role descriptors for different positions in the sector. Sport coaching is one such mapped area. Interestingly, despite its sizeable role within the sector historically and in management terms, sport development is not a single 'professional standard'. Perhaps this is due to it not covering one but straddling many diverse areas in sport and leisure including youth work, community development, sport management, project management, and coaching. The Professional Standards Framework is defined as, "The CIMSPA Professional Standards Framework outlines occupations and job roles within the sport and physical activity sector, by defining what knowledge and skills an individual must understand and demonstrate to undertake a particular role" (CIMSPA, 2020: online).

They now have, for example, Assistant Coach, Coach, Senior Coach, Coach in a High Performance Environment professional standards, which are also mapped onto CIMSPA documents (CIMSPA, 2020: online) and sit alongside the existing vocational and educational UKCC packages that NGBs and SGBs have in place. So, for example, if you already have a level 1 FA educational qualification, you can approach CIMSPA to see where this and your experience 'fits'. Assuming that perhaps you have 'Coach' you can apply for CIMSPA level Senior Coach. This sounds simple, but the reality is that in the complex world of community and elite sport, NGBs will hold true their interest in a 20-year-long established educational qualification system. As it stands, NGB systems, UKCC, and CIMSPA professional standards are running in parallel. Making sense of this is important as for many it is simply a case of carry on as normal with use of the UKCC system with 'their sport' and 'their setting' the most important factor.

What may emerge from this is that having formalised qualification systems for many of the population that make up the 3 million community and grass roots coaches is far from critical to their existing and the opportunities they provide. However, as people move from volunteering in localised provision that is about getting people active, having fun, and engaging with participants into more advanced performance-led work qualifications, training, and the nature of the education shifts (Burt and Morgan, 2014). It is also critical that we acknowledge that new policy at national level (DCMS, 2015; Sport Scotland, 2019; Sport Wales, 2020: online) is starting to ask the volunteer coach and paid coach to work in diverse areas such as crime prevention, youth rehabilitation, mental health, and community development planning. Traditional coach education is not well placed to deliver these goals, and perhaps NGBs and SGBs are not the best organisations to embed training for volunteers here. Partnerships in some cases are emerging with national mental health charities (MIND, 2020: online) in their projects Get Set to Go for working with those with more complex mental health needs. In the case of Mind, they trained over 325 sports coaches specifically in working with mental health communities with around 1000 participants over a two-year period (Mind, 2017). Such coaches were branded as sports coordinators and had a package of online, peer, and community support built into the programmes. It is thus clear that this model for delivery acknowledges a highly complex and nuanced 'coaching' model that does not deliver a standard benefit for all (Mind, 2017). Sport development delivery needs to be aware of, therefore not making across the board assumptions about, the role of coaching. This study independently evaluated the impact of this tailored sports coaching and the process around mental health. It can be seen that it is early days for this major area of sport development national policy in this domain. Furthermore, a Ministry of Justice Review undertaken by Professor Rosie Meek (Meeks, 2018) of the role of sport and physical activities in the criminal justice system identified similar findings. Training and coach education here does not have to be just those that work with sport in settings that are criminal justice-based. It could also be where sport development project and initiatives targeting say deprived communities may need the associated coaches to have skills in behaviour management.

Beyond two binary professional fields

Where sport development and coach development have a long-established historical cross over is in the work of the various agencies Active Partnerships, Sports Councils, local government sport development teams and NGBs/SGBs working with the voluntary sector. The previous chapter illustrated the sizeable scope, breadth, and importance of such volunteers. With an estimated 151,000 clubs and an estimated third of those being involved in coaching in clubs (Sport England, 2018), it is fundamental to make clear that whilst high performance elite sport is where much of the media focus lies, it is community-based work in clubs where the higher proportion of sport development activity is. To consider sport development activity in this space, we can perhaps look at the day-to-day lived realities of the local government SDO (Bloyce, 2008; Mackintosh, 2012), NGB SDO organisational change (Thompson, Bloyce, and Mackintosh, 2020), and sub-regional strategic SDO partnerships (Baker, 2017). In all these cases, several words seem to emerge from the organisational landscape fragmentation, change and increased complexity. Into this mix we must also add in the diversifying settings in which coaching is now expected to operate and with this the more nuanced and sensitive awareness reflective coaches must operate. For example, Morgan and Batlle (2019) in their study of sport-for-development landscape suggest that coaches and youth workers abilities need to clearly mapped out, but also understood not as a fixed set of skills. Students, graduates and established SDOs that are working in such community development roles to re-engage disaffected youth, prevent drug misuse or other social justice-led campaigns must consider how 'coaching' is less about sport and more about development. Training volunteers and working across this divide is a new and exciting space for those in sport development, but as Morgan and Batlle (2019) warn it can easily be a myopic panacea that fails to deliver and offers many veiled benefits.

Ethnicity and community coaching is also an area in which advocacy and campaigning organisations such as Sporting Equals focus. The subtle localised differences between communities and within supposedly bounded group of individuals are critical here. For example, in their work around British Muslim youth, Mackintosh and Dempsey (2017) identify that assumptions are made, beliefs held, and stereotypes set around the Islamic faith communities. If an agency is looking to support community development in such a way around, say, sport coaching development and youth engagement, it is necessary to build not just coach development links. This approach would have sat comfortably in the 1980s national pilot projects (Houlihan and White, 2002).

Instead, what is required is more of a global lens for those engaged in sport development and parallel community development processes. Long, Fletcher, and Watson (2017) argue for this in their study of sport and leisure and social justice, where they argue for placing the 'researched' centre stage, specifically their experiences and understanding. Such insights into marginalised youth, 'the disengaged', inactive, and other minority groups can arguably shed more light on wider society too.

A theme within this book is that of the diversification of sport development away from its historical 'traditions', original activity bases set out in the 1970s facility boom of the UK and golden era of leisure centre and sport facility provision. This reshaping of a backdrop to sport development came from the need to, simply put, get communities using sport facilities. Often, these were classified as target groups (women, low income, and so on). As we move forward 40 years, it seems intriguing that with a profession potentially of over 10,000 individuals alongside ever expanding infrastructure in delivery and development, the coach is not given more attention. Community coaches sit, it has been argued, at the very intersection of where community sport development has failed. Community sport is the embodiment of public policy narratives and agendas, it reflects how sports clubs and coaches resist and embrace government intentions and plans. But, perhaps most simply, the coach who works with other volunteers, participants, parents, and wider local partners (schools, clubs, and agencies) is uniquely positioned to instil change from the bureaucratic policy level at the 'street level' (Lipsky, 1979).

As a sense of scale, around 3000 sport coaches undertook a UKCC coaching qualification in Scotland in 2017–2018 (Davidson, 2017). Across the sports that have an established qualification framework and accreditation system linked to the UKCC, this shows that community through to elite sport coach education is an important area of Scottish sport development. In England, no numbers were able to be obtained, the same for Northern Ireland and Wales. Indeed, Scotland is also an interesting case study because it shows a genuinely UK 'reach' to the UKCC and unified system. For many university students, school pupils, sixth formers, adults in clubs, and youth sport settings the UKCC remains the key system for enabling coach education. This said, other channels of coach reflection, development and enterprise are starting to emerge. Many of these are positioned on platforms such as Vimeo, You Tube, and individual SGB websites. Where historically a regional officer for a local government agency in Scotland might solely have pushed the UKCC pathway, now some coaches would actively engage with these emerging online platforms for more personalised and flexible coach development activities. This also alters practice links with sport development. Social media, for example, is a way a rural agency can link sport clubs into such work and offer far reaching marketing of the coach development 'offer'. Through Instagram, Facebook, and Twitter this can build sizeable coverage of a SGB 'push' to recruit more people into the first tier of community coaching. Having an online offer then becomes increasing critical as opposed to a traditional two-day courses in a clubhouse or community centre. It can also open up new avenues of possibility for previously under-represented community sport development coaches such as the disabled, lower socio-economic classes and specific individuals from ethnic groups. Whilst this is set within the context of Scotland, many of the core principles apply to each of the other three home nations. It brings with it a challenge for the future of sport coaching frameworks across the UK (CIMSPA, 2020: online; Mackintosh and Carter, 2018). As it stands, there is no clear direction for the UKCC, the decision around its future; potential transition into future arrangements remains with home nations and individual NGBs and SGBs. It seems Scotland has made decisions on its future based on the review of the UKCC but exact details at the time of writing remain unknown. In England there is a similar story. As with other themes in this book, it is also worth recognising that whilst macro policy drivers such as the above are important, in many cases the local coach will adapt, resist, and transform policy regardless (Gale and Ives, 2019; Ives et al., 2019) (Figure 13.1).

Figure 13.1 illustrates how any sport coach in any sport development setting will have a complex and multi-faceted range of support, enablers, and potential barriers to delivering what we might think of as 'just coaching'. This visual representation is meant as a model to be drawn upon when considering a starting point for exploring community sport coaching and how it overlaps with sport development. In this visual model there are five key aspects. First, the

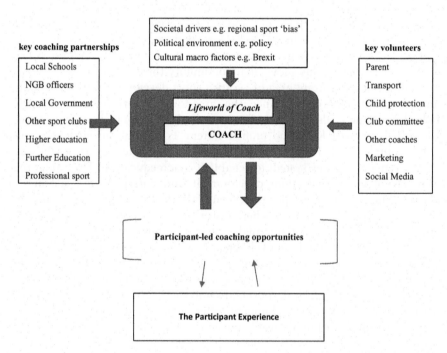

FIGURE 13.1 Diagram illustrating the influences on a coach's lifeworld positioned within the sport development policy context

participant experience – much of the coaching literature has shaped the view in recent years that sport is not about what the coach wants, needs, or demands (Ives et al., 2019; Potrac, Jones, and Armour, 2002). It also locates the coach as not just an entity in existence themselves but within their *Lifeworld*. This essentially acknowledges that, conceptually, a coach is influenced and shapes their own lived world they inhabit. This is a growing realm of social science research in coaching (Cronin and Armour, 2018; Hughes, 2021 forthcoming). For example, in considering coaching with community groups and disabilities, the first step could be to adopt an *ableism* approach and view people as socially 'able' as opposed to disabled. This alters provision, need, and approach (Ives et al., 2020). If we start from the position of participant needs first, this is a long way from the view that locates government policy and the state as central. Second, there is the coach, here we should now view this as a diverse set of people around themes of age, gender, sexuality, and ethnicity in multiple contexts where some of these impressions of, say, a Muslim female coach challenges norms and long-held assumptions. Interactions between this are the coaching opportunities that are designed. Again, these are now often 'co-produced' as opposed to coach-led. It may even be that the coach facilitates the sessions and the participants steer, manage, and coach themselves. Finally, it could be considered helpful to students new to this area to analyse the final three strands of this model. The first strand is the macro influences that overarch the whole sphere and lived experience of community coaches. This covers socio-political, economic, and cultural factors that are often beyond the influence and control of a coach but shape their everyday. Good examples in recent years include the Covid-19 virus breakout, austerity measures since 2010 by various Conservative governments, Brexit, and planned new Sport England policy in 2021. All influence coaching but perhaps outside of the 'world of coaching' and the lived experience of daily life. See a study of RFU community coaches for more detail on this type of approach to studying policy on sport development and coaching. Finally, the final two elements are *key coaching partnerships* and *key volunteers*. These are aimed at helping students to conceptualise the community sport coaching process within the wider sport development structures, environments, and volunteering influences. For example, it suggests whether a club coach, the opportunities they provide, and the participant experience is supported or 'enabled' by wider partnerships from perhaps higher education (supporting coaches or volunteers in a club), funding support for equipment and to buy time in a local authority facility from Active Partnerships. Finally, the section on key volunteers is to establish that the position of coach-participant needs to be set within the supportive environment of multiple volunteers roles. Child protection is a great example here, where it still remains a little considered aspect of those that facilitate core coaching activities (Lang et al., 2018). A vast quantity of the volunteers in the UK provide this human capital infrastructure that is the bedrock of coaching. Interactions across these multiple variables and the dynamic factors that can change show how, if we value the welfare of the player, participant, and coach as central to sport participation (Brackenridge, 1999; Lang et al., 2018), we have to embed reflect practice within both coaching and sport development. This is a broader theme that will be considered in more depth later. The purpose of the framework is to provide a starting point at level 4 for beginning to see the overlaps of coaching, development, volunteering, and community aspects of provision. This could be done for an individual sport, a specific community targeted approach (LGBTQ+, BAME, disability sporting provision) or geographical communities.

▓▓▓ CASE STUDY 13.1 ▓▓▓

Coaching workforce modernisation in the Rugby Football Union (RFU)

The developing formats for coach education and how those working in sport development settings, be they NGBs or local government, are becoming increasingly diverse. Professionals operating in this domain will need to be increasingly flexible about how they deliver, what, to who and the methods they use to reflect upon approaches utilised. The issue of workforce modernisation within NGBs and 'outside' in community partners and amongst volunteers and other professionals will be considered in this case study. It has be consistently argued that a evidence-based programme for coaching is beneficial to coach and participant (Griffiths, Armour, and Cushion, 2018). For others, the direct use of reflective practice when they have undertaken a level 1 or 2 RFU coaching award based within a local rugby club (Burt and Morgan, 2014) is a complex and variable process. Rich analysis of community sports coaching settings in periods of austerity have also identified a complex interplay between individual identity, political context, and sport pedagogy (Ives et al., 2019). In examining a number of coaches, it was also seen that issues around trust played out due to the fractured nature of aspects of community provision (Gale et al., 2019). Not all this research relates directly to Rugby Union in England. But it is meant as a precursor to this case study and shows that a growing literature is forming where sport development and coaching intertwine with policy actor decisions.

In an extension of this broad point, Hughes (2021) in her study of RFU community coaches over the whole sport plan (WSP) funding cycle 2017–2021 considered the lived experiences of coaches using a phenomenological methodology. This approach to research values and prioritises the lifeworld and view of the coach. It targets a very small number of research participants and explores how individuals develop and redevelop meanings and beliefs around community sport development, coaching and policy. This was a period of consistent change for the RFU, which at one point had up to 350 development staff and coaches employed nationally. Sport coaching plays a key role in delivery of broader social policy roles (Hughes, 2021, forthcoming).

In 2013, the RFU secured £20 million pounds with just over £15 million being ring-fenced for sport participation outcomes. Furthermore, they highlighted the aim to use the Rugby World Cup in 2015 as a legacy for participation (RFU, 2013). In relation to community sport coaching and development it has been argued that, their key strategic priorities comprised of enhancing their brand, reputation and relationship maintenance, increasing revenue, securing success at all levels and increasing adult participation from 190,000 to 215,000 through their 'rugby for everyone' initiative (RFU, 2013). The development arm of the organisation, made up of Rugby Development Officers (RDOs) and Community Rugby Coaches (CRCs), were accountable for translating and implementing these priorities to an estimated 2,000 rugby clubs, together with more than 100,000 volunteers (RFU, 2017).

(Hughes, 2021, forthcoming)

In this research, undertaken with community coaches that are located at the cross roads with development work, they identify a number of challenges in their professional practices. For them, their lived experiences illustrate complex identities having to manage and shape working as a community development coach with wider political and social environments. Specific challenges include the requirement to meet targets set by Sport England and measured internally by the NGB. Further to this, they talked of the significance of the RFU organisational restructure in 2011. Since publication of this work, a further RFU restructure of the development team of 350 personnel has also been implemented. One telling quote that is given is this,

When I originally came into post there were five of us working in [disclosed area] and I looked after three clubs. We then went through a redundancy round and we went from five of us to two of us, so I now look after I think fourteen clubs within the county … so coverage is quite big.

('Harry', Community Rugby Coach, cited from
Hughes, 2021, forthcoming)

This is a powerful individual quote, which illustrates how changes at national level influence coaching, sport development, and, ultimately community provision within RFU clubs. Other areas of concern highlighted included the mainstreaming of contemporary business management practices within 'their world' of coaching and frustration with coaching delivery format as the geographical spread of clubs has increased.

Seminar questions and task

You are a Rugby Union development officer for a single county, covering 24 clubs of variable standard in competition terms and scale of volunteering ranging from 20 volunteers to 86 volunteers. In community coaching terms, the RFU wants you to deliver sessions to try and attract 25 new junior and 5 adult volunteers to the county.

1. How will you establish current levels of volunteering in the county (in rugby and other sports)?

2. Why might this information be useful to you as a development officer with a clear remit in sport coaching?

3. Where are the areas of overlap in sport development, community coaching, and volunteering for your role and the NGB the RFU?

References

Baker, C. (2017) *Coordination of Community Sport Development in Wales: An Investigation of Stakeholder Perspectives Concerning the Organisation and Structure of Community Sport in Wales*, Gloucester: University of Gloucester.

Bloyce, D. (2008) Playing the game (plan)': A figurational analysis of organizational change in sports development in England, *European Sport Management Quarterly*, 8:4, 359–378.

Brackenridge, C. (1999) Managing Myself: Investigator survival in sensitive research, *International Review for the Sociology of Sport*, 34:4, 399–410.

Burt, E. and Morgan, P. (2014) Barriers to systematic reflective practice as perceived by UKCC level 1 and level 2 qualified Rugby Union coaches, *Reflective Practice*, 15:4, 468–480.

Cassidy, T., Jones, R., and Potrac, P. (2009) *Understanding Sports Coaching: The Social, Cultural and Pedagogical Foundations of Sports Coaching Practice*, London: Routledge.

CIMSPA (2020) *Professional Standards: Employer-led Standards for Every Job Role in Sport and Physical Activity*, Loughborough: CIMSPA, available at: www.cimspa. co.uk/standards-home/professional-standards [accessed on 01 June 2020].

Cronin C. and Armour K. (2018) *Care in Sport Coaching Pedagogical Cases*, London: Routledge.

Davidson, R. (2017) *Personal communication with Ruari Davidson, Head of Coaching in Scotland*, June 2017.

DCMS (2015) *Sporting Nation*, London: DCMS.

Gale, L. and Ives, B. (2019). Emotional struggles and troubled relationships, in Gale L. A. and Ives B. (eds), *Sports Coaching in the Community: Developing Knowledge and Insight*, Manchester: Metropolitan University.

Gale, L. A., Ives, B. A., Potrac, P. A., and Nelson, L. J. (2019) Trust and Distrust in Community Sports Work: Tales From the "Shop Floor", *Sociology of Sport Journal*, 36:3, 244–253.

Griffiths, M. A., Armour, K. A., and Cushion, C. J. (2018) 'Trying to get our message across': Successes and challenges in an evidence-based professional development programme for sport coaches, *Sport, Education and Society*, 28:3, 283–295.

Houlihan, B. and White, A. (2002) *The Politics of Sports Development: Development of Sport or Development Through Sport?*, London: Routledge.

Hughes, A. (2021), forthcoming Unpublished PhD thesis, Manchester: Manchester Metropolitan University.

Ives, B. A., Gale, L. A., Potrac, P. A., and Nelson, L. (2019) *Uncertainty, shame and consumption: Negotiating occupational and non-work identities in community sports coaching, Sport, Education and Society*, 1–17.

Ives, B., Clayton, B., Brittain, I., and Mackintosh, C. (2020) 'I'll always find a perfectly justified reason for not doing it': Challenges for disability sport and physical activity in the United Kingdom, *Sport in Society*, iFirst 1–19.

Lang, M., Mergaert, L., Arnaut, C., and Vertommen, T. (2018). Gender-based violence in EU sport policy: Overview and recommendations, *Journal of Gender-Based Violence*, 2:1, 109–118.

Lipsky, M. (1979) *Street-Level Bureaucracy: Dilemmas of the Individual in Public Services*, New York: Russell Sage Foundation.

Long, J., Fletcher, T., and Watson, B. (2017) *Sport, Leisure and Social Justice*, London: Routledge.

Mackintosh, C. (2012) The shifting dynamics of local government sports development officer practice in England: New identities and hazy professional boundaries, in Harris, S., Bell, B., Adams, A., and Mackintosh, C. (eds) *Sport for Sport? Theoretical and Practical Insights into Sports Development*, Brighton: Leisure Studies Association, 113–130.

Mackintosh, C. and Carter, J. (2018) *The Review of the United Kingdom Coaching Certificate (UKCC): A shock to the Coaching System?*, Manchester: Manchester Metropolitan University.

Mackintosh, C. and Dempsey, C. (2017) The British Asian Muslim male sport participation puzzle: An exploration of implications for sport development policy and practice, *Journal of Youth Studies*, 20:8, 974–996.

Meek, R. (2018) *A Sporting Chance: An Independent Review of Sport in Youth and Adult Prisons*, London: Ministry of Justice.

Mind (2017) *Get Set to Go Evaluation Summary 2014–2017*, London: Mind.

Mind (2020) *Get Set to Go: Being active can change your life*, 'www.mind.org.uk/about-us/our-policy-work/sport-physical-activity-and-mental-health/get-set-to-go/ [accessed 01 June 2020]

Morgan, H. and Batlle, C. I. (2019) 'It's borderline hypocrisy': Recruitment practices in youth sport-based interventions, *Journal of Sport for Development*, 7:13, 1–14.

Potrac, P., Jones, R. and Armour, K (2002) 'It's All about Getting Respect': The Coaching Behaviors of an Expert English Soccer Coach, *Sport, Education and Society*, 7:2, 183–202.

Rugby Football Union (RFU). (2013) *Seizing the Opportunity: The RFU Strategic Plan 2012/13 – 2016/17*, Twickenham: Rugby Football Union.

Rugby Football Union (RFU). (2017) *Annual Report: 2017*, Twickenham: Rugby Football Union.

Sport England (2018) *Working in an Active Nation: The Professional Workforce Strategy for England*, London: Sport England.

Sport England (2017) *A Coaching Plan for England*, London: Sport England.

Sport England (2019a) *Sport for Life: A vision for sport in Scotland*, Glasgow: Sport Scotland.

Sport England (2019b) *A Vision for Sport in Wales*, Cardiff: Sport Wales.

Sport Scotland (2019) *The Sport Scotland Business Plan 2019–2021*, Glasgow: Sport Scotland.

Sport Wales (2020) *Vision for Sport in Wales*, Cardiff: Sport Wales.

Thompson, A., Bloyce, D., and Mackintosh, C. (2020) 'It is always going to change' – managing top-down policy changes by sport development officers working in national governing bodies of sport in England, *Managing Sport and Leisure: An International Journal*, iFirst, 1–20.

UK Coaching (2019) *Coaching in the UK 2019: Coach Survey*, Leeds: UK Coaching.

CHAPTER 14

Schools and sport development

Sport development has for a long time worked at the complex dividing line between school and community sport work. Houlihan (2000) famously described it as a 'crowded policy space'. Houlihan said this over 20 years ago, this remains true for the sport development sector. The chapter will predominantly provide an overview of primary, secondary, and tertiary education sport development policy and practice in the UK. It will not touch upon the HE sector, which will receive attention as a chapter in itself. The next chapter will consider HE institutions and British Universities and Colleges Sport's (BUCS) strategic role in sport development and position within regional and local sport systems as a little researched, but increasingly significant, partner in sport development for the post-18-year-old sport policy landscape.

As new school policies in the UK reflect different central government priorities, this chapter will examine national background to PE, school sport, after-school (and increasingly before-school day sport) in what has been termed 'youth sport' policy by some. This theme will cross over with further advancement of the background on school sport development policy in recent years including School Sport Partnerships (SSPs) and the Youth Sport Trust programmes that also include the School Games legacy of London 2012 Olympics programme. Students will get an overview of the sector, how it shapes and is shaped by sport development policy, and the professional skills that working in this complex sector involves. Further wider themes will be explored including the contractualisation and outsourcing of traditional in-house physical education (PE) and school sport provision and the implications this has for new providers in sport development. It will also aim to tease out some of the different political, social and contextual differences between the four home nations.

Sport development and school sport: a congested space?

Sport development has always been closely linked in both policy and practice terms next to school physical education and school sport. It is important to acknowledge the definitional differences between these areas as this is key to showing the role (and not) of sport development in the school policy space. First, schools in each of the home nations have *curricular* physical education (PE) areas of provision and policy that in most cases individual schools implement their own interpretation of the national PE curriculum. Physical education and how it came to exist is beyond the scope of this text, but further details can be found in Griggs (2016) if this is of interest. For a sport development practitioner, it is important to be aware of what we might term the macro position of a government on PE or increasingly physical literacy of a young population. Perhaps ten years ago, traditions of sport development were to put in place pathways for the progression of children from primary into secondary school and beyond as part of a panacea for lifelong participation. However, as this became increasingly convoluted, various governments changed their approaches to this mass participation and healthy lifestyle vision (Mackintosh and Liddle, 2015; Griggs, 2016). Second, *after-school sport* is an increasingly changing area of provision, previously the domain of multiple NGBs and local authorities, but in more austere times this is a space the private coaching sector have moved into, particularly in England in the case of the Primary School Sport and PE Premium. It is, however, still important given the scope and potential of this area. Finally, the other area sometimes referred to is *school sport*; this is not curricular, or compulsory PE within the curriculum but other areas of provision that sit in the space of the school facilities. Examples could be provision by providers external to the school (e.g. NGBs or charities) or intra-school sport (e.g. Youth Sport Trust work around the Youth Games in England). It may also embrace informal recreational sport and physical activity that occurs during school time, on educational spaces and places.

Houlihan (2000) identified three sectors of policy influence at the 'micro' or local level. First, that of elite sport development such as NGBs, UK Sport Institute (now English Institute of Sport) and UK Sport. Second, he argued for a specific 'sport development' policy influence on education service including local government, Sports Councils and Chief Leisure Officers Association (CLOA). The final sector was 'education' in UKPEA (now deemed Association for PE – AfPE) and Youth Sport Trust. At the heart of his conceptualisation of these sectors was school sport, for which he specifically noted the boundaries are challenging to clearly determine. As far back as 20 years ago, he also identified the growing intersection with an increasingly powerful private sector voice in the lobby and advocacy for the choices of young people in school. As we consider the position of the school sector and how it overlaps with PE, after school-sport and elite sport in school settings it seems that the way policy has been interpreted and re-interpreted is increasingly fragmented with a multitude of understandings. For a detailed map of the period preceding 2020, see Houlihan and White (2002) and Houlihan and Lindsey (2013). In this chapter we turn away from the historical context, itself highly complex and entwined in the political turns of government and various lobby groups of each era (e.g. YST, AfPE, DfE, Sports Councils).

Sport development practice aligned with schools has changed immeasurably. During the pre-2010 period of financial austerity, when sizeable proportions of activity, funding, and initiatives were driven through local government, it would have been about local sport units in councils having relationships with 'their schools'. By covering this network of primary and secondary schools, they offered support for after-school sport, coach development, and developing links between schools and clubs. They also acted as a networking point for regional officers in NGBs looking to launch programmes of 7–11 years, 11–16 years and 16–18 years activity. In England this was further embedded in the School Sport Partnership (SSP) network, a series of over 400 networks of primary schools linked to secondary hubs of expertise. This was removed in 2010 by Education Minister Michael Gove with a partial reinstatement but ultimate winding up of the national programme, in part set up to deliver a participation legacy from London 2012 (Mackintosh, 2014; Mackintosh and Liddle, 2015). This produced in England what some have termed a 'patchwork quilt' provision for support in community sport development around primary and secondary schools (Mackintosh and Liddle, 2015). What remains unclear is whether this policy decision limited the critical potential participation legacy for this one-off investment of £9.3 billion over two weeks in London in 2012 (Weed et al., 2015).

Scotland has Active Schools, a different approach to sport development based within the school setting. It has shown good success with developing more active lifestyles and addresses issues in sport participation (Sport Scotland, 2015). It is also useful as an example to show the devolved different approach to a key policy area in sport development practice across national boundaries. For example, SGBs can now tap into the benefits from this; they can potentially support the platform in sport and activity so that national Scottish government visions (Scottish Government, 2020; online; Sport Scotland, 2015) can overlay their own SGB plans. This may be in diverse areas such as volunteering, talent development, coach education, and leadership as well as more traditional areas such as targeted sport participation. In contrast, in England where there is now a heavily fragmented system for sport development support around schools, there arguably have been sizeable gaps left. Graduates will find themselves navigating these spaces in policy and practice. If you end up working for an Active Partnership, in an isolated geographically dispersed region such as Lincolnshire or Devon and Cornwall, you will be really challenged in being able to support schools. In terms of 'remit', school sport (not PE) is an area that was central to the work of many in sport development. Now it has fallen between the tracks.

A specific shift in approach, operations, and philosophy is in the PESSP implementation in England (Griggs, 2005; Griggs, 2016). It could be argued that this replaced the SSP system brought in under New Labour and was the outcome of the ministerial removal of support in 2010. Here individual primary schools can access financial support for the delivery of after-school sport provision. The directive here is that "the premium must be spent by schools on making additional and sustainable improvements to the provision of PE, physical activity and sport for the benefit of all pupils to encourage the development of healthy, active lifestyles" (YST, 2020: online).

At first glance, this seems a positive development. However, emerging research has begun to identify that this contracting out of PE and after-school sport is creating a new tier of effectively privatised provision (Griggs, 2005). In many cases, delivery is outsourced to coaching consortiums, without educational outcomes. If, for example, it is an aspiration to deliver sport and physical activity to meet the DCMS (2015) outcomes around wellbeing, social, and individual development much more would be needed than a sporting 'child minding' session with low qualified coaches. There is a diversity of quality, and recent research by DfE (2019) has illustrated the variable role of the PESSP across England. Some coaching companies have now reached over 700 coach employees in size. These private companies are highly profitable and are gaining considerably from this shift towards outsourcing of after-school PE for 7–11-year-olds.

It is not all bad news though, as a discerning head teacher can shop around for different providers and may not decide based solely on price in this now free market for sport development. Some companies and individuals that were sole traders and limited companies have now set up as social enterprises and charities. By their very nature, they have to have a social impact in their mission statement and vision for what they wish to achieve. They are also, in many cases, not about profit but about re-investment in quality of what they offer, and the alignment to government and regional Active Partnership goals (inactivity and inclusion).

A key national agency that has been a long-standing pillar of sport development policy advocacy, campaigning and programme design and delivery is the Youth Sport Trust. In their previous strategy they set out to "to give 1 million primary and 2.5 million secondary-aged students the opportunity to participate in sport and physical activity whilst transforming the perception and practice of disability in PE and sport among 250,000 young leaders, volunteers and teachers" (YST, 2013). In their more recent strategy, they have positioned themselves to work across 16 core programmes of activity ranging from *Breaking the Boundaries* to *Girls Active* and a number of national local government pilots (mental health in schools) and NGB pilots (girls football) (YST, 2020: online). In the strategic document *Strategy 2018–2022 Believing in Every Child's Future* they identify the paradox of £1.24 billion invested in PESSP primary PE provision but a 38% cut in curricular PE (YST, 2018). They have a membership network of 4000 schools and their work reaches a wider network of 20,000 (YST, 2018).

In terms of scale, they are a major national sport development policy and advocacy implementer, for example, in terms of scale. Many of the YST products and services are delivered through the *YST Learning Academy*. This encompasses 100 tutors, 70 development coaches, 80 mentors, and 22 team leaders. In addition, the YST has numerous senior managers, sport development staff, a board, research and insight team, and wider business function staffing. This positions the YST at around the size of a top-five NGB in the UK. As a charity this is a significant factor in the work it undertakes but also how it is positioned in the sport development landscape. The organisation does correspond closely to Sport England, UK Sport and NGB relationships as well as the overarching DCMS strategy. This can be seen in the recent emergence of national pilot work in Greater Manchester's healthy minds project around school PE and sport as well as intergenerational work and work with young women of colour (YST, 2020: online). As stated above, with the removal of other support (Mackintosh, 2012), decline in scope and size of local government (King, 2014; Widdop et al., 2017), and evolution of PESSP contracting out of PE (Griggs, 2005), now more than ever is a time when the community sport development role for the YST must come to the fore. Awareness of their strategy, role, and remit is fundamental to a level 4 students building their knowledge and understanding of the sport development landscape, not only in terms of educational settings themselves but also in relation to how they mesh with NGBs across England. No agency like this charity is present within the other three home nations and this is an important distinguishing characteristic in the infrastructure across comparing countries.

Scale of physical education: a key sport development resource

In total, there are 4.72million primary-aged children educated in 16,769 primary schools and 3448 secondary schools with 3.327 million secondary-aged pupils in England (DfE, 2019). A further educational policy change in recent years in England has been the move towards academies. This area of provision in PE and sport development terms gives schools the ability to opt out of local authority control. To date, in England 5180 primary schools and 2315 secondary schools have academy status (DfE, 2019). If you overlay the contractualisation and privatisation of primary PE where organisations such as the YST have estimated a 38% decrease in curricular PE, it is perhaps an important factor to consider the fact that around a third of all primary schools in England are now academies. The full picture of the implications of these policy processes for local sport and PE are yet to be fully established. It also shows that around 10 million children aged 7–18 are educated in schools in England out of the 67 million population, which gives a sense of the population that NGBs, Active Partnerships, and other agencies such as charities and professional sport club community organisations have available to target. The skills of the development officer lie in how to engage, partner, and build links with such educational stakeholders.

It is also critical to consider that sport development is also focused as a profession on those excluded from society. In the case of England, for example, 125,000 children are at special schools and a further 47,000 of these children get access to free school meals (DfE, 2019). The free school meals measure is an indication of a proxy measure for social deprivation. In this educational setting, students have physical and/or potential intellectual disabilities and over 37 per cent are also socially deprived. In secondary schools this figure is 14 per cent with access to free school meals. Thus, in terms of policy priorities, it may be that certain schools nationally, regionally, and locally should be our sport development priority. As Fitzgerald (2005) has argued, many disabled young people are tired of feeling like a 'spare piece of luggage'. Ohers have suggested that disability sport development must confront the complex barriers and enablers of participation in their work with leading disability charities (Ives et al., 2020). The Disability Alliance could, for example, access students located in such schools and indirectly target an English population of around 150,000 young people. A number of other young people also have places in what has been termed 'mainstream' education. In the interest of not 'othering' such young people by casting them as a binary category against people without a disability, it is perhaps better to consider those that are included and integrated into the curriculum, school, and sport through support and accessibility packages. School can also provide a powerful pathway into elite sport for those that self-identify as disabled or with learning difficulties. This then starts with the development of a talent pathway that is highly specialised from PE departments progressing through to supportive sport clubs with the capacity, interest, and inclination to reassure participants from schools. Encouraging empathetic specialist clubs and non-specialist clubs with strong inclusion backgrounds or sections is vital (Brighton and Williams, 2019).

Whilst considering school sport in the past, we have focused on secondary and primary schools. Instead, a new range of provision should perhaps be prioritised now given current policy around accessing the 'hard to reach' (DCMS, 2015; Sport England, 2016; Sport England 2017). Few studies have analysed sport and physical activity patterns of young people accommodated in Pupil Referral Units (PRU). These facilities are educational in nature, but also accommodate children that have been excluded from mainstream education but require the provision of education. In England from 2011 to 2019 this population of young people grew from just over 14,000 to just over 16,000. These are some of the most challenging, disadvantaged, and at-risk individuals (Medcalf and Mackintosh, 2019). In working alongside such groups, this also illustrates the changing nature of the sport development skill set where managing individuals or small groups of 'at-risk' individuals needs a re-conceptualised approach to provision. Sport and physical activity choice is important but more fundamental is how you are adapting delivery, the programme, and evaluation of a project to achieve social outcomes (Coalter, 2007; Meeks, 2018; Morgan and Batlle, 2019). A good example of a fundamental paradigm shift in approach is illustrated by that of Quarmby (2019) in his exploration of the use of puppets with highly vulnerable children. Crucially, a little like the example of PRUs, Quarmby (2014) examines a hidden group of vulnerable children living in care. The context is different, but does have parallels and the professional shift is towards power being given to the participant, to build rapport and trust. Similar principles could be taken for building relationships with other excluded groups in the sport development context that are starting to emerge due to the social policy direction of national visions.

In Table 14.1, we can see the breakdown of schools by type in Wales that accommodates around 468,000 pupils. This is a significantly smaller market than the educational sector in England, but reflects the overall population size. The Welsh Government (2020: 6) identified that,

TABLE 14.1 Change in school type in Wales between 2018 and 2019

	2018	2019
LA maintained schools	1,521	1,494
All schools	1,591	1,569
Nursery	11	9
Primary	1,261	1,238
Middle	13	19
Secondary	195	187
Special	41	41
Independent	70	75

Source: Welsh Government, 2020

the number of qualified teachers has remained fairly steady over the long term, peaking at 28,461 in 2006. However, this has decreased over the last 5 years to a low of 25,802 in 2019. This is largely due to school closures and amalgamations.

PE in Wales offers the opportunity to link projects between NGBs and Sport Wales to address national policy priorities (Sport Wales, 2020). Sport development in the intersection between school sport (after school, inter-school, and intra-school) and daytime curricular PE will vary by local authority region. There is no PESSP system in Wales for the primary sector and no link directly to the YST. However, it is also worth acknowledging that Disability Sport Wales leads in the area of advice and provision for disabled young people. They are, however, a national organisation without local officers across the regions and local authorities. In total, there were 136,826 reports of SEN classification type made with an average of 1.3 per pupil with SEN (Welsh Government, 2020). In a small country, the most common SEN was 'general learning difficulty' at around 40,000 pupils. Provision for PE, sport, and competitive opportunities across these 130,000 individuals with special needs, many of which are clustered and overlap showing the sport development challenge for schools, SDOs, NGBs, charities, and professional sports clubs that need to engage with this public policy space.

Table 14.2 illustrates an overview of school sector provision in Northern Ireland. Again, the important clustering is around the divide between grammar and non-grammar schools with regards to free school meals. This also applies in an even more stark way to the nearly 6000 children in what DENI (2020) refer

TABLE 14.2 Breakdown of number of schools by category and pupil enrolment numbers in 2018–2019

No. of schools		Enrolments	Entitled to free school meals
Primary (Y1–Y7)	813	174,523	29.5%
Grammar	66	62,862	14.1%
Non-grammar	130	79,377	39.2%
Special schools	39	5,959	52.0%

Source: 2018/19 School Census, DfE, 2019

to as 'special schools' where 52 per cent of pupils have access to a free schools meal. How sport development is shaped in relation to this is underpinned national by policy and strategy in Sport Northern Ireland (Sport NI, 2013a). Likewise, this governs and encourages NGBs in Northern Ireland and sport development teams based in local government. The country had a total of 19,764 teachers across approximately 1000 schools. A range of curricular PE is provided, with associated after-school clubs at secondary and primary. Perhaps more fundamental is the use of pathways to support participants into lifelong participation, which is stressed in national policy through school-club links (Sport NI, 2013b).

A good example of this is the Belfast City Council *On The Right Track* project, which has three strands of activity for young people (Belfast City Council, 2020: online): participation encouragement, club development, and developing young champions. It targets 13–16-year-old pathways to build lifelong participation as opposed to a short-term initiative. They also support Belfast *Club Mark*, a club accreditation system that signposts young people and their parents to clubs with gold standard child protection, high-quality coaching and appropriate ethos to facilitate enjoyable opportunities. The final example of sport development links with education through sport development is the pathways built by Belfast City sport development team and the income they have won in the form of a £1.5 million grant from the UK National Lottery Funding to deliver Sport Northern Ireland's *Every Body Active* 2020 programme (Belfast City Council, 2020: online). Specific focus groups here, which could link directly to primary and secondary schools, as well as special schools include: women and girls, people with a disability, and those in areas of greatest social need.

These are also useful examples to illustrate how one single organisation can, and does, sport development. In this case whilst often focused on young people in schools NGBs, local government sport development, local government, and school facility providers, charities ('social need' and disability) as well as perhaps professional sports clubs all have to shape delivery, evaluation, and scoping of what *Every Body Active*'s outcomes will be for local communities.

Recently, Sport Northern Ireland has established a five-year corporate plan 2015–2020 (Sport Northern Ireland, 2015), which uses the SPLISS model and

Lifelong Involvement in Physical Activity and Sport (LIPAS) model as core components to evaluating and sustaining their approach to sport development. Specifically, they identify that through the use of SPLISS (2012) elite success system there are key components of the system that illustrate key gaps in the system. Talent development pathways from school to club, facility infrastructure and coaching are examples of gaps in such provision that may limit the participation and performance pathways that Sport Northern Ireland is striving to embolden (Sport Northern Ireland, 2015). The clear vision from wider public service provision is the delivery of benefits to wellbeing, addressing social exclusion of disadvantaged groups and improving the economy (Sport Northern Ireland, 2015). In 2019, as an example of a sport development and community coaching programme illustrative of this endeavour, a £600,000 programme working with 7–11-year-olds in 300 schools was established with the GAA and the Irish FA (Sport Northern Ireland, 2020: online). It will specifically target girls and replaces the former *Curriculum Sports Programme*, which ended at the end of 2018 (Table 14.2).

Scotland has 2,004 primary schools, 358 secondary schools, and 114 special schools with a total populations of children aged 7–18 of just under 700,000. This is, as with each home nation, a useful figure to consider the scope, size, and potential impact of sport development within the educational sector. PE, school sport, and inter-school competitions are, in the case of Scotland, heavily underpinned by the Active Schools programme, a well-established domain of sport development provision targeting lifelong activity and the transition into sport club 'hubs' (Table 14.3).

Furthermore, disability in the school sector is a good starting point for understanding the lived experiences and scale of those with different learning

TABLE 14.3 Breakdown of Scottish pupils by special needs and additional support requirements (ASN)

	Female	Male	Total
CSP (Co-ordinated Support Plan)	639	1,068	1,707
IEP (Individualised Education Programme)	11,306	24,350	35,656
Child Plans	15,613	27,168	42,781
Assessed/declared disabled	5,873	12,592	18,465
Other	73,554	97,081	170,635
All pupils with ASN (additional special needs)	89,709	126,188	215,897
All pupils with ASN (excluding Other type)	**26,497**	**48,813**	**75,310**

and physical needs aged 7–18 in Scotland. Table 14.3 above shows individuals by gender and by category of Scottish disability or additional support needs (ASN). In England this is referred to as Special Educational Needs (SEN), with different classifications and systems of acknowledging disability and use of language. In the context of this chapter it is illustrative of the importance to build a coherent system for disability youth sport in a country, where, for example, in Scotland there are over 215,000 pupils that have an ASN. Capacity, inclination, and technical skills in delivery of inclusive sport is a challenge (Fitzgerald, 2005; Brighton and Williams, 2019; Medcalf and Mackintosh, 2019; Ives et al., 2020).

CASE STUDY 14.1

PE, NGBs, and designing an 'extra-curricular offer' – a crowded space of negotiation

The provision of pathways between school activity and wider community provision in sports club and third sector provision is at the core of traditional teaching of sport development. This chapter has begun to question and unpick the foundations of such assumptions given the considerable changes in education sector in the UK and how sport development agencies works alongside schools. At times, schools have become a 'forgotten delivery partner' in the sport development policy landscape. But, arguably one that is considerable in its national size, scope, and policy independence from national government due to funding regimes in the UK. This case study will consider the case of primary school education in England where schools receive a PE and School Sport Premium (PESSP) to supplement delivery of curricular and extra-curricular PE as well as competitive and informal sports participation (perhaps during lunch and other break times for primary school children). However, the distribution is centralised with government and spent at the very local level.

Imagine you are an NGB development officer for a sport of your choice with a regional area that encompasses a number of local authorities – consider how you would approach designing a project to support extra-curricular provision given many schools may already have opted into a contract with a 'provider'.

- Step 1: Consider the needs of the children and young people – are there any equality and diversity issues to think of (and how should you include this in your project)?

- Step 2: What gaps in provision might primary schools have? What needs might they want plugging?

- Step 3: What existing NGB products (coaching, programmes and so on) could you link into your planned idea?

- Step 4: who else might be useful to involve for your club, activities, or project that you are aiming to run?

- Step 5: How much will it cost to run for an academic year and what might the school pay? (breakdown costs)

- Step 6: Plan into the project sustainability – how might it bring longer-term benefits (2–5 years) for the NGB, school, other network of schools, sports clubs, and volunteer networks.

Be prepared to present this idea back to your peers as a group. Ask your tutor to act as the Regional NGB Officer to assess the best planned project idea link to the PESSP sport development policy.

Further reading

Griggs, G. (2010) For sale – primary physical education. £20 per hour or nearest offer, *Education 3–13: International Journal of Primary, Elementary and Early Years Education*, 38:1, 39–46.

References

Belfast City Council (2020) On the right track!, available at: [accessed on 01/06/2020]

Brighton, J. and Williams, T. L. (2019) Using interviews to explore experiences of disability in sport and physical activity, in Medcalf, R. and Mackintosh, C. (eds) *Researching Difference in Sport and Physical Activity*, London: Routledge, 25–40.

Coalter, F. (2007) *A Wider Social Role for Sport: Whose Keeping the Score?*, London: Routledge.

DCMS (2015) *A Sporting Nation*, London: DCMS.

Department for Education (DfE) (2019) *Primary PE and Sport Premium Survey: Research Report*, London: DfE.

Department for Education Northern Ireland (2020) *Schools and Pupils in Northern Ireland 1991–92 to 2019–20*, available at: www.education-ni.gov.uk/publications/school-enrolments-northern-ireland-summary-data [accessed on 01/06/2020].

DfE (2019) *Main Text: Schools, Pupils and their Characteristics*, London: DfE.

Fitzgerald, H. (2005) Still feeling like a spare piece of luggage? Embodied experiences of disability in physical education and school sport, *Physical Education and Sport Pedagogy*, 10:1, 41–59.

Griggs, G. (2016) Spending the primary physical education and sport premium: A West Midlands case study, *Education 3–13*, 44:5, 547–555.

Houlihan, B. (2000) Sporting excellence, schools and sports development: The politics of crowded policy spaces, *European Physical Education Review*, 6:2, 171–193.

Houlihan, B. and Lindsey, L. (2013) *Sport Policy in Britain*, London: Routledge.

Houlihan, B. and White, A. (2002) *The Politics of Sports Development: Development of Sport or Development Through Sport?*, London: Routledge.

Ives, B., Clayton, B., Brittain, I., and Mackintosh, C. (2020) 'I'll always find a perfectly justified reason for not doing it': Challenges for disability sport and physical activity in the United Kingdom, *Sport in Society*, iFirst, 1–19.

King, N. (2014) Local authority sport services under the UK Coalition government: Retention, revision or curtailment, *International Journal of Sport Policy and Politics*, 6:3, 349–369.

Mackintosh, C. (2014) Dismantling the school sport partnership infrastructure: Findings from a survey of physical education and school sport practitioners, *Education 3–13*, 42:4, 432–449.

Mackintosh, C. and Liddle, J. (2015) Emerging school sport development policy, practice and governance in England: Big Society, autonomy and decentralisation, *Education 3–13*, 43:6, 603–620.

Medcalf, R. and Mackintosh, C. (2019) *Researching Difference in Sport and Physical Activity*, London: Routledge.

Meeks, R. (2018) *A Sporting Chance: An Independent Review of Sport in Youth and Adult Prisons*, London: Ministry of Justice.

Morgan, H. and Batlle, C. I. (2019) 'It's borderline hypocrisy': Recruitment practices in youth sport-based interventions, *Journal of Sport for Development*, 7:13, 1–14.

Quarmby, T. (2014) Sport and physical activity in the lives of looked after children: 'A hidden group' in research, policy and practice, *Sport, Education and Society*, 19:7, 944–958.

Quarmby, T. (2019) 'No strings attached': Reflections on using puppets in focus group interviews with vulnerable children in sport and physical activity, in Medcalf, R. and Mackintosh, C. (eds) *Researching Difference in Sport and Physical Activity*, London: Routledge, 41–54.

Scottish Government (2020) *Active Scotland Delivery Plan*, available at: www.gov. scot/publications/active-scotland-delivery-plan/ [accessed on 29/4/2020].

Sport England (2016) *Towards an Active Nation*, London, Sport England.

Sport England (2017) *Sport Volunteer Strategy*, London: Sport England.

Sport NI (2013a) *The Northern Ireland Strategy for Sport & Physical Recreation 2009–2019*, Belfast: Sport NI.

Sport NI (2013b) *The Northern Ireland Strategy for Sport & Physical Recreation 2009–2019*, Belfast: Sport NI.

Sport Northern Ireland (2015) *Sport Northern Ireland: Five-year corporate plan 2015–2020*, Belfast; Sport NI.

Sport Northern Ireland (2020) *8th Progress Report 01 Oct 2016 to 30 Sept 2017*, Belfast: Sport NI.

Sport Scotland (2015) *Raising the Bar: Corporate Plan 2015–2019*, Glasgow, Sport Scotland.

Sport Wales (2020) *Vision for Sport in Wales*, Cardiff: Sport Wales.

Weed, M., Coren, E., Fiore, J., Wellard, I., Chatziefstathiou, D. Mansfield, L. and Dowse, S. (2015) The Olympic Games and raising sport participation: A systematic review of evidence and an interrogation of policy for a demonstration effect, *European Sports Management Quarterly*, 15:2, 195–226.

Welsh Government (2020) Schools and teachers, available at: https://statswales.gov. wales/Catalogue/Education-and-Skills/Schools-and-Teachers [accessed on 01/06/2020].

Widdop, P., King, N., Parnell, D., Cutts, D. and Millward, P. (2017) Austerity, policy and sport participation in England, *International Journal of Sport Policy and Politics*, 10:1, 7–24.

Youth Sport Trust (YST) (2013) *Youth Sport Trust: Sport Changes Lives Strategic Plan 2013–2018*, Loughborough: YST.

YST (2018) *Strategy 2018–2022 Believing in Every Child's Future*, Loughborough, YST.

YST (2020) YST: Our Strategy – believing in every child's future, available at: www. youthsporttrust.org/our-strategy, [accessed on 01/06/2020].

CHAPTER 15

Higher education sport development

Change has been a constant theme in the last two decades in the sport development landscape. This chapter examines the growing role of the higher education sector, a wider sector of which has underdone considerable structural, financial, and arguably philosophical change in the UK. Admittedly, it is predominantly targeting the 18–25-year-old population, but this is a significant proportion of the UK population and in line with many other sectors that have been considered in this book. This is not to say that it also does not encompass a sizeable international population of students, mature individuals (over 25 years of age) and diverse strata that cut across gender, sexuality, ethnicity, faith, and social class. Perhaps most significant is acknowledging how the size, scope, and remit of sport development staff teams in Higher Education Institutions (HEIs) is vastly broader than what it was ten years ago. In many cities, for example, the human resources staffing sport development teams across, say, two to three universities in a large metropolitan city are greater than that of the city and county council. The role of the sport development function of HEIs also remains under researched with a few exceptions in student–community volunteering projects (De Souza, 2004; Hayton, 2016), impact of sport engagement on graduate employability (Allen et al., 2013, national HEI sport policy (Brunton and Mackintosh, 2017), and enhancing the student experience through sport (BUCS, 2017). Only as recently as 2011 did funding get allocated nationally in England towards the Active Universities programme and later the Sport Activation Programme in 2014 to drive recreational sport and physical activity in the 41 universities that were part of the Active Universities Project (Sport England, 2015). The work that operates in this sector of the sport development national landscape is overseen by British Universities and Colleges Sport (BUCS) the association that represents and strategically steers the work across its member universities and colleges. The next section will outline the recent changing role for BUCS and how it is emerging as a key player in sport development in a highly globalised, competitive, and changing higher education market (Department of Business Innovation and Skills, 2011; HM Government, 2013).

164

The changing purpose of university sport for BUCS

The purpose of university sport has changed noticeably over its history across the world, with many histories illustrating the huge growth over the centuries (BUCS, 2017; Georgkakis, 2006). In England, this can be seen clearly when looking at the changes to BUCS strategies. The developments more recently are seen within the most recent strategic plans where there is a broader agenda than inter-varsity sport competition that was once the main focus, to one that widens the definition and aims of university sport. In the strategy period 2011–2015, sport was to focus on competition, participation, and performance, with objectives of getting more people playing and taking part in physical activity as well as improving the quality of the student and staff experience in sport offered through intra-mural sports programmes; in addition to a focus on the provision of competitions, regional, national, and international. In 2010, sport development was incorporated into the role of BUCS and a strong relationship with Sport England was developed, creating a formal partnership for the first time. A new BUCS *Sport Development Strategy for England 2013–16* was produced that also recognised the government white paper *Higher Education: Students at the Heart of the System* (Department of Business Innovation and Skills, 2011) and the focus for institutions to deliver a high-quality student experience. The role sport plays in the student experience varies across universities as does the importance that universities place on sport to help support the achievement of the broader areas of university business, as discussed earlier. BUCS have made it their responsibility to continue to make the case for sport as a tool to help support universities to achieve their core objectives (BUCS, 2013); however, this is a big ask and is one that is ongoing and needs greater investment in research to help BUCS to realise this aspiration. Subsequent strategies were developed in 2013–2017 and more recently updated in 2015–2018, where the student sport offer incorporated more elaborated social and participation levels in addition to competitive sport. BUCS do include areas of core university business within their purpose with a clear headline of the 2013–17 strategy stating: "BUCS' vision is to enhance the student experience through sport" (BUCS, 2013, p. 9) and that members wanted to measure the relationship between sport and graduate employability that was referred to earlier. Most recently BUCS have released a Mental Health Charter for sport in Higher Education (BUCS, 2019).

Wellbeing and the use of sport, but more widely physical activity to engage, support, and retain students in HEIs is an emerging trend on the university campus in the UK (Brunton and Mackintosh, 2017). In evaluating a number of university campuses, policy documents, and through undertaking in-depth interviews with senior 'non-sport' HEI management, the authors identified this as a core theme for sport development on campus given the size of the UK market, which includes a total number of HE students of 2,383,970 in 2018/19 (HESA, 2020). This is useful to compare against the UK market of secondary school children of around 3.3 million. As a target population for healthy lifestyles, engagement with wellbeing, and also use of sport for addressing health concerns (e.g. mental health), this population overseen by BUCS and constituent universities does sound very significant. Yet, close attention to all recent sport development texts sees minimal, if any, reference to process, policy, and programmes in the sector (Bloyce and Smith, 2010; Hylton, 2013; Girginov, 2008). A good, if now dated, example of this is Thorpe and Collins (2010) who examined sport participation and elite performance at Loughborough University. Excluding academic, postgraduate, and undergraduate students (at this time approximately 1060), the Sport Development Centre (SDC) had over 150 staff servicing community, elite, and student needs. There is also a close relationship with the student union and associated sports clubs.

In 2008 Sport England noted that the 'sporting estate' of HEIs was worth £20 billion (Sport England, 2008). The recent expansion of sport facilities on many modernised campuses is part of the 'campus wellbeing trend' and a senior management need to offer an increasingly marketable brand to students in a competitive HEI marketplace. It is likely that expansion has grown considerably further since this 2008 audit of sport facilities. No information across the UK is available on this. In the 2008 Sport England strategy the then Chair of BUCS was quoted as saying, "universities are a vital part of the community in which they are located and sport plays a vital role in creating those community connections through students acting as volunteers and coaches … sport helps to develop 'life skills'" (Sport England, 2008: 17).

As we reflect on the changing market and role for sport development, it is clear that volunteering on internal and external projects remains a core focus on many degrees (Hayton, 2016). But, as Hayton (2016) has determined, such partnership and community collaborations are not without their challenges. If you are a level 4 volunteer, beginning to consider your career in sport coaching and volunteering the landscape remains unnerving. Furthermore, whilst we assume that sport is inevitably positive as a volunteer, attending sessions in disadvantaged areas, managing children with complex behavioural needs, or working in a project that exposes the volunteer to mental health issues are still new domains for HEI and wider sport development.

The HE campus: an under-exploited sport development resource?

On campus, universities are also incredibly diverse, as are our student populations. When Thorpe and Collins (2010) examined Loughborough campus over ten years ago, they painted a picture quite dissimilar to many other campuses, metropolitan universities, and smaller rural universities. For example, over 400,000 students are 30 years and older. A further 331,000 have a known disability (HESA, 2020). Just across these two factors alone we can see that there would be a diversity of experiences in terms of engaging with HEI sport development. It will also vary across institutions where some have outstanding inclusive provision (perhaps due to the staff and facilities); in other areas, historical and cultural attitudes might leave less engagement with disability inclusion in sport and wellbeing.

Central government has specifically identified the role of HEIs in community wellbeing (Universities UK, 2013). Similarly, whilst the UK has begun a journey to develop provision around wellbeing, research suggests that in other countries HEIs have acknowledged the role of 'campus recreation' in retention, satisfaction, and even learning (Elkins, Forrester, and Noel-Elkins, 2011; Henchy, 2011; Kampf and Teske, 2013; Moffitt, 2010; Sturts and Ross, 2013; Tsigillis et al., 2009). Such debates are well established in the USA and emergent in parts of Australia (Knapp, 2011), Turkey (Sarac and McCullick, 2015), Hong Kong (Chung, Liu and Chen, 2013), Iran (Mirsafian, Doczi, and Mohamedinejad, 2014), and Nigeria (Shehu, 2010). The overarching theme is what Moffitt (2010) outlines as 'recreating retention'; in other words, can we build campus provision that is designed to engage, retention, and develop lifelong interest in a healthy lifestyle? This is far removed, I would argue, from a campus that is designed to provide elite performance sport spaces and opportunities.

If we are addressing wellbeing, university spaces and their sport development and wider student support, staff must also address concerns with unhealthy practices. For example, multiple studies have highlighted heavy drinking culture at university (Partington et al., 2013; Ward and Gryyczynski, 2007) and what others have deemed 'hazing' around initiation ceremonies (Groves, Griggs, and Leflay, 2012). Even recognition of such activities problematises the sport 'solves all social ills' formula. Sport development therefore perhaps has a role to play in liaising with student services, the student union, and other service providers to ensure sport does actually provide wellbeing, positive outcomes, and intended social aspects it is either funded to deliver or that the HEI indirectly supports via clubs and societies. As critical sport development graduates that may enter this workplace in the future, we should also recognise that the wider macro challenges around a global campus (different faiths, religions, and identities), gender (how sport is presented and represented to men and women), and hidden minority communities (LGBTQ, older parents) are also offered support in engaging.

As with all national strategies in the home nations, whether in England, Scotland, Northern Ireland or Wales, inactive and less physically healthy social groups are a body of people that HEIs can engage with. It is particularly vital as the transition from school, college, or work into HEI life (and onwards into work) can provide two vital steps in habit formation and patterns and physical (in) activity (Roberts, Reeves, and Ryrie, 2014). Indeed, meta-studies on university students have illustrated that between 40 and 50 per cent are physically inactive (Keating et al., 2005). In contrast, Haase (2004) established it could be as high as 70 per cent that are not participating in regular free-time physical activity or recreation. This then moves the goal in sport development terms to a physical activity 'activation' goal. Very little is known about exercise motivation for UK populations of students (Roberts, Reeves, and Ryrie, 2014). This is a good example where the approach of sport development staff arguably needs to shift from traditional sport development initiative development to a more public health intervention focus (Franks et al., 2011). Here, rather than having standardised projects on national scale Franks et al. (2011: 12) argue for how "interventions and evaluations must be flexible, evolve in partnership with local communities, and reflect local need and context". It is perhaps these last two components of the review around behaviour change and public health interventions that could be critical for HEIs. Many have diverse and different populations, facility and staffing mixes, and ethos and policy drivers in relation to sport, physicality, and health (Brunton and Mackintosh, 2017).

University sport is also about more traditional student sport societies, clubs, their committees that govern them, and the competitive structures that are part of the BUCS national system. Increasingly, a number of sport development staff are positioned in working alongside performance sport development systems in respective HEIs. First, sport scholarship teams offer support to the high-performance students that meet requirements of elite standards of performance. This could be anything from a full scholarship where an individual represents at Paralympic or Olympic level through to lower level acknowledgement for, say, national clubs standard athletics. The power of all these scholars is that they can perform for the university in BUCS against other universities and by winning points raise the university in the league table. Universities that offer sport and non-sport courses are constantly competing each year to be the number one HEI for marketing and sporting kudos. Second, there are officers that support elite players from niche strength and conditioning through to, say, female football development officers. Such officers may be part funded by the university, and, say, a county Football Association (FA) so have some remit for volunteer recruitment from the university, deployment of new coaches into junior girls clubs, and development activity on campus (women's mental health, BAME engagement, and so on). Finally, there are the more typical sport development teams responsible perhaps for student and (in some cases) staff-focused sport, fitness, and wellbeing activities. These projects may be as simple as the designing of a timetable of campus recreation activities in partnership with the HEI sport facilities team. Or, it could be more wellbeing-led work at exam time such as yoga, pilates, and walking campus projects.

Universities can no longer remain an isolated organisation in a city or region, they must embed themselves within the infrastructure and partnerships of sport development they find themselves located in (Brunton and Mackintosh, 2017). For a university that is based in, say, Glasgow, it will have a range of organisational and individual staff relationships and networks. This could encompass strategic partnerships with aspects of the NHS, major employers that want to develop sport programmes for their staff, placement providers in leisure trusts, sport development teams, and professional sports club community interest charities. Staff in HEIs also undertake a comprehensive range of sport development research, evaluation, and monitoring with agencies such as Sport Scotland or Glasgow City Council. This work can involve undergraduate and postgraduate students, multiple staff and considerable resources and intellectual input from the HEI.

In other examples, HEIs have developed unique partnerships that feed a workforce of students into local communities. A good example of this is the University of Glamorgan students who delivered extra-curricular 7–11 primary sport as part of the Sport Wales Dragon Sport project (Griffiths and Rainer, 2009). This was a direct result of a teaching unit design called 'Community Sport Development' put in place to meet the needs of local and national agendas and enhance future employability. It was a yearlong unit, applying theory to practice, over a 20-week practical, 15 hours of Dragon Sport delivery, a subsidised NGB coaching award, and a period of placement preparation (Griffiths and Rainer, 2009). In total, sessions were delivered to 4300 participants , 1200 volunteer hours contributed in 25 schools. This is a good example of a typical unit that inhabits many of the sport development and wider sport management degrees (with a community focus). For further more contemporary insights to a similar project see Hayton (2016) for the role of university volunteers in a local community sport development context.

CASE STUDY 15.1

The English HEI sport development context – exploring your own campus

Locate Table 1 in the recent article by Brunton and Mackintosh (2017), which provides an overview of the two strands of policy influence over HEI sport development. First, there is a main thread of their work around education, research, innovation, and civic engagement (Universities UK, 2013). For example, this is where the 'core business' of student recruitment, teaching and learning, and staff and institutional research is positioned. Sport does have an influence here across all four areas, in terms of assets such as facility infrastructure being accessible to local sport groups, coaches and NGBs. Further to this, if a university has a strong volunteering programme in sport development, this adds to the human capital in a city or region. In this case study, explore how these policy documents overlap with your university provision. What areas of sport development provision can you identify in your courses, infrastructure, and BUCS provision.

Focusing on the right-hand side of the table listed in the article, which looks at key strands of national policy, try and map where sport development is emerging on your campus. The column on the left sign posts you to the macro policy issues for HE in the UK. This is really beyond the scope of this task, but it is good to be aware universities are not driven primarily by Sport England, UK Sport, and DCMS but by their 'core work' in delivery of HE goals (Universities UK, 2013). This activity is also about you locating a research paper independently, finding a model within it, understanding it, and the context it is written for (HE sport) and then applying it to your university campus sport and wellbeing setting.

Seminar questions

1. What volunteering is available in sport development in your university?
2. What sport development work is undertaken by student volunteers in clubs and your university sport development team?
3. Are there any elite sport development pathways, systems, support, or vehicles for improving BUCS performance at your university?

Seminar group task

External partnerships, relationship, and stakeholder involvement in sport development are critical to those working in HEI but also in reverse for community-based groups and organisations.

1. Designing a table to help establish how many external partnerships you can identify in your university in sport development. On the left list the organisation, on the right list the type of activity and what area or theme of national policy it relates to.
2. All this is under your nose – stop and reflect upon the area that interests you the most. If you were to approach the relevant internal department or external organisation what skills and knowledge would they be looking for?

Seminar reading to locate model of HE sport policy (Table 1 in article).

Brunton, J. and Mackintosh, C. (2017) A study of higher education sport development policy in England – where next?, *International Journal of Sport Policy and Politics*, special edition editorial, 9:3, 377–395.

References

Allen, K., Bullough, S., Cole d, Shibli S., and Wilson J. (2013) *The Impact of Engagement in Sport on Graduate Employability*, Sheffield: Sports Industry Research, Sheffield Hallam University.

Bloyce, D. and Smith, A. (2010) *Sport Policy and Development*, London: Routledge,

British Universities and Colleges Sport (BUCS). (2013) *BUCS Sport Development Strategy 2013–2016*, London: BUCS.

British Universities and Colleges Sport. (2017) *BUCS Strategy 2017–2021*, London: BUCS.

Brunton, J. A. and Mackintosh, C. I. (2017) Interpreting university sport policy in England: Seeking a purpose in turbulent times?, *International Journal of Sport Policy and Politics*. 9:3, 377–395.

Chung, P. K., Liu, J. D., and Chen, W. P. (2013) Perceived constraints on recreational sport participation: Evidence from Chinese university students in Hong Kong, *World Leisure Journal*, 55:4, 347–359.

Department of Business Innovation and Skills (BIS). (2011) *Higher Education: Students at the Heart of the System*, London: BIS.

De Souza, A. (2004) *An Investigation into the Role of Higher Education in Developing Volunteering*, unpublished MSc thesis, Loughborough: Loughborough University.

Elkins, D. J., Forrester, S. A., and Noel-Elkins, A. V. (2011) The contribution of campus recreational sports participation to perceived sense of campus community, *Recreational Sports Journal*, 35, 24–34.

Franks, H., Hardiker, N. R., McGrath, M., and McQuarrie, C. (2011) Public health interventions and behaviour change: Reviewing the grey literature, *Public Health*, 126, 12–17.

Georgkakis, S. (2006) The place and function of sport in Australian Universities: Sport at the University of Sydney, *Change: Transformations in Education*, 9:1, 39–48.

Girginov, V. (2008) *Management of Sport Development*, Oxford: Butterworth-Heinemann.

Griffiths, R. and Rainer, P. (2009) Supporting high-quality extra-curricular primary school sport in Wales: An evaluation of a university/community partnership initiative, *Managing Leisure*, 14:4, 286–301.

Groves, M., Griggs, G., and Leflay, K. (2012) Hazing and initiation ceremonies in university sport: Setting the scene for further research in the United Kingdom, *Sport in Society: Cultures, Commerce, Media, Politics*, 15:1, 117–131.

Haase, A., Steptoe, A., Sallis, J., and Wardle, J. (2004) Leisure-time physical activity in university students from 23 countries: Association with health beliefs, risk awareness and national economic development, *Preventative Medicine*, 39, 182–190.

Hayton, J. (2016) Plotting the motivation of student volunteers in sports-based outreach work in North East England, *Sport Management Review*, 19: 5, 563–577.

Henchy, A. (2011) The influence of campus recreation beyond the gym, *Recreational Sports Journal*, 35, 174–181.

Her Majesty's Government (HM Government). (2013) *International Education – Global Growth and Prosperity: An Accompanying Analytical Narrative*, London: HM Government.

Higher Education Statistics Authority (HESA). (2020) *Higher Education Student Statistics: UK, 2018/19 – Student numbers and characteristics*, available at: www.hesa.ac.uk/news/16-01-2020/sb255-higher-education-student-statistics/numbers, [accessed on 02 June 2020].

Hylton, K. (ed.) (2013) *Sport Development: Policy, Process and Practice* (3rd Edition), London: Routledge.

Kampf, S. and Teske, E. J. (2013) Collegiate recreation participation and retention, *Recreational Sports Journal*, 37, 85–96.

Keating, X. D., Guan, J. Piñero, J. C., and Bridges, D. M. (2005) A meta-analysis of college students' physical activity behaviors, *Journal of American College Health*, 54: 2, 116–125.

Knapp, D. (2011) *The Case for University Sport*, Queensland: Australian University Sport.

Mirsafian, H., Doczi, T., and Mohamedinejad, A. (2014) Attitude of Iranian female university students to sport and exercise, *Iranian Studies*, 47:6, 951–966.

Moffitt, J. (2010) Recreating retention, *Recreational Sports Journal*, 34, 24–33.

Partington, S., Partington, E., Heather, N., Longstaff, F., Allsop, S. Jankowski, M., Wareham, H., Stephens, R., and Gibson, A. S. (2013) The relationship between membership of a university sports group and drinking behaviour among students at English Universities, *Addiction Research & Theory*, 21:4, 339–347.

Roberts, S., Reeves, M., and Ryrie, A. (2014) The influence of physical activity, sport and exercise motives among UK-based university students, *Journal of Further and Higher Education*, 39:4, 598–607l.

Sarac, L. and McCullick, B. (2015) The life of a gay student in a university physical education and sports department: A case study of Turkey, *Sport, Education and Society*, 22:3, 338–354.

Shehu, J. (2010) Sport in higher education: An assessment of the implementation of the national sports development policy in Nigerian universities, *Assessment and Evaluation in Higher Education*, 25:1, 39–50.

Sport England. (2008) *Sport England Strategy 2008–2011*, London: Sport England.

Sport England. (2015) *Active Universities Year 2 Report: Qualitative Findings*, London: Sport England.

Sturts, J. R. and Ross, C. M. (2013) Collegiate intramural sports participation: Identified social outcomes, *International Journal of Sport Management, Recreation and Tourism*, 11, 25–41.

Thorpe, R. and Collins, M. (2010) Sport and higher education: Participation and excellence, in Collins, M. (ed) *Examining Sports Development*, London: Routledge, 105–119.

Tsigillis, N., Masmmanidis, T., and Koustelios, A. (2009) University students' satisfaction and effectiveness of campus recreation programs, *Recreational Sports Journal*, 33, 65–77.

Universities UK. (2013) *Patterns and Trends in UK Higher Education: Higher Education – A Diverse and Changing Sector*, London: Universities UK/HESA.

Ward, B. W. and Gryyczynski, J. (2007) Alcohol use and participation in organised recreational sports among university undergraduates, *Journal of American College Health*, 56:3, 273–280.

CHAPTER 16

The sport-for-development sector
A role in social justice?

Alongside a landscape with growing focus on marketisation and professionalisation of the sport development workforce in a decade of austere public expenditure, has come a renewed request for agencies and volunteer organisations to focus on social justice (DCMS, 2015; Meek, 2018; Morgan, Parker, and Marturano, 2020). Social justice is the addressing of social inequalities that exist within society. This is, for example, the levelling of the playing field for individuals, families and communities that lack access to sport and recreation. The drivers of such access inequality are well documented and could be around inter-related factors such as 'race and ethnicity' (Fletcher and Swain, 2016; Fletcher and Walle, 2015; Long and Hylton, 2005), faith and religion (Mackintosh and Dempsey, 2017; The Inter Faith Network for the UK/ Sporting Equals, 2017), gender (Norman, 2019; Norman, Rankin-Wright, and Allison, 2018; Hill, Roberts, and Andrews, 2017) and disability (Fitzgerald, 2005; Ives et al., 2020). Historically, in sport development these groups represented designated 'target groups' around which specific programmes might be designed and deployed in packages across the country by local government, schools, and/or NGBs. However, in more recent times a new doctrine has also emerged, that is subtlety, but, crucially different to these targeted interventions. This has become entrenched in public policy and sport development narrative and discourse as 'sport-for-development'.

This term is equally loose in definition to sport development itself. However, Houlihan (2011) argues that there are three areas of sport development policy of 'sport-for-sports sake', sport-for-development, and elite sport performance development. He clearly is acknowledging a moving object in an evolving landscape of policy reacting to government directives and the responses to agencies, communities, and individuals to such viewpoints. In trying to map out this landscape, it is critical to start to explore the conceptual territory. This starts with some of the origins of the field of sport development itself with Action Sport in 1982. The detailed background of the evolution of this work is well documented in historically rich textbooks

173

(see Houlihan and White, 2002; Houlihan and Lindsey, 2013). What is important to acknowledge is that as recently as 40 years ago professionals in the guise of sport development officers (SDOs) were deployed to use sport as a vehicle in urban riots across England. In essence, whilst the scope has changed, the principal marker remains the same. This is the use, tailoring, and deployment of sport and physical activity-led programmes to address complex nuanced social issues. The exponential growth in the range of such issues that sport has been employed to address has led to a number of academic authors questioning the viability of the underlying rationale (Coalter, 2007; Morgan and Batlle, 2019). It is therefore to understand from a first insight to this area, that this is one of the more complex areas you are likely to study on a sport development degree. This doesn't mean that you should not be exposed to studying it at levels 4 and 5 as you need a foundation to your later more theoretical challenging approach to its study as a field of professional practice. It is also a domain in which the profession is growing thanks to respective home nation policies (DCMS, 2015; Sport England, 2016; Sport Northern Ireland, 2015; Sport Scotland, 2019). The overarching words that are sometimes used in this field are sport being used in 'community cohesion' (Coalter, 2007; Platts, 2018). As already stated with origins in Margaret Thatcher's government investment in the 1980s through to some investment by John Major in the 1990s, varied governments have seen a role for this. However, it was perhaps with the 1997–2010 New Labour government period that social inclusion and community cohesion saw a new heyday (Coalter, 2007; Houlihan and Lindsey 2013). This has, however, followed through on alternative opposing political party lines with the emergence of the DCMS (2015) and Sport England (2016) strategies. For example, both claim that sport and physical activity has scope to deliver outcomes related to mental health challenges, those at risk of criminal offending, and associated factors such as youth disengagement and alcohol and drug misuse (Sport England, 2016).

Sport-for-development: definition and contested origins?

Coater (2015) questions whether the diversification of the work of traditional sport development agencies is all positive. He notes that interventions are often based on ill-defined objectives and outcomes with poorly thought through monitoring and evaluation. Sandford, Armour, and Warmington (2006) agree with Morgan and Batlle (2019) that evidence, monitoring and the theoretical base for much of the claims made are questionable. Griffiths and Armour (2014: 308) argue the field is, put simply, "under-researched and poorly understood". For sport development agencies working in this landscape they face a dual paradoxical pressure. First, policy from government is offering money, resources, and political will to support social inclusive projects that address community cohesion development. But, second, the knowledge base for working in these areas is pushing people into spaces that are stretching them at best, and at worst are way outside their skill set. In a study of 12 local government SDOs in three counties in the East Midlands, respondents expressed concern then as to how they now had to understand evidencing crime prevention projects (Mackintosh, 2012). Skip forward around a decade and new research illustrates that evidence of how activities develop individuals is equally poorly conducted (Coater, 2015; Griffiths and Armour, 2014; Morgan and Batlle, 2019).

However, it is not all to be viewed negatively, but should be evaluated critically. For example, in 2019, a major review was undertaken by Prof Rosie Meek at the request of the Ministry of Justice around the role of sport and physical activity in the criminal justice system. In this review, emergent findings of good practice, steps in undertaking evaluation, and implementation of such cohesion work are present. Where it is possible to move beyond simplistic solutions and instead problematise the role of sport development, it is likely that agencies will find discrete evidence-led positions that they can adopt (Spaaij, MaGee, and Jeanes, 2014). For graduates in this area, understanding in this domain will increasingly be about stretching beyond the 'traditions' of sport development narratives and seeking out the very latest research on highly complex issues. Teaching and learning will be inter-disciplinary and move outside the comfortable boundaries of management, sociology, and politics. For example, criminology has been used to explore sports role in crime prevention already (Nichols, 2004; Nichols, and Crow, 2004; Meek, 2020; Morgan et al., 2019). But, we need students to engage with criminology-led dissertations to become the next generation of trainers, educators, and workforce support in sport development. No longer can we simply put a project in place for knife crime with general aims and objectives and a loose evaluation system. We need to understand the sociology of gangs, criminology around knives, and youth and youth work approaches to delivery of projects. I suspect that this work, when aligned with the key role for social media, is an area of huge appeal for the more innovative motivated students that wish to work at the cutting edge.

Of the sport development landscape that operates in this social justice driven field encapsulated by 'sport-for-development', some conceptualise it as a three-field area (Darnell and Hayhurst, 2011). First, there are projects that deliver what is known as *Traditional Sport* where there is an assumption that sport has natural developmental properties. Second, Darnell and Hayhurst (2011) identify *Sport Plus* where sport is adapted to maximise developmental outcomes. Finally, *Plus Sport* are those projects that use sport as the hook to attract participants into education or training initiatives; here, the development of sport is not the main aim. Most projects in sport development that have an underlying commitment to social justice driving a sport-for-development ethos and vision can be conceptualised in one of these three categories. The substantive focus of projects is highly varied and embraces diverse and eclectic target populations (Jump and Smithson, 2020; O'Hanlon et al., 2020; Sport for Development Coalition, 2020).

Organisations in the field and amongst their communities

In the UK, a number of key national organisations dominate this space who have sizeable staffing, resources, and presence across the UK. Two to start with include *Street Games* and *Active Communities Network*. Both charities are organised around social justice and, arguably, a community development and youth work perspective. Both have a strong leaning towards developing youth in their communities, particularly areas of complex social deprivation and disadvantage. Here, staff adopt different approaches to traditional sport development processes when establishing clubs, sessions, and participation opportunities. The principles of these two major charities are slightly different as *Street Games* are so large scale. They are the largest sport charity in the UK with global partnerships with brands such as Coca-Cola. They have also accessed considerable central government funding and developed ongoing regional stakeholder partnerships that overlay their work in programmes that they run such as *Active Girls* and *Doorstep Sports Clubs* (Street Games, 2020: online). As a mass provider of opportunities for youth in disadvantaged areas, they have a clear vision for improving lives since 2007 when they were established. They specifically use BAME, women and girls, and people with disabilities as their 'target groups' but also argue for a general vision for sport being used as a tool to engage and develop young people in areas of social disadvantage. At its core this is a 14–25-year-old focus in national programmes such as Doorstep Sport Clubs (DSC).

We now go back to the conceptualisation of sport-for-development containing three typologies of sport development projects. Arguably DSCs use a focused bottom-up, community development-influenced approach. In this policy space DSCs draw on use of role models, an awareness that sport can divide and the need for leaders and coaches to be known to the community. If projects are targeting a theme such as gender, or crime prevention and antisocial behaviour, they are tailored so that DSCs and Active Girls 'fit' more with a *Plus Sport* categorisation.

Active Communities Network is another charity, of smaller scale, that works in six cities with a core staff that drive their youth work-led bottom-up philosophy to sport development (Active Communities Network, 2020: online). They work in complex communities but, in general, do not run national programmes that they roll out. Instead, there is a focus on understanding the needs of a group of individuals and young people. This is very much an asset-based community development (ABCD) model of delivery and development (Schulenkorf, Sherry, and Rowe, 2016). This is a model that in this sector of sport development will likely expand in the next evolution of policy and programmes. A challenge for non-bespoke projects is that youth and young adults needs are not met. Coaches, leaders, and sport development officers and managers will also see that for the most complex needs sport needs to be more than just a 'hook' as it is often simplistically referred to (Coater, 2015). The ABCD model essentially starts off by understanding the human, physical, and cultural assets present within a community. For example, does a village, city, or town have existing leaders 'hidden' in a community, have young people already volunteered at a mosque or Hindu temple? Are there sport-specific regional assets in terms of interests? For example, in areas such as Leicester and Bradford where there are very diverse BAME groups, can this be utilised and acknowledged as a core asset in programme and project design? In establishing working groups and starting to shape a programme, local populations are embedded in this process. Then there is a mapping of the community assets and needs, followed by building a plan for the community vision and its assets. Final steps involve mobilising and 'activating' the community an interaction between organisations such as ACN, youth services, Active Partnerships, local government, NGBs, and probably most fundamentally local schools and sports clubs. The very last step is referred to as leveraging activities and resources. This sees the sport being deployed alongside the required needs-led activities to meet the programme vision.

ACN charitable organisation have around 65 staff across their five hubs in the UK in Portsmouth, Belfast, London and Manchester as well as an international 'spoke' to their work in South Africa. They are also a good example of a growing volume of charities and agencies that are working in this policy space in either niche remits (mental health, prisoner education, sport/physical activity, elite athlete 'transition' out of sport careers, drug misuse). It is important as students of this subject area to recognise that sport is not a panacea. Put simply, sport is not the solution to all societal ills. Sport development is not always well designed, sport development is not always evidence-led, sport development projects can be established to chase income for an increasingly cash poor organisation, or sport-for-development acts as a helpful public relations vehicle. As Coalter, Long, and Duffield argued in 1988 in *Recreational Welfare*, this statement probably does have some grounds. A recent evidence review by Sport England (Sport England 2017) has benchmarked the DCMS (2015) five characteristics against robust academic and grey literature evaluations and research. In this work the field of sport-for-development came out as requiring considerably more research before a certainty to link can be made between sport, physical activity, and social policy outcomes such as mental health, individual development, and community development. The spheres of economic development and physical and physiological benefits seemed well established in both reviews. Both reviews are also a useful starting point for students beginning to explore the evidence base for areas that to date they have assumed exist.

Most recently, the Sport-for-Development Coalition was established (Sport-for-Development Coalition, 2020). They have positioned themselves as:

> The Sport for Development Coalition is a movement of organisations who all believe in the power of sport and physical activity to act as effective tools for intervention when generating positive social outcomes. We aim to provide evidence of this, especially to other sectors – such as health, criminal justice or education – and to funders or investors seeking more efficient solutions for society's biggest problems.

> The Coalition has three strategic goals: Advocacy – showcasing the sector; impact – demonstrating the sector's impact and making the case for investment; investment – securing new funds for the sector.
>
> (Connect Sport, 2020: online)

The Coalition encompasses 66 organisations (at the time of writing) including agencies such as *Comic Relief*, *The Laureus Foundation*, *Women in Sport*, *The Youth Sport Trust*, *The Laurence Dallaglio Foundation*, *Active Partnerships Network*, *Alliance of Sport in Criminal Justice*, *Street League* and *Dame Kelly Holmes Trust*. This is a typical network seen in the sport development sector, which has been founded on such advocacy coalitions of interests since the 1960s (Houlihan and White, 2002; Houlihan and Lindsey, 2013; Zehndorfer and Mackintosh, 2017). The group of organisations are essentially a lobbying group, political policy advocacy partnership, and way for agencies to share knowledge and understanding. Most interestingly, they operate largely virtually, with some board meetings through the online media portal *Community Sport*. Community sport shares knowledge through its web-led mailing list and 'members', an innovative vehicle for positioning community sport within the hands of the community. Perhaps a sign of things to come for the sector moving forward in terms of where the power lies for those deploying 'the power of sport'. As it stands, the Sport-for-Development Coalition retains its strength from the size and authority of various key policy stakeholders. But, the impact of the Coalition is still to be determined. They plan to grow the sector from around 60 to over 400 organisations. They go on to state,

> Across the UK, it is estimated there are at least 2500 organisations intentionally using sport and physical activity to generate positive social outcomes. The Charity Commission has registered 1942 charities with sport in their name, activities or objectives, with 356 citing 'sport for development', 33 'sport for change' and 117 'sport for good'.
>
> (SFDC, 2020: 1)

It is clear that this policy space is one that will continue to expand as more agencies innovate to stake a claim in the role they can play to deliver social justice goals. For graduates emerging into the job market it will be a new set of horizons, skill sets and theoretical underpinning that sport development will require in this domain. Alternative patterns of delivery exist across local communities, regional conurbations, and major stakeholders such as NGBs and the four national Sports Councils. Since the promise of delivering 'recreational welfare' (Coalter, Long, and Duffield, 1988), post-1980s urban riots and the formation of many original sport development units, it appears sport development has gone a long lumbering full policy circle. The difference is that as local government has undergone cuts and reorganisation, and NGBs have refocused on the core market of a traditional 'sport for sport' delivery sector, new agencies have emerged in the sport for development sector currently epitomised by the metaphorical umbrella of the Sport for Development Coalition.

CASE STUDY 16.1

Sport development and crime prevention – a seminal reading

Every now and then, students ask 'why am I reading this "really old" article?' It is a fair question and one that we fail to explain clearly as academic staff involved in teaching and learning. Around 2004–2005, Geoff Nichols undertook his seminal research exploring sport, leisure, and crime prevention strategies in a number of case studies. This research, whilst 15 years ago, acts as my 'go to' for understanding sport and crime prevention. In this case study, I will provide an overview of the paper and essential why it matters. The implications are significant for you if you want to work in this growing area of sport-for-development. Most crucially, many of those engaged in delivery of programmes, design of projects, and research and evaluation may not have read this body of substantive (means–subject specific) work.

The reading below is taken from the West Yorkshire Sports Counselling (WYSC) evaluation work that was undertaken between 2004 and 2005 (Nichols, 2004; Nichols and Crow, 2004). In the UK context, when we consider our original understanding of why sport can, and cannot, play a role in engaging disengaged youth the epicentre in policy terms lies with the WYSC. Furthermore, when others have shaped writing and ideas in more recent times models and frameworks for understanding, the challenges have come from the book Nichols delivered. In this book he offered an overview of the policy sector at this point, of which there were some fledgling movements given the New Labour government use of sport in social inclusion (1997–2010).

A reading of this 'old' article now will offer three fundamental things. First, students will see how policy has subtly changed through history in the sport development context. Secondly, perhaps most fundamentally it offers a critical lens on what seems like a straightforward *Sport Plus* concept of a programme. Finally, it can provide lessons for evaluating what are currently being 'presented' as sport-for-development projects now, which in many cases are simply *Traditional Sport* conceptual frameworks (Darnell and Hayhurst, 2011). The chapter selected explores how factors such as individual self-esteem and self-control are influenced by a project based in West Yorkshire. Like more contemporary projects that have used sport in this sphere the use of counselling is fundamental to delivery of outcomes of the programme.

Guided reading

Nichols, G. (2008) West Yorkshire Sports Counselling, in Nichols, G. *Sport and Crime Reduction*, London: Routledge, 59–74.

Top tip: note taking

Whether online on a e-book, or hard copy notes and annotations in the margin of the photocopied chapter, good note taking is an essential skill. For me, it provides a summary of what I have read, a focus whilst I am reading, and the start of the writing process. Generally, I look for theoretical ideas, key statistics, themes, and links to wider reading as well as great quotes (and their page). As a level 4 student, you will need to develop this skill set. It is not easy and for many it is a new skill.

Key seminar questions

1. Although over 15 years old, what principles and lessons can be learnt from this seminal piece of reading?
2. Are there any key themes that the author argues are important?
3. What limitations may be present within an existing sport-for-development programme? (Choose any from within the 66 organisations in the Sport-For-Development Coalition.)

Reflection

Consider what your initial thoughts were when asked to read an old, dated, and dusty journal article. Now reflect on what you have learned individually and as a class. How might you approach this task differently in future? What would the impact of this be on:

- Your academic learning
- Your professional practice
- Your knowledge and understanding of nuanced topics.

References

Active Communities Network (ACN). (2020) *How we started*, available at: www. activecommunities.org.uk/ourstory [accessed on June 03 2020].

Coalter, F. (2007) *A Wider Social Role for Sport: Who's Keeping the score?*, London: Routledge.

Coater, F. (2015) Sport-for-change: Some thoughts from a sceptic, *Social Inclusion*, 3:3, 19–23.

Coalter, F., Long, J. A., Duffield, D. S. (1988) *Recreational Welfare: A Rationale for Public Leisure Policy*, Aldershot: Avebury.

Connect Sport. (2020) *Sport for Development Coalition*, available at: www.connectsport.co.uk/coalition [accessed on June 03 2020].

Darnell, S. C. and Hayhurst, L. M. C. (2011) Sport for decolonization: Exploring a new praxis of sport for development, *Progress in Development Studies*, 11:3, 183–196.

Department of Culture, Media and Sport (DCMS). (2015) *Sporting Nation*, London: DCMS.

Fitzgerald, H. (2005) Still feeling like a spare piece of luggage? Embodied experiences of disability in physical education and school sport, *Physical Education and Sport Pedagogy*, 10:1, 41–59.

Fletcher, T. and Swain, S. (2016) Strangers of the north: South Asians, cricket and the culture of 'Yorkshireness', *Journal for Cultural Research*, 20:1, 86–100.

Fletcher, T. and Walle, T. (2015) Negotiating their right to play: Asian identified cricket teams and Leagues in Britain and Norway, *Identities: Global Studies in Culture and Power*, 22:2, 230–246.

Griffiths, M. and Armour, K. (2014) Volunteer sport coaches as community assets? A realist review of the research evidence, *International Journal of Sport Policy and Politics*, 6:3, 307–326.

Hill, C., Roberts, S., and Andrews, H. (2017) 'Why am I putting myself through this?' Women football coaches' experiences of the Football Association's coach education, *Sport, Education and Society*, 23:1, 28–39.

Houlihan, B. (2011) Introduction: Government and civil society involvement in sport development, in Houlihan, B. and Green, M. (eds) *An International Handbook of Sport Development*, London: Routledge, 51–54.

Houlihan, B. and Lindsey, I. (2013) *Sport Policy in Britain*, London: Routledge.

Houlihan, B. and White, A. (2002) *The Politics of Sports Development*, London: Routledge.

The Inter Faith Network for the UK/Sporting Equals. (2017) *Using the Power of Sport to Build Good Inter Faith Relations*, Leicester: The Inter Faith Network for the UK/ Sporting Equals.

Ives, B., Clayton, B., Brittain, I., and Mackintosh, C. (2020) 'I'll always find a perfectly justified reason for not doing it': Challenges for disability sport and physical activity in the United Kingdom, *Sport in Society*, iFirst 1–19.

Jump, D. and Smithson, H. (2020) Dropping your guard: The use of boxing as a means of forming desistance narratives amongst young people in the criminal justice system, *The International Journal of Sport and Society*. 11:2, 55–69.

Long, J. and Hylton, K. (2005) Reviewing research evidence and the case of participation in sport and physical recreation by black and minority ethnic communities, *Leisure Studies*, 33:4, 379–399.

Mackintosh, C. (2012) The shifting dynamics of local government sports development officer practice in England: New identities and hazy professional boundaries, in Harris, S., Bell, B., Adams, A. and Mackintosh C. (eds) *Sport for Sport? Theoretical and Practical Insights into Sports Development*, Brighton: Leisure Studies Association, 113–130.

Mackintosh, C. and Dempsey, C. (2017) The Muslim male youth sport participation puzzle: An examination of the role of identity, religion and ethnicity in determining involvement in sport, *Journal of Youth Studies*, 20:8, 974–996.

Meek, R. (2018) *A Sporting Chance: An Independent Review of Sport in Youth and Adult Prisons*, London: Ministry of Justice.

Meek, R. (2020) The use of sport to promote employment, education and desistance from crime: Lessons from a review of English and Welsh prisons, in Ugwudike, P., Graham, H., McNeill, F., Raynor, P., Taxman, F. & Trotter, C. (eds) *The Routledge Companion to Rehabilitative Work in Criminal Justice*, London: Routledge, 409–418.

Morgan, H. and Batlle, C. I. (2019) vIt's borderline hypocrisy': Recruitment practices in youth sport-based interventions, *Journal of Sport for Development*, 7:13, 1–14.

Morgan, H., Parker, A., and Marturano, N. (2020) Community-based intervention and marginalised youth: Inclusion, social mobility and life-course transition, *Journal of Education and Work*, iFirst, 1–17.

Morgan, H., Parker, A., Meek, R., and Cryer, J. (2019) Participation in sport as a mechanism to transform the lives of young people within the criminal justice system: An academic exploration of a theory of change, *Sport, Education and Society*, iFirst, 1–14.

Nichols, G. S. (2004) Crime and punishment and sports development, *Leisure Studies*, 22:3, 177–194.

Nichols, G. and Crow, I. (2004) Measuring the impact of crime reduction interventions involving sports activities for young people, *The Howard Journal of Criminal Justice*, 3:43, 267–283.

Norman, L. (2019) 'I don't really know what the magic wand is to get yourself in there': Women's sense of organizational fit as coach developers, *Women in Sport and Physical Activity Journal*, (forthcoming), 1–12.

Norman, L. , Rankin-Wright, A. J. and Allison, W. (2018) 'It's a concrete ceiling; it's not even glass' : Understanding tenets of organizational culture that supports the progression of women as coaches and coach developers, *Journal of Sport and Social Issues*, 42:5, 393–414.

O'Hanlon, R., Mackintosh, C., Holmes, H.-L., and Meek, R. (2020) Moving forces: Using sport and physical activity to support men and women in the military to civilian transition, *Managing Sport and Leisure: An International Journal*, iFirst, 1–22.

Platts, C. (2018) Including the excluded: Community cohesion through sport and physical activity, in Wilson, R. and Platts, C. (eds) *Managing and Developing Community Sport*, London: Routledge, 67–80.

Sandford, R. A., Armour, K. M., and Warmington, P. C. (2006) Re-engaging disaffected youth through physical activity programmes, *British Educational Research Journal*, 32:2, 251–271.

Schulenkorf, N., Sherry, E., and Rowe, K. (2016) 'Sport for development: An integrated literature review', *Journal of Sport Management*, 30:1, 22–39.

Spaaij, R., MaGee, J., and Jeanes, R. (2014) *Sport and Social Exclusion in Global Society*, London: Routledge.

Sport England. (2016) *Towards an Active Nation*, London: Sport England.

Sport England (2017) *Review of Evidence on the Outcomes of Sport and Physical Activity: A Rapid Review*, London: Sport England.

Sport-for-Development Coalition. (2020) *Sport for Development Coalition 2020–2024 Business Plan*, London: SFDC.

Sport Northern Ireland. (2015) *Sport Northern Ireland: Five-year corporate plan 2015–2020*, Belfast: Sport NI.

Sport Scotland. (2019) *Sport For Life: A Vision for Sport in Scotland*, Glasgow: Sport Scotland.

Street Games. (2020) *About Street Games*, available at: https://network.streetgames. org/about-us/about-streetgames [accessed on June 03 2020].

Zehndorfer, E. and Mackintosh, C. (2017) The Olympic Bid Cycle as a form of irrational investing: An application of Minskyian theory, *Cogent Social Sciences: Sport, Leisure & Tourism*, 3:1, 1281466, 1–8.

CHAPTER 17

The private sector

A considerable policy change in sport development is the increasing role of the private sector (sport providers and non-sport commercial sponsors) who have become increasingly significant. This chapter will address the potential sphere of sport development agencies that encompass the private sector that engage in purported community sport development implementation and delivery. The consideration of sponsorship and non-sport agencies as key vehicles for sport development funding in the UK will also be analysed. A key sub-sector within this sphere is that of the professional sports club, many of which now engage with corporate social responsibility or other community-facing activities. Football, cricket, and rugby are now major deliverers of activities, and have responded to the move from government-led to networked governance patterns of delivery and policy design. Students will be supported in developing their understanding of this sector through engagement with differentiation between, and collaboration with NGB sport development practices. The different ideological and philosophical tensions will be considered to give students an introductory overview of the contested nature of private provision of what was historically a 'public good' (sport and leisure) delivered predominantly by public-owned agencies (government). Links can also be made back to the previous chapters that have considered primary school sport development pathways that are in some areas of the UK dominated by providers that are private sector orientated (David Lloyd Gyms, Boxing Products, Virgin Health). This is a complex and nuanced sector but one that too often is left out of traditional textbooks examining sport development due to its supposedly parallel market orientated philosophy.

The distinction between public and private is not always easy. For example, Sheffield United Football Club and Sheffield Hallam club have a project called Football Unites Racism Divides (FURD). It is a trust managed by a board of trustees. In 1995, when the Premier League exploded onto the global platform, this brought with it financial and commercial gains for clubs. Alongside partnering Kick It Out, the national ant-racism campaign, the orientation of the FURD programme was a social justice wing of a growing private commercial venture. The work undertaken here is most definitely that of the sport development officer.

The above is a good microcosm of wider Football in the Community programmes (FiTC) that have been in place for 25 years in the sport development landscape of the UK (Sanders et al., 2020; Stone, 2018). The projects were launched with six pilots in the North West of England of England: Bolton, Bury, Manchester City, Manchester United, Oldham, and Preston. The goals included aiming to address unemployment, build links between football and its communities, BAME target group work, reduce hooliganism, and maximise use of club facilities. Numerous authors over the first ten years of such provision called for greater clarity in terms of the social impact of the FiTC departments (Coalter, 2007; Tacon, 2007).

Seminal research by Brown (2008) underpinned recommendations for FiTC, principally the need for separate independent community organisations, which saw 'clubs' divide from 'the community department'. More recently, the aspirational research vision of Coalter (2007) has been picked up by academics shaping evidence in this arena (Curran et al. 2017; Krustrup and Parnell, 2019; Bingham et al., 2014). Specifically, Krustrup and Parnell cultivate the concept of 'football as medicine'; whilst not a new term, the origins of this debate lie in the long-standing position of private professional clubs within their local communities over the last 25 years (Sanders et al., 2020). This must also be further related to more recent moves away from outputs (numbers of young people, women, BAME participants, 'disengaged' youth) towards outcomes of the project (progress towards improving self-esteem, recidivism). These are now significant vehicles for the implementation of sport development goals locally, regionally, and nationally (DCMS, 2015). Major FiTC operators can have as many as 50 staff. This vastly swamps the size of an Active Partnership and Local Government sport development unit in a major metropolitan area. Manchester City FiTC works in areas across multiple sports; it engages with diverse markets such as challenging youth groups, primary coaching, and secondary and FE educational programmes. Recently, in 2018, it began the delivery of the Manchester City FC degree and foundation degree where students spend a considerable proportion of their degree within the FiTC programmes. As stated earlier in the book, there are 'hidden' populations and the Pupil Referral Unit (PRU) is one such space for excluded children from school. Here, MCFC FiTC staff engage with you in these settings to deliver sport-led activities that are adapted to engage with them and deliver fun educational tools that draw heavily on football.

There is not sufficient space to consider all the 300 or so NGBs in the UK and the role their professionalised organisations and leagues play in community sport development. An automatic area to acknowledge is that of the player pathway function, sometimes considered a part of the 'old' paradigm of 'traditional sport development'. Exploring this, it clearly is located in the juncture of what Houlihan (2011) designated as 'elite performance sport'. Within this it is perhaps useful to try and encapsulate the breadth of activities that are located in Figure 17.1.

Figure 17.1 illustrates that whilst Houlihan (2011) argued for sport development having three clear areas of professional practice and policy, the elite performance strand could perhaps be better conceptualised as having three areas in the new era of highly professionalised sport development. In terms of

---

Elite Performance Sport model

High elite (Olympic, professional) – national/international players
- Elite centres
- Coaching (permanent, paid and high professional qualifications)
- Sport Science (linked to national Institutes in HEIs)
- Sport Psychology (embedded in teams, squads or 1-2-1 from HEIs)
- Lifestyle advisor –careers, mental health, education
- Nutrition and sports medicine/physiotherapist
- Welfare
- Agents, legal and sponsorship

Talent identification and development
- Players in player performance pathway
- Scouting systems
- First contact with agents
- Sub-national coaching (variable degree of professionalisation
- Academy structures (professional sports)
- Nutrition and sports medicine/physiotherapist
- County performance structures *club, school
- Welfare and child protection officers
- BUCS elite athlete scholarships

'Sport for sport' becomes 'talent' and performance
- Participant ethos vs elite pathway for individuals
- Trials, county representation, coach recommendations
- Parental support, travel requirements and financial resource
- Private 1-2-1 coaching
- School to higher regional representation
- Youth Sport Trust *School Games* national-regional representation

---

FIGURE 17.1 Outline of the three tiers of elite sport performance that shape experiences of performers in a sport development 'pathway'

the talent development area, this varies considerably by sport, in part based on ethos, tradition, and approach but also on fiscal resources available to individual clubs and sports (Baker, Cobley, and Schorer, 2012). For example, in Till et al.'s (2012) study of the junior talent identification, selection, and development pathway and process in Rugby League, players only go to professional clubs after U-16s. Prior to this, there is use of regional performance camps progressing through to a 'national carnival' and a final step into a national camp and preparation. Clearly, there is a considerable infrastructure of selectors, coaches, administrators, and professional club staff around this system. It is a useful insight to the vast elite sport development system that is present within sports in the UK (and beyond). If we then take the UK's football, cricket, and Rugby Union academy systems in addition with this, we have five sizeable systems that sit across regional and local infrastructure in sport development. Most people working in community sport development would most probably not overlap too heavily with the elite domain of provision, although the original scope of the FiTC to share facilities is still an aspirational one where clubs may share their sport facilities with local community clubs where appropriate.

Rugby in Scotland can also provide a good insight into how professional sport provides both opportunities, infrastructure, and sport development job opportunities. The case of Glasgow Warriors RFC is illustrative of the large vehicle for participation and engagement in regional and local youth in a series of three core programmes. They run *Wee Warrior Clubs* and *Warrior Camps* targeted at 5–17-year-old children across the Glasgow area in holiday periods (Glasgow Warriors, 2020: online). Club sessions have been running since 2015. This can be seen to be largely a community arm of the professional club, generating income for the club and making sport participation possible through the deployment of level 1 and 2 coaches. In contrast, other professional sports clubs have taken a more *Plus Sport* approach (Darnell and Hayhurst, 2011) where they have built a portfolio of activity programmes that are aiming to use the 'sport as a hook' vehicle for genuinely challenging wider societal issues. A good example of this can be seen in Glamorgan Cricket Club in their *Beyond The Boundaries* (BTB) project, which offers workshops for diverse agencies in partnership with their staff (Glamorgan Cricket Club, 2020). Activities in these workshops use cricket law and the game's sense of fair play to explore complex issues including: role models, belonging and conflict (Syrian Disaster), famine, differences in ethnic perspectives, and intolerance. In this BTB the professional club has worked with local prisons, charities working with young people not in education or employment (NEET), and the Barnardo's charity. This focused work is part of the philanthropic focus of a private sports club, but one that has a community-led arm to its operations. Glamorgan CC also engages with more traditional sport development processes through its *All Stars Cricket* (ASC) roll out project, which began in 2017 in 100 clubs with 2300 individuals signing up aged five to eight years for eight-week cricket coaching programmes. This grew to 130 clubs or cricket centres in 2020. Just by size of participant footprint and scale of coaching implementation resource, this should clearly show how a professional sports club becomes one of the fundamental stakeholders in cricket development. Indirectly, by targeting disability participants, BAME groups, areas of social disadvantage, and women and girls, it is also contributing heavily to the Sport Wales (2019) vision for a more active and healthy Wales.

The private sector does not only need to be recognised as the realm of private, commercial sports clubs. It is also the domain of the private sports coaching organisation. It is very hard to estimate how many paid, full time, and part time coaches there are within the UK, although UK Coaching argue that there are 3 million individuals engaged in sport coaching in the UK (UK Coaching, 2019). What is clear is that since 2010 and the removal of the English School Sport Partnership (SSP) system supporting primary PE through secondary PE specialists, and the implementation of the Primary PESSP, there has been a boom in private coaching companies accessing school provision. Such companies are employed in varied amounts, scope, and remits but typically deliver after-school sports clubs.

Private sector involvement also sits within the sport development sector in terms of sponsorship from commercial organisations. This often facilitates community sport programmes. A very simple example is the use of MacDonald's fast food retailer financial support to support the Football Association (FA) kit and community club initiative. Likewise, HSBC Bank has a close relationship with British Cycling and uses the profile of the sport in terms of elite and community cycling clubs to its own benefit. This said, the fiscal resources that a major sport like HSBC can offer make programmes and initiatives possible that would sit outside the resourcing of Sports Councils and regional government. Other sports like the LTA NGB have a wide-ranging and diverse set of headline financial partners and key collaborators. These range from food nutrient bar providers and gin suppliers through to technical tennis and footwear equipment global suppliers. This is also another good example of stopping to acknowledge the globalised landscape of sport development. Flows of information, marketing relationships, TV rights, and global mega events also combine to support very localised sport-for-development projects, strategic planning around the tennis club, and the event workforce. We can no longer consider a sport development project solely as an isolated local programme.

Similarly, private health club providers such as Pure Gym (UK's largest 'budget' provider) through to more luxury brands in David Lloyd and an expanding middle territory of leisure providers such as Virgin Health Clubs arguably are positioned very closely to government targets across the country in each of the four home nations. If local authority gyms are not being consumed and subscribed at the rate they used to be, then this has significant implications for the physical stock of facilities but also for sport development staff. There is now evidence that organisations such as Virgin are exploiting relationships with schools, PE departments, and parental 'offers'. Furthermore, the traditional work of an SDO to work solely with public stock, public staff alone, and in a silo manner is long gone. The future skill set of staff in the field will be to develop synergies in governance around sponsorship, shared resources, and opportunities for developing sport, and physical activity. Arguably, the weakest element of the private 'offer' lies in how they would service low-income groups and minority needs that cost more to accommodate at the expense of profit. Where a corporate social responsibility model can be applied in a sustainable manner, there are opportunities. Reliance upon the public purse has been shown to have significant limitations when Sport England or other Home Nations turn their head away from funding organisations towards a new whim of policy or selective performance indicator. A good example here is in the UK sporting system where funding regimes in formalised elite sport (e.g. UK Sport/NGB) contrast with the ad-hoc philanthropic gifts that can enable professional sports clubs to deliver multiple programmes of community sport development (HSBC, McDonald's and so on).

████████████████ CASE STUDY 17.1 ████████████████

Football academies in the UK – elite sport pyramid pinnacle or home of rejection for the talented?

An example will be used in the case of football youth academies in England that are part coaching, part youth development, and part participation focused in their outlook. Whilst largely operating outside the traditional pathways and conceptualisation of sport development, they provide a powerful and rich vehicle for introducing the ideas of ethics and applied professional values. Links will also be made with the notion of the virtuous cycle of mega events and mass participation stemming from elite events (the World Cup and mass TV exposure) relating to the myth of 'trickle down' effects.

Football academies have received attention in recent years in terms of how players move through and transition the system they find themselves in (Conn, 2017; Green, 2005; Platts and Smith 2009). In particular, as an ethical and welfare issue, a number of academic authors have highlighted the transition from youth football to academy as a critical issue (Bullough and Jordan 2017; Mills et al. 2014). In each of these studies, different research and theoretical approaches are taken to examining the transition process. But, what is clear is that, for young footballers, this is a complex and at times challenging life experience and transition. The central figures in the 'lifeworld' of players here are often highly polarised between educational and welfare officers and the professional football coaching staff. A further layer of complexity is from the wider interest and in some cases pressure from parents and other role models. Locate the two paper above and choose one that appeals to you (but also think why it appeals – the theory, the evidence, or the language of the author, is it accessible for example?).

Commercialisation in sport (Slack, 1997) has shaped, and been shaped by increasing forces from globalisation in football (and other sports). Some clubs are keen to invest in 'the finished product' over developing talent (Green, 2005). Equally, the Premier League clubs are now part of a global monopoly on the elite tier of football talent workforce in football. This said, training, developing, and transitioning players between 'host clubs' and others has become an increasing trade for some. Agents, firmly located in the mercenary trading of human capital, offer little resistance to the global forces of sports juggernaut.

In some cases, football academies are now overseen by Directors of Sport (AoFD, 2020). With appointed football directors, comes an overview responsibility for the welfare of youth players and all that encompass the regimes of training, diet, selection, and competitive fixtures. As suggested by previous studies, the ethics of welfare surrounded such football academies is complex, nuanced, and, at times, deeply ethical by nature (Bullough and Jordan 2017; Platts and Smith 2009). Amidst the talk of 'transition' remains the white elephant of the many thousands of players that do not make it to play at the highest level in English professional football. Many of these cross cutting issues were picked up in the 2017 Duty of Care in Sport Review conducted by Baroness Tanni Grey-Thompson. This is an additional resource that you can access an extend this activity.

Seminar questions

1. Who is in charge of the welfare of the young people (16 years plus)?

2. How do child protection regimes differ for those aged, say, 7–15 that encompass activities within the academy?

3. If you were employed as a welfare officer what challenges do you think you would face from different individuals, in different roles in the academy?

Further reading

Parnell, D., Cope, E., Bailey, R., Widdop, P. (2017) Sport policy and English primary physical education: The role of professional football clubs in outsourcing, *Sport in Society*, 20:2, 292–302.

Rowe, K., Karg, A., and Sherry, E. (2018) Community-oriented practice: Examining corporate social responsibility and development activities in professional sport, *Sport Management Review*, 22:3, 363–378.

References

Association of Football Directors (2020) *Home*, available at: https://associationofsportingdirectors.com/ [accessed on 03 June 2020].

Baker, J., Cobley, S., and Schorer, J. (2012) *Talent Identification and Development in Sport*, London: Routledge.

Bingham, D. D., Parnell, D., Curran, K., Jones, R., and Richardson, D. (2014) Fit fans: Perspectives of a practitioner and understanding participant health needs within a health promotion programme for older men delivered within an English Premier League Football Club. *Soccer & Society*, 15:6, 883–901.

Brown, A. (2008) *How Can We Value the Social Impact of football Clubs? Qualitative Approaches*, The Social Value of Football Research Project for Supporters Direct: Working Papers, Manchester: Substance.

Bullough, S. and Jordan, J. (2017) Youth academy player development in English football: The impact of regulation since 2006, *Sport, Business and Management: An International Journal*, 7:4, 375–392.

Coalter, F. (2007) *A Wider Social Role for Sport: Who's Keeping the score?*, London: Routledge.

Conn, D. (2017) 'Football's biggest issue': The struggle facing boys rejected by academies, available at: www.theguardian.com/football/2017/oct/06/football-biggest-issue-boys-rejected-academies, [accessed on 06 June 2020].

Curran, K., Rosenbaum, S., Parnell, D., Stubbs, B., Pringle, A., and Hargreaves, J. (2017) Tackling mental health: The role of professional football clubs, *Sport in Society*, 20:2, 281–291.

Darnell, S. C. and Hayhurst, L. M. C. (2011) Sport for decolonization: Exploring a new praxis of sport for development, *Progress in Development Studies*, 11:3, 183–196.

DCMS. (2015) *Sporting Nation*, London: DCMS.

Glamorgan Cricket Club. (2020) *Cricket in the Community'*, available at: www.glamorgancricket.com/beyond-the-boundaries [accessed on 03 June 2020].

Glasgow Warriors. (2020) *Wee Warriors Club*, available at: www.glasgowwarriors.org/community/community-programmes/wee-warriors-club [accessed on 03 June 2020].

Green, C. (2005) Building sport programs to optimize athlete recruitment, retention, and transition: Toward a normative theory of sport development, *Journal of Sport Management*, 19:19, 233–253.

Houlihan, B. (2011) Introduction: Government and civil society involvement in sport development, in Houlihan, B. and Green, M. (eds) *An International Handbook of Sport Development*, London: Routledge, 51–54.

Krustrup, P. and Parnell, D. (2019) *Football as Medicine: Prescribing Football for Global Health Promotion*, London: Routledge.

Mills, A., Butt, J., Maynard, I., and Harwood, C. (2014) Examining the development environments of elite English football academies: The players' perspective, *International Journal of Sport Science and Coaching*, 9:6, 1457–1472.

Platts, C. and Smith, A. (2009) The education, rights and welfare of young people in professional football in England: Some implications of the White Paper on Sport, *International Journal of Sport Policy and Politics*, 1:3, 323–339.

Sanders, A., Keech, M., Burdsey, D., Maras, P., and Moon, A. (2020) CEO perspectives on the first twenty-five years of football in the community: Challenges, developments and opportunities, *Managing Sport and Leisure: An International Journal*, iFirst, 1–20.

Slack, T. (ed.) (1997) *The Commercialization of Sport*, London: Routledge.

Sport Wales. (2019) *A Vision for Sport in Wales*, Cardiff: Sport Wales.

Stone, C. (2018) Community engagement through elite sport, in Wilson, R. and Platts, C. (eds) *Managing and Developing Community Sport*, London: Routledge, 93–108.

Tacon, R. (2007) Football and social inclusion: Evaluating social policy, *Managing Leisure*, 12:1, 1–23.

Till, K., Chapman, C., Cobley, S., O'Hara, J., and Cooke, C. (2012) Talent identification, selection and development in UK junior rugby league: An evolving process, in Baker, J., Cobley, S., and Schorer, J. *Talent Identification and Development in Sport*, London: Routledge, 106–118.

UK Coaching. (2019) *Coaching in the UK 2019: Coach Survey*, Leeds: UK Coaching.

PART III

Conclusions, future directions, and debates

Part III will provide an opportunity to pull together cross-cutting strands and themes that have run through the textbook. It will give students space to understand the emerging priorities for their subject area, profession, and research agendas in sport policy and development. All four home nations have been considered in this text, intentionally to problematise the sometimes 'hidden voices' of those in sport policy outside England. As the dominant political power based around Whitehall government and DCMS (2015) visions for the role of sport policy and sport development, it is useful to be aware of how this may differ subtly from Wales, Scotland, and Northern Ireland. Even at levels 4 and 5, it is also imperative to locate sport development practices within a globalised context (Cuskelly, Hoye, and Auld, 2006; Palmer, 2013; Sherry, Schulenkorf, and Phillips, 2017). A view beyond our localised context is a real aspirational goal for those studying sport development. In encountering challenges in the field, whilst on placement or volunteering in sport, many such circumstances can be experienced through a lens of globalisation. Speed of change of circumstances, routes to changes in societal views and the development and sharing of new ways of working are facilitated through global connections and interactions in sport development.

In this next section, the aim is to provide a combination of overview and a vision of next steps and future challenges for sport development. Previous collections of research and studies of sport development have arguably examined the dual binary (and often opposing) sport development policy goals of mass participation in sport and elite performance (Collins, 2010; Bloyce and Smith, 2010; Harris, Mori, and Collins, 2009; Houlihan, 1994; Houlhan and White, 2002). However, as this book has illustrated across multiple sectors such as local government, central government, and regional agencies, alongside NGBs, charities, and trusts this 'divide' and professional bifurcation seems far more nuanced than in the last 40 years in the UK. Certainly, the emergence of policy agendas that are clustered around other thematic debates and arguments to justify expenditure in sport and physical activity have become more mainstream, whilst academic authors acknowledge a long-standing recognition for the role of sport in crime prevention and recidivism (Coalter, 2007; Nichols,

191

2008), mental health (DCMS, 2015; Smith et al., 2016; Everton FC, 2020; online) and educational attainment linked to PE, sport and physical activity (Griffiths, Armour, and Cushion, 2018). Such strands of policy and their associated sport development communities are gaining in momentum, with further sub-clusters such as those interested in sport and prison population physical activity and mental health (Meek and Lewis, 2012; Meek, 2020), use of sport to support military war veterans (O'Hanlon et al., 2020), and work with refugee populations as a response to growing global crises in locations such as the Middle East (Long, Hylton, and Spracklen 2014; Spaaij, 2015; Spracklen, Long, and Hylton, 2015).

As there seems to be a fork in what Houlihan (2011) defined as the three pathways of sport development policy: 'sport for sport', sport for social good, and elite performance development, we can see other nuances beginning to shape the landscape of agencies, organisations, and professional practice in the UK. For example, schools remain a major player in delivery of physical education and after-school, intra-school, and inter-school sport provision. The sporting 'diet' of those in this vital landscape from 7–16 and 16–18 including FE and sixth forms is fundamental to shaping and inculcating a lifelong interest in sport. How activities supported by the PE profession are linked to additional wider community provision is also a matter for policy and an area that has undergone vast change since the 2010 change in government (Pitchford and Collins, 2010; Mackintosh, 2014; Zehndorfer and Mackintosh, 2017). Equally, initiatives that cut across into other national context provide fertile spaces for exploring alternative ways in which sport development is implemented. Active Schools in Scotland is a good example, alongside Dragon Sport in Wales. Both have different focuses and different policy agendas to service and operate in geographically unique sport development contexts. Further to the school setting, the voluntary sector remains a lifeblood of UK sport development (Findlay-King et al., 2018; Nichols et al., 2019) supporting over an estimated 151,000 sports clubs. With suggestions that there are also around three million sport coaches operating across these and other settings, we begin to see that the organisational workforce of the country is complex, sizeable, and a powerful potential vehicle for achieving policy goals of government. Sport England recently published a workforce strategy where it was acknowledged that various 'glass ceilings' existed, with barriers for women, those of BAME background, and other drivers around inequality (Sport England, 2018). With local government, NGB, SGB, charities, national sport development agencies, and professional sport also layered onto the sport development infrastructure, it illustrates how as a student you enter an exciting, but also complex domain.

So how to make sense of this? Is it all located in a single book, a set of journal articles, or your course reading list? Like any professional practice setting, it is a combination of factors that will help you make sense of such agencies, organisations, and very subtle cultural nuances that divide them (yet they operate in the same agenda, environment, and policy space). A useful tip at this point is to try and virtually or, even better, physically explore the context of the exciting field of sport development. Such experience varies in terms of *length of duration* and *scale of involvement*. This spectrum of learning opportunities with examples of potential learning opportunities shows where students can embed, explore, and build up understanding. Most crucially, it will give students access to professionals tacit knowledge and skills in sport development. Tacit is defined as where a professional individual (nurse, doctor, teacher, sport coach) such as a sport development manager, project officer, or researcher draws on skills and knowledge naturally, in an implicit, unacknowledged manner to deliver their daily routines, job, and outcomes of sport development. An example of tacit knowledge would be 'just knowing' how to explain national NGB policy to a local volunteer in a friendly, accessible way. This translation is critical for national policy to ever work at the local level (Harris, Mori, and Collins, 2009; Mackintosh, Hughes, and Daniels, 2021).

A range of opportunities are available to you as an individual to build a better contextual understanding of the sport development organisations you will need to grapple with when you enter professional practice. In particular, the key facets of this are that you can either aim for short or long-term contacts or placements. Likewise, the scope and size can vary in the organisation you approach. It is the view of this author that nothing can help you understand and experience policy like 'doing it', living the experience and seeing how it has multiple meanings for those involved (Bevir and Rhodes, 2016; Wagenaar, 2011). For example, by being a community sports club volunteer on a core committee you will be exposed close up to child protection procedures, financial statements, marketing strategies for junior recruitment, and debates about whether 'the latest' government gimmick (their view possibly) is even worth reading. That policy could be a £40 million investment in a 'key' agenda but if local people are not engaged by it and NGBs don't communicate effectively around why it may be of use or interest then these sport development makers are the ones that really 'make' policy.

Many students have the option to do mini (two- to six-week placements) in levels 4 and 5. Alternatively, those on a foundation degree, perhaps do units in professional practice. This has become a growth domain for sport development, and part of arguably the professionalisation of the sector (CIMSPA, 2020: online; Dowling, Edwards, and Washington, 2014; Hylton and Hartley, 2012). This is a first opportunity to explore an NGB, coaching setting, PE provision, or a charity that you know little about other than it was the short placement offered to you. Such opportunities are fundamental to finding your way through to what career you may choose. It is also a space to begin to shape your skills in being a reflective practitioner (Gibbs, 1988; Johns, 2017) in acknowledging the experiences, learning, and challenges you face. The ability to consider where you sit reflexively in your placement, their operations, and the work they do with wider agencies and communities is critical. For example, perhaps until you attend the first two-week placement in school as a potential school-based PE or school-sport worker ,you didn't realise the challenge of class room management, or how many meetings a regional football development officer has, and how they spend their life on their mobile phone, laptop and based in service stations and coffee shops. This learning is key, as is the core fundamentals of changing sport development officer changing professional practice, which we can then revisit the literature around. Whether it is sport and crime prevention (Meek, 2018), NGBs (Thompson, Bloyce, and Mackintosh, 2020; Mackintosh, Hughes, and Daniels, 2021), Football in the Community programmes (Sanders et al., 2020), local government (King, 2009; King, 2014; Widdop et al., 2017), or primary and coaching (Griggs, 2018; Parnell et al., 2016) academic literature coming together with personal professional experience is a powerful co-production of learning.

References

Bevir, M. and Rhodes, R. (2016) *Routledge Handbook of Interpretive Political Science*, London: Routledge.

Bloyce, D. and Smith, A. (2010) The emergence and development of sport policy, in Bloyce, D. and Smith A. *Sport Policy and Development: An Introduction*, London: Routledge, 29–55.

Chartered Institute for the Management of Sport and Physical Activity (CIMSPA). (2020) *Occupations, job roles and specialism*, available at: www.cimspa.co.uk/standards-home/occupations-job-roles-and-specialisms [accessed on 22/04/20].

Coalter, F. (2007) *A Social Role for Sport: Who's Keeping the Score?*, London: Routledge.

Collins, M. (2010) From 'sport for good' to 'sport for sport's sake' – not a good move for sports development in England?, *International Journal of Sport Policy and Politics*, 2:3, 367–379.

Cuskelly, G., Hoye, R. and Auld, C. (2006) *Working with Volunteers in Sport: Theory and Practice*, London: Routledge.

Department of Culture, Media and Sport (DCMS). (2015) *Sporting Future a New Strategy for an Active Nation*, London: DCMS.

Dowling, M., Edwards, J., and Washington, M. (2014) Understanding the concept of professionalization in sport management research, *Sport Management Review*, 17:4, 520–529.

Everton Football Club. (2020) *Everton FC in the community: Tackling the blues*, available at: www.evertonfc.com/community/health-and-wellbeing/the-projects/tackling-the-blues. [accessed on 29/4/2020].

Findlay-King, L., Nichols, G., Forbes, D., and Macfadyen, G. (2018) Localism and the Big Society: The asset transfer of leisure centres and libraries–fighting closures or empowering communities? *Leisure Studies*, 37:2, 158–170.

Gibbs, G. (1988) *Learning by Doing: A Guide to Teaching and Learning Methods*, London: Further Education Unit at Oxford Polytechnic.

Griffiths, M. A., Armour, K. A., and Cushion, C. J. (2018) 'Trying to get our message across': Successes and challenges in an evidence-based professional development programme for sport coaches, *Sport, Education and Society*, iFirst, 1–18.

Griggs, G. (2018) Investigating provision and impact of the primary Physical Education and Sport Premium: A West Midlands case study. *Education 3–13*, 46:5, 517–524.

Harris, S., Mori, K., and Collins, M. (2009) Great expectations: The role of voluntary sports clubs as policy implementers, *Voluntas International Journal*, 20:4, 405–423.

Houlihan, B. (1994) *Sport, Policy and Politics: A Comparative Analysis*, London: Routledge.

Houlihan, B. (2011) Introduction: Government and civil society involvement in sport development, in Houlihan, B. and Green, M. (eds) *An International Handbook of Sport Development*, London: Routledge, 51–54.

Houlihan, B. and White, A. (2002) *The Politics of Sports Development*, London: Routledge.

Hylton, K. and Hartley, H. J. (2012) Sports development: A profession in waiting?, in Harris, S., Bell, B., Adams, A., and Mackintosh, C. (eds) *Sport for Sport? Theoretical and Practical Insights into Sports Development*, Brighton: LSA, 4–22.

Johns, C. (2017) *Becoming a Reflective Practitioner* (5th Edition), Oxford: Wiley Blackwell.

King, N. (2009) *Sport Policy and Governance*, Oxford: Butterworth-Heinemann.

King, N. (2014) Local authority sport services under the UK Coalition government: Retention, revision or curtailment, *International Journal of Sport Policy and Politics*, 6:3, 349–369.

Long, J., Hylton, K., and Spracklen, K. (2014) Whiteness, blackness and settlement: Leisure and the integration of new migrants, *Journal of Ethnic and Migration Studies*, 40:11, 1779–1797.

Mackintosh, C. (2014) Dismantling the school sport partnership infrastructure: Findings from a survey of physical education and school sport practitioners, *Education 3–13*, 42:4, 432–449.

Mackintosh, C., Hughes, A., and Daniels, J. (2021) Community coaching management through an interpretivist lens: From community participation to modernisation and business practices, *European Journal of Sport and Society*, iFirst, forthcoming 1–20.

Meek, R. (2018) *A Sporting Chance An Independent Review of Sport in Youth and Adult Prisons*, London: Ministry of Justice.

Meek, R. (2020) The use of sport to promote employment, education and desistance from crime: Lessons from a review of English and Welsh prisons, in Ugwudike, P., Graham, H., McNeill, F., Raynor, P., Taxman, F., and Trotter, C. (eds) *The Routledge Companion to Rehabilitative Work in Criminal Justice*, Routledge: London, 409–418.

Meek, R. & Lewis, G. (2012) The role of sport in promoting prisoner health, *International Journal of Prisoner Health*, 8:3/4, 117–131.

Nichols, G. (2008) *Sport and Crime Reduction*, London: Routledge.

Nichols, G., Hogg, E., Knight, C., and Storr, R. (2019) Selling volunteering or developing volunteers? Approaches to promoting sports volunteering, *Voluntary Sector Review*, iFirst, 1–16.

O'Hanlon, R., Mackintosh, C., Holmes, H.-L., and Meek, R. (2020) Moving forces: Using sport and physical activity to support men and women in the military to civilian transition, *Managing Sport and Leisure: An International Journal*, iFirst, 1–22.

Palmer, C. (2013) Social theory, globalization and sports policy in a Risk Society, in Palmer, C. *Global Sports Policy*, Sage, London.

Parnell, D., Buxton, S., Hewitt, D., Reeves, M. J., Cope, E., and Bailey, R. (2016) The pursuit of lifelong participation: The role of professional football clubs in the delivery of physical education and school sport in England. *Soccer & Society*, 17:2, 225–241.

Pitchford, A. and Collins, M. (2010) Sports development as a job, career and training, in Collins, M. (ed.) *Examining Sport Development*, London: Routledge, 259–288.

Sanders, A., Keech, M., Burdsey, D., Maras. P. and Moon, A. (2020) CEO perspectives on the first twenty-five years of football in the community: challenges, developments and opportunities, *Managing Sport and Leisure*, iFirst 1–16.

Sherry, E. Schulenkorf, N. and Phillips, P. (2017) What is sport development? In Sherry, E. Schulenkorf, N. and Phillips, P. (eds) *Managing Sport Development: An International Approach*, London: Routledge, 3–11.

Smith, A., Jones, J., Houghton, L., and Duffell, T. (2016) A political spectator sport or policy priority? A review of sport, physical activity and public mental health policy, *International Journal of Sport Policy and Politics*, 8:4, 593–607.

Spaaij, R. (2015) Refugee youth, belonging and community sport, *Leisure Studies*, 34:3, 303–318.

Sport England. (2018) *Working in an Active Nation: The Professional Workforce Strategy for England*, London: Sport England.

Spracklen, K., Long, J., and Hylton, K. (2015) Leisure opportunities and new migrant communities: Challenging the contribution of sport, *Leisure Studies*, 34:1, 114–129.

Thompson, A., Bloyce, D., and Mackintosh, C. (2020) 'It is always going to change' – managing top-down policy changes by sport development officers working in national governing bodies of sport in England, *Managing Sport and Leisure: An International Journal*, iFirst, 1–20.

Wagenaar, H. (2011) *Meaning in Action: Interpretation and Dialogue in Policy Analysis*, London: Routledge.

Widdop, P., King, N., Parnell, D., Cutts, D., and Millward, P. (2017) Austerity, policy and sport participation in England, *International Journal of Sport Policy and Politics*, 10:1, 7–24.

Zehndorfer, E. and Mackintosh, C. (2017) The Olympic bid cycle as a form of irrational investing: An application of Minskyian theory, *Cogent Social Sciences: Sport, Leisure & Tourism*, 3:1, 1281466, 1–8.

CHAPTER 18

Where next for sport development in the UK?

The textbook has provided at this stage a window into introducing the organisations, agencies, and key policy domains of community sport development. This chapter will reflect on the sector wide challenges, future directions, and professional issues that are facing organisations in community sport development. It will return to the theoretical windows and conceptual frameworks outlined in Chapters 4, 5, and 6 to consider future evolving landscapes of provision and the implications this has for how we study sport development. Theory is central to how students of this policy arena and domain of professional practice understand and analyse sport development. However, it is in the organisational settings that many who gain future employment and begin their own development that such understanding will play out. This chapter will consolidate learning, refresh, and remind learners of the key debates from earlier in the book but also begin to look towards next steps in learning.

Sport development emerged from the 1960s Wolfenden Report landscape of the UK. What followed over the next 60 years has been an exponential rise in the growth of recreation and sport sector per se (Mackintosh, Griggs, and Tate, 2019). In the 1960s, before the birth of the first local authority leisure centres, and fledgling sport, recreation, and leisure department, what existed were a number of NGBs, largely run in a code of amateurism and voluntary sector sports clubs. Furthermore, facilities that did exist were those attached to private 'big business' employee recreation clubs, or the Victorian legacy of parks and open spaces in the form of playing fields. Sport development emerged as investment in leisure facilities, swimming pools, playgrounds and Sports Council home nation infrastructures began. It was deemed a necessary function to address engagement, activate the use of facilities and begin to embolden mass participation. As already stated, a number of texts cover this in far greater depth than there is space here in an introductory text (see Houlihan and White, 2002; Houlihan and Lindsey, 2013).

Continuity and change: the parallel paths of sport development practice

However, what is fundamental is to revisit how policy has changed and followed various paths over this period. As identified by Collins (2010), each government has its own particular vision, goals for the use of sport (and sport development). This is a driver of how sport development plays out in the organisations in this book. The gap that this text has aimed to close is between recent policy and contemporary organisation, agencies, and practice to bring students a sense of closeness to their subject. For example, as leisure centre 'booms' occurred in the 1970s what followed was a focus on procurement, performance management, and target setting for those working in sport facility management and development (King, 2009). Whilst now 50 years ago, and arguably for many students a period of time far too removed from 'their studies', this era of conservative power in government parallels that of the 2008–2020 era that has a focus on austerity (cost cutting, performance, and measurement of NGB delivery of WSP targets). Other authors have identified that culture and organisational change in NGBs reflect the business and marketisation of sport development functions (Thompson, Bloyce, and Mackintosh, 2020). Here, volunteer management is a good example to recognise how volunteers are being recruited, retained and developed in the mode of paid staff (Findlay-King et al., 2018; Nichols et al., 2019; Mills and Mackintosh, 2021). History therefore remains a rich area of understanding for us, and should not be forgotten as a contextual space for learning.

In 1995, Collins undertook research to establish the scope, size, and workforce structural health of the sport development industry (Collins, 1995). At this point it was estimated that there were around 2500 and 3000 jobs in sport development. Skills Active (n.d.) ten years later estimated there was between 4000 and 5000 people in full or part-time employment in the sport development sector. In this research a survey was undertaken with 900 sport development staff. Regional workshops were also undertaken that identified the most common job titles. An adaption of the results is shown in Table 18.1.

In addition to the general information seen in Table 18.1, it is also clear that around 50 per cent of job titles are 'other' or are represented by small percentages of the respondents to the research undertaken. What can be seen is that some areas that were just emerging and starting to take a stand in the workforce such as football in the community (0.4 per cent) will likely have expanded considerably given the last 15 years of expansion of provision in this sport (Sanders et al., 2020), and, other sports such as rugby (RFU, 2020; online; Glasgow Warriors, 2020: online). In 2005, 39 per cent of sport development posts were hosted in local government, 11 per cent within sport clubs, 9 per cent in charitable trusts, 6 per cent NGB, 6 pe cent school-based, 5 per cent County Sport Partnership (now 'Active Partnership' in England) and 2 per cent Leisure Trust. Collins (2010) identified how this

TABLE 18.1 Job titles in sport development in 2005 (adapted from Pitchford and Collins, 2010)	
Job title	**%**
Other	31.2
Sport development officer (including youth and community)	18.9
Sport coach/leader	10.9
Sport-specific development officer (e.g. netball)	9.7
Sport development manager (LA, NGB)	9.6
Programme manager	3.1
Teacher, tutor, lecturer	2.5
Sport officer	2.1
Assistant sport development officer	2.1
(Adapted from Pitchford and Collins, 2010)	

drop to 40 per cent in local government was a sizeable drop from research undertaken in 1995.

Table 18.2 illustrates that there are a proposed five types of job role functions. This can also be referred to as a taxonomy. In this framework the five categories of job functions parallel much of the emerging CIMSPA (2020) professional standards. There are, in this sense, levels of sport development roles that have been identified back in 2005 by Collins (2005). But, what the table does, is brings this up-to-date with reference to changing patterns of sport development professional delivery and management of policy experienced in the last 15 years. Two new tiers of the taxonomy have been adapted to include research functions and activity with sport development that are increasingly core categories of job function to the field (Mackintosh, 2012; Rowe, 2009) and funding and governance (King, 2014; Widdop et al., 2017). This final sphere of activity is related to the notion that with income being increasingly fragmented compared to 20 years ago, and there being an era of austerity in the public sector, senior sport development staff must also be aware of funding. This is also represented in the work of the junior face-to-face delivery staff, who may also be operating in an increasingly fragile funding environment.

This chapter has set out to shape your understanding of some of the major challenges facing the sector, but also provide some learning frameworks to help you address your own learning. The following case study is not intended to contextualise this learning in shaping your understanding of the emerging profession of sport development.

TABLE 18.2	Reconceptualising core sport development job functions (includes adaption of Collins, 2005 table, cited in Pitchford and Collins 2010)	

Job function area	Collins (2010) features	Mackintosh (2020) features
Coaching	Direct delivery of sport	Thematic considerations in mental health provision, crime prevention and community engagement
Leadership Face-to-face delivery	Session planning requires child protection, equity and managing behaviour	Use of community ABCD delivery style Renewed focus on child protection agenda
Facilitation or coordination	Enabling and management of face-to-face sport partnership work: project planning, M/E, and budget control Inter-agency 'micro' working and marketing	Increased use of volunteer workforce management Increased use of diverse partners to deliver Increased sophistication of M/E – partnerships with national and regional partners for evidence base Heavy role for social media-led marketing, e.g. Twitter, Instagram, online event booking tools, Facebook
Management	Strategic resource management focused on staff, budgets, HR employee relations	Increased use of individuals with non-sport background to address complex challenges Use of non-executive directors to challenge representation on boards *UK Sport A Code for Sport Governance* used to challenge roles of organisational boards
Research, insight, and evidence management	New function since 2005 typology	To deliver evidence-bed projects clear deployment and design of M/E systems Use of national and regional secondary data sets (e.g. Active Lives and Active People Surveys) Use of specialists within organisations Increased links with more HEIs (UKSDN, AfPE, YST)
Funding and governance	New outright function since 2005	Societal and political changes mean that senior sport development staff work within changing governance structurers (e.g. social enterprise, CiC, and asset transfer policies)

CASE STUDY 18.1

Tokenism vs professionalisation in sport development – the realm of community sport

In this case study we will take on two major debates within the field of sport development policy head-to-head. Throughout the book, we have explored emergent key themes such as equity for disabled people, improving mental health through physical activity, and supporting young people in endeavours to prevent them engaging with criminal activity through sport. In the specific context of community sport in the UK, I'd like you to develop your own evidence, arguments and be able to start to build an argument to present based on research. First, we need to revisit two concepts raised in this book to provide a theoretical position for your debate. Examples and web references to projects and schemes are great. But, as you have moved through this book you should now starting to be seeing the importance of evidence, theory, and concepts. Remember, concepts are just the bright ideas that go to make up bigger macro theory. In the case of this book, pick a country of the four we have looked at (so you have clear policy and programme context), pick a sector that appeals (primary PE, sports clubs, Football in The Community, for example ...), then we are going to look at two concepts when we use them as a lens to examine that area of sport development. Ultimately, the final few chapters of the book aim to test how well you can use concepts and explore issues. If you do not use theory or concepts, work is what is referred to as 'atheoretical'. It is likely to be highly descriptive and lack real analysis, with the recipient of your debate, ideas, and sport development understanding being limited often to anecdotes and personal opinion. Theory helps us to understand, have a higher level of analysis, and ultimately offers rich insights your university subject. Whether that theoretical paradigm is sociological, that of business management, or political will vary on different units and research projects.

In this case study, one concept we can use is that of *community development* (Hylton and Totten, 2013; Sherry, Schulenkorf, and Phillips 2017). Work in this area in the UK is starting to emerge again as significant in adopting this philosophy to working with local communities. The agencies that work in this area often drive a 'bottom up' position as opposed to a top-down policy driven stance. As a NGB, for example, it would involve consulting your clubs, volunteers, players, and members to establish their needs and wants. Then it is about considering what skills and knowledge they bring to the NGB as opposed to imposing a programme, project, or idea onto clubs. Partington and Totten (2012) also offer a good case study of such an approach to sport development in Rochdale in England. Larger national Sport Wales, Scotland, England, and Northern Ireland agencies often drop major policies and it is how they play out in regional spaces that can limit their worth.

Second, we can return to the concept *professionalisation* as mentioned earlier in the book. It is a constant thread to work in sport development. Professionalised approaches to workforce endeavours, whether with volunteers, other sport partnerships or young people in a youth club. The natural implication of this can be a catch-all term for many facets of the sport industry (Taylor and Garrett, 2010).

More recent work has also illustrated that analysis of the conceptual terrain around this is useful for exploring dynamics within the sport development sector (Dowling, Edwards, and Washington, 2014). In this case study, consider how the process of an organisation becoming more professionalised (voluntary clubs are a great example) may have wider implications for things like community sport ethos, commitment to volunteering, age profile of volunteers, and disability. Try and 'unpick' what might be understood by professionalisation. Think of employees, volunteers, organisations and how they operate, process policy from stakeholders like NGBs and Sports Councils. It can be very day-to-day features (these can be positive and negative) or more large-scale aspects of an organisational approach to marketing, communications (individual agency or structural ways of operating).

Seminar task

Select a country, then perhaps an NGB or regional agency and try and undertake an analysis that starts to use the two conceptual tools to explore what insights and ideas you gain from using them:

1. Community development
2. Professionalisation.

Seminar extension task

In building this initial insight, now try and read one of the two articles that relate to the initial conceptual ideas. In particular, note:

• How is the article fleshed out in terms of its scope and remit around your concept?
• How is the conceptual ground used, explained, and examined?
• What could you now do as a student using that more detailed conceptual set of ideas?

Further readings

Dowling, M., Edwards, J., and Washington, M. (2014) Understanding the concept of professionalisation in sport management research, *Sport Management Review*, 17:4, 520–529.

Sherry, E. Schulenkorf, N., and Phillips, P. (2017) What is sport development?, in Sherry, E. Schulenkorf, N. and Phillips, P. (eds.) *Managing Sport Development: An International Approach*, Routledge, London, 3–11. * Note you have read this back in Chapter 3 – how has your conceptual and professional understanding of community sport development evolved?

References

Chartered Institute for the Management of Sport and Physical Activity (CIMSPA). (2020) *Occupations, job roles and specialism*, available at: www.cimspa.co.uk/standards-home/occupations-job-roles-and-specialisms [accessed on 22 April 2020].

Collins, M. (1995) *Sports Development Locally and Regionally*, Reading: Institute of Leisure and Amenity Management (ILAM).

Collins, M. (2010) *Examining Sport Development*, London: Routledge, 259–288.

Dowling, M., Edwards, J., and Washington, M. (2014) Understanding the concept of professionalisation in sport management research, *Sport Management Review*, 17:4, 520–529.

King, N. (2009) *Sport Policy and Governance*, Oxford: Butterworth-Heinemann.

King, N. (2014) Local authority sport services under the UK Coalition government: Retention, revision or curtailment, *International Journal of Sport Policy and Politics*, 6:3, 349–369.

Findlay-King, L., Nichols, G., Forbes, D., and Macfadyen, G. (2018) Localism and the Big Society: The asset transfer of leisure centres and libraries – fighting closures or empowering communities?, *Leisure Studies*, 37:2, 158–170.

Glasgow Warriors. (2020) *Wee Warriors Club*, available at: www.glasgowwarriors.org/community/community-programmes/wee-warriors-club [accessed on 03 June 2020].

Houlihan, B. and Lindsey, L. (2013) *Sport Policy in Britain*, London: Routledge.

Houlihan, B. and White, A. (2002) *The Politics of Sports Development: Development of Sport or Development Through Sport?*, London: Routledge.

Hylton, K. and Totten, M. (2013) Community sport development, in Hylton, K. (ed.) *Sport Development: Policy, Process and Practice* (3rd Edition), London: Routledge.

Nichols, G., Hogg, E., Knight, C., and Storr, R. (2019) Selling volunteering or developing volunteers? Approaches to promoting sports volunteering, *Voluntary Sector Review*, iFirst, 1–16.

Mackintosh, C. (2012) The shifting dynamics of local government sports development officer practice in England: New identities and hazy professional boundaries, in Harris, S., Bell, B., Adams, A., and Mackintosh, C. (eds) *Sport for Sport? Theoretical and Practical Insights into Sports Development*, Brighton: Leisure Studies Association, 113–130.

Mackintosh, C., Griggs, G., and Tate, R. (2019) Understanding the growth in outdoor recreation participation: An opportunity for sport development in the United Kingdom, *Managing Sport and Leisure: An International Journal*, 23:4, 315–335.

Mills, C. and Mackintosh, C. (2021 forthcoming) Categorising sports club volunteering by goal focus and activity: The case of English golf clubs, *Sport in Society*, iFirst, 1–20, forthcoming.

Partington, J. and Totten, M. (2012) Community sports projects and effective community empowerment: A case study in Rochdale, *Managing Leisure*, 17:1, 29–46.

Pitchford, A. and Collins, M. (2010) Sports development as a job, career and training, in Collins, M. (ed.) *Examining Sport Development*, London: Routledge, 259–288.

Rowe, N. (2009) The Active People Survey: A catalyst for transforming evidence-based sport policy in England, *International Journal of Sport Policy and Politics*, 1:1, 89–98.

Rugby Football Union (RFU). (2020) *Get Involved*, available at: www.englandrugby.com/participation/playing/get-involved [accessed on 04 June 2020]

Sanders, A., Keech, M., Burdsey, D., Maras, P, and Moon, A. (2020) CEO perspectives on the first twenty-five years of football in the community: Challenges, developments and opportunities, *Managing Sport and Leisure: An International Journal*, iFirst, 1–20.

Sherry, E., Schulenkorf, N., and Phillips, P. (2016) *Managing Sport Development*, London: Routledge.

Sherry, E., Schulenkorf, N., and Phillips, P. (2017) What is sport development? in Sherry, E. Schulenkorf, N., and Phillips, P. (eds) *Managing Sport Development: An International Approach*, London: Routledge, 3–11.

Skills Active. (n.d.) *Briefing Note: A Summary of Community Sport Development Research Report*, London: Skills Active.

Taylor, B. and Garrett, D. (2010) The professionalisation of sports coaching: relations of power, resistance and compliance, *Sport, Education and Society*, 15:1, 121–139.

Thompson, A., Bloyce, D., and Mackintosh, C. (2020) 'It is always going to change' – managing top-down policy changes by sport development officers working in national governing bodies of sport in England, *Managing Sport and Leisure: An international journal*, iFirst, 1-20.

Widdop, P., King, N., Parnell, D., Cutts, D. and Millward, P. (2017) Austerity, policy and sport participation in England, *International Journal of Sport Policy and Politics*, 10:1, 7–24.

CHAPTER 19

New policy pressures and new delivery models in unstable times

Policy encompasses a diverse philosophical and ideological landscape in sport development. By this we mean different organisations (say, governments) have alternative visions for what sport development should do and how it is delivered and to whom. However, the majority of those working in sport development do not do so in policy making in central government, or even traditional arm's length strategic agencies (CSPs, quangos, and national agencies). Thus, this chapter aims to try and sketch out the professional field of sport development as it stands, with previous estimates of only 5000 professionals (Collins, 1995) now dated and there have been considerable changes in policy and practice, and the organisations that are tasked with delivery have never been as diverse. This chapter will then move on to establish the skills, values, and professional knowledge that are valued in the field and by sectors within the sport development profession. It will also examine contested debates around evidence-based practice in the field, the growth of the 'insight' industry and demand for rigorous academic research skills as part of a portfolio of graduate skills in sport development.

Research, monitoring and evaluation in sport development

Since the 1980s, there has been a gradual expansion of a sub-industry within sport development, that of those individuals and organisations engaged in sport development research. As graduates in sport development and individuals with an understanding in sport policy and management at a community level, you will be embedded within a sphere of daily professional practice. This could be as a football development officer for a national football NGB that is working to increase female engagement quality experiences in the game. Here, you may have two to three key programmes from coach education through to targeted initiatives with professional Scottish top tier clubs and their Football in the Community Trusts. Part of your role here is to be able to evaluate whether such different schemes deliver their intended outcomes. Traditional sport development delivered between 1980s and the late 1990s was arguably easier to evaluate as it was based around sporting outcomes. Equally, many historical research approaches were output-led, in that they were keen to know the numbers of coaches, volunteers and participants that were recruited, trained, and engaged (Coalter, 2007; Coalter, 2015). Since the mid-1990s and the emergence of sport's identified role with community social exclusion (crime prevention, youth engagement, literacy, drug misuse, and individual personal development), evaluation became more nuanced and complex. Indeed, many have critiqued the role of such initiatives and, furthermore, the associated monitoring and evaluation supporting the delivery and quest for insight into 'what works' (Coalter, 2007; Sport England, 2017).

For those now positioned in the field, organisational change is a constant motif of our times due to the funding cycles and associated performance targets in strategic sport development (Baker, 2017; Mackintosh, 2011; Thompson, Bloyce, and Mackintosh, 2020). In addition, the daily lives and lived experiences of an SDO are now far more research-led (Bloyce et al., 2008; Mackintosh, 2012). Here, individuals are required to work towards a gold standard of 'evidence-based' policy (Cairney, 2016). What this means for those working with NGBs, clubs, volunteers, coaches, parents, participants schools and charities is that research must now be central to decision-making. Organisational sectors mentioned in this book each have their own cultures around research, their own bias, and their own positioning and use of research for their own agendas. As students we need to remain aware and open to such critique, not just assume that a report that says a project that has used cricket to engage refugees in an 'inner city challenging area' has been a success actually has delivered its goals and outcomes. The way to unpick and examine this is through building an understanding of the research process.

The research process in sport development is largely no different to elsewhere in the social sciences (Armour and MacDonald, 2012; Medcalf and Mackintosh, 2018; Smith and Sparkes, 2016). Any of these texts provide a good starting point for examining the research process that you will engage with at levels 4–7 and possibly into a PhD beyond masters level 7. Clear research questions, project aims, and robust research objectives that feed into a robust methodology, and well delivered research data collection and analysis are what any evaluation in sport development requires. This text will not be explaining the detail and focus of design, methods and so on. However, suffice to say, many of the industry reports you might read in this book, within units, and across your degree will assume a level of understanding. For now, the principal scope of this book is to introduce you to the sphere of research and evaluation in sport development. To do so, a useful vehicle for this is to consider examples, as opposed to the complex definitions and ideas that you will explore in more depth at level 5.

Let's return to the example of the SGB officer working with a series of five professional clubs. Designing evaluation should start before the project, not afterwards or in the worst case at the end. Retrospective evaluation misses all the 'process' evaluation learning (Coalter, 2007; Belfiore and Bennett, 2010) that is happening 'live' as the project is going on. Indeed, Belfiore and Bennett (2010) argue convincingly to move away from a single tool kit of evaluation props towards more bespoke design to embrace the individual nuances of cultural programmes often which contain hard to 'measure' soft outcomes. Ten years on from this plea, sport has consistently moved toward a need to quantify, measure, and count aspects of 'value'. The industry around evaluation is itself divided into multiple schools of thought. Again, it is not useful to be listing and exploring all these here. Safe to say, that is far beyond offering a starting point for understanding the field. At its most simplest they might fit into the three categories of research and evaluation tradition in sport development (see Table 19.1).

Table 19.1 illustrates how each of the three broad categories as 'tradition' have associated methods or ways of conducting research. Likewise, each of these three traditions have an inclination towards different areas of research in sport development. This is not intended to be an exhaustive (or complete) list of interests. Instead, the Scottish FA in their work with 11–16-year-old girls

TABLE 19.1 Outline of the characteristics of three broad research and evaluation traditions in sport development

Research and evaluation tradition	Method	Sport development outcome interests
Quantitative	Surveys Secondary data sets, e.g. Active Lives data, Office for National Statistics Physical activity measurement	Measuring levels of satisfaction, motivation, participation Changes in patterns of behaviour over time Establishing gaps in provision
Qualitative	Interviews Focus groups Online visual methods Observational	Understanding emotions Explaining non-engagement Accessing little explored worlds Accessing 'life worlds' of SDOs, sport coaches, volunteers, and users
Mixed methodology	Survey feeding into undertaking depth interviews Secondary data to support focus groups and observations	Testing ideas and exploring motivations and understanding Test policy ideas

working in Football Trusts at professional clubs to be better understand experiences, attitudes, and behaviours for example might employ qualitative
research. A quantitative survey might instead be used to measure satisfaction
more precisely over time, and motivation to attend and count the numbers
engaged across five clubs. Finally, a mixed methodology may use secondary
analysis of football participation data for 11–16-year-olds in Scotland and
study past reports and literature to then inform a series of six to seven interviews with key staff at each of the football clubs and a focus group of
11–16-year-olds. This paints a picture of the different approaches.

What is most significant, is that the remit of undertaking this research was
at one time that of the 'researcher', whether from a university, external consultancy company, or internal evaluation officer. But such is the scope and requirement of monitoring and evaluation now that this is core professional work for
most SDOs now (Mackintosh, 2012; Gregory and Wilson, 2018; Sport
England, 2018).

New models of delivery

When Collins (2010) reflected on the changing nature of sport development
ten years ago, drawing on his own work from 1995 and earlier, it was clear
that the notion of local authority sport development as 'king' was long gone.
Such pessimistic visions of local governance administration for sport policy
were supported at the time by others (Bloyce and Smith, 2010; Bloyce et al.,
2008; King, 2009). In his analysis of Liverpool community sport programmes,
King (2009) identified significant budget constraints and new, but sometimes
contradictory, ways of working in local government. Here, this was specifically
around the need to find new ways of working between local–national partnerships around policy agendas. In more recent times Widdop et al. (2017) have
explored the post-2008 period of ten years of austerity for sport policy and
development in the UK with its impact on local government delivery, funding,
and sport provision. As we move from a model of 'big government' into new
models of enabled governance through networks and partnerships, this leaves
the platform for sport development delivery with a very different 'look'.

First, there is more diverse landscape of providers on what we might term the
supply-side of sport development. These are the agencies, organisations, and
individual people that meet the needs of a population of 67 million in the UK.
This book has tried to map out some of these new providers and long-established agencies that are redefining their role. In recent times, use of virtual online
spaces is perhaps the least well-explored space of sport development practice as
we have tended to assume 'it' can only occur in sports club venues, leisure facilities, and pools. However, it has been clear that there are virtual instructors,
clubs, and online spaces where young and old can meet, interact. and develop
sport. Young people are using YouTube, Vimeo, and other visual tools to share
ideas, lessons, and ways of playing. This was particularly apparent in the
COVID-19 pandemic period from March 17th 2020 when much of the community sport sector went into lockdowns. Furthermore, agencies such as NGBs,

SGBs, and UK Coaching are offering virtual lessons, coach education, and self-taught e-learning units for coaches (UK Coaching, 2020: online). Linked to this, we are starting to see change in the wider workforce education processes; for example, virtual sport development apprenticeships are targeting 16–23-year-olds to give them access to SDO work with VLUK partners such as Powerleague, Essex Cricket Club, and Portsmouth FC (VLUK, 2020: online).

Second, funding is shifting and how it is allocated, spent, and withdrawn is changing at great speed. Other authors have positioned sport development as a non-statutory service in local government territorial areas (King, 2009; Mackintosh and Liddle, 2015). As cuts took place after the global crash in 2008, many such services over the next ten to 12 years saw significant reductions in both staffing, facilities, and programme budgets. Where sport development had been used to deliver social policy goals, these cuts now shone a light on under-provision in local communities and money moving through the UK in different ways. For example, schools saw cuts in centralised budgets for learning support and teaching assistants whilst other schools moved from local authority control to academy status (Gunter and Rayner, 2007). These two strands of policy impact alone had a considerable impact on school sport and PE. In primary schools, the primary PESSP income that schools received saw a boom in new coaching companies delivering post-school 'clubs'. Many have criticised such clubs for the quality of this contracted-out provision (Griggs, 2010, 2016). Funding moved between agencies' sport development supply and demand is affected, and much of it is underpinned by ideology. In addition, the philosophical views and standpoint of a government becomes increasingly central to the sport development policies, process and practice embedded in society (Hylton, 2013; Bloyce and Smith, 2010).

Others have argued for the emergence of sport development policy impacts around the Conservative government's 2010 mantra of 'Big Society' (Devine, 2012; Mackintosh and Liddle, 2015). Here, the broad consensus for what this represented was a calling for individuals to play their part in civic society, but also running, administering, and developing public services (Griffiths, Kippin, and Stoker, 2015). It is no surprise that this occurred alongside major cuts to the same public services in the UK. For example, local leisure facilities such as libraries began to be seen as suitable facilities to be 'run' and managed solely by community volunteers. Equally, some sport facilities and the development opportunities that were present within them were effectively contracted out (a little like the primary PE and after-school sessions). For example, a cricket or rugby club may use local government playing fields and a changing room that is owned by the council. However, they may be encouraged to hand over in trust the club, grounds, and its maintenance to the club as a *Community Interest Company*. The club then has to run the sport development programmes out of the pitch, but then also take over all maintenance from the council. This saves council budget and reduces workload for a shrinking sport workforce who can perhaps signpost to the NGB. Since 2005, over 13,000 such Community Interest Companies have been founded, showing the growth of the movement. These are not all in the sport sector.

Perhaps the fastest growing market in the UK is social enterprise and the associated practices of social investment and social value. It has been suggested that there are "around 70,000 social enterprises in the UK, contributing £24 billion to the economy and employing nearly a million people" (SEUK, 2017: 6). Furthermore, research conducted by NCVO for Big Society Capital independently identified 67,000 'asset-locked social companies', which shows a similar triangulated number of such agencies (SEUK, 2017: 6). Ratten (2011a) argues for the important role sport can play in terms of social enterprises delivering outcomes through entrepreneurs. In relation to the major study above, around 7 per cent of social enterprises were classified as 'leisure' and 12 per cent as educational. For the sport coach this might straddle the two. But even a conservative estimate would locate 7 per cent of 70,000 UK social enterprises at just under 5000. These range from major regional and national employers to sole individuals. Since the global 2008 recession and arguable push into a period of public sector austerity (Widdop et al., 2017), there have been a record number of sport businesses/social enterprises running in the UK (ONS, 2017). Specific shifts include a boom of 70 pe cent in PE, sport, and education social enterprises and businesses since the alteration of PSPES in 2012, until 2017 (ONS, 2017).

Reid (2017) has also argued that the definitions around social enterprise are not agreed. He analysed the case study of a football club and social enterprise work around it that centres on community development and youth work. In this case study he shapes clear insights into some of the concerns for working in this way, but also potential real gains to sport development. The line between entrepreneurship, commercial acumen, and contracting out of public 'goods' is a fine line. Ratten has written extensively on enterprise and entrepreneurship (Ratten, 2011a; Ratten, 2011b; Ratten and Ferreira, 2016); in her work it is important to relate this back to the professional values, principles, and process of sport development. Communities, equality, and social justice need to be core to the work of the agencies and individual working together as part of the new networks and partnerships in delivery of social policy and sport policy outcomes through sport development. If we are not careful, the structure of the organisation or the income they generate become a vehicle for providing an alternative ideological footing for sport development.

In the worst cases, for example, we see traditional and well-established partners such as NGBs, Youth Sport Trust, and national charitable partners with long histories in sport development moved aside by a fragmented delivery system business or social organisation with far less accountability. Indeed, accountability is a little researched topic in sport development. It is also essential that long-learned lessons in the two spheres of child protection (Brackenridge, 1999; Gleaves and Lang, 2017) and legal issues (Hartley, 2009; James, 2017) must be upheld. As new graduates into this job market, the world of 2010, and before this 1995 as discussed by Collins (2010) offers little clear point of reference for comparison. However, what it does teach us is that macro changes at the national and global scale will continue to shape the very 'micro', local experiences of the SDO and the coaches they employ, clubs they work with and volunteers they train. Social enterprises and Community Enterprise Companies may perhaps be growing (SEUK, 2017; ONS, 2017; ONS, 2020) but in the next ten years a new set of challenges will have been set for you as graduates. New organisations, issues and new roles that were not present before will be on the meeting agenda of the SDO.

Conclusion and a call to arms: stubborn societal inequalities, fragmented communities, and physical inactivity

Sport development has long had an interest and propose role in the social welfare agenda of the UK (Coalter, 2007; Coalter, 2015; Coalter, Long and Duffield, 1988). As discussed already in this chapter, the changing shape and landscape of the organisational and sport policy environment in the UK is crucial for students to understand. Such understanding offers the platform for reading, analysing, engaging with through placement, and using volunteering to better appreciate the complexities of where they work. Differences between the four home nations are subtle, but only through studying up close can you appreciate how, say, mental health and sport features differently in England and Scotland. Likewise, the role of professional sports clubs is different across national boundaries, part due to financial resources, part due to political interest groups. If we assume that sporting organisations are changing (Brunton and Mackintosh, 2017; Mackintosh and Liddle, 2015; Ratten and Ferreira, 2016; Reid, 2017), this book has hopefully started to provide a bedrock for you to explore where, who, how and why agencies are engaging with local, regional and national sport development processes in the UK.

In a call to arms to the next generation of those that will work in sport development, I urge you to exploit this opportunity whilst studying your subject at university to see the potential a wide variety of conditions, activities, and formats of sport policy have to contribute to the wider government agendas of the UK. For the first time, the DCMS strategy for England (DCMS, 2015) was written as a cross governmental document, and in parallel national settings in Wales, Scotland, and Northern Ireland the pleas around public health and social welfare policy are positioned differently but across similar debates. The emergence of a sport-for-development coalition (Sport For Development Coalition, 2020) a coalescing of 66 major sport charities, social enterprises, and organisations with shared welfare goals in the UK shows an increasing maturity to this part of the sector. However, this is not the end of a story, the major charity Street Games has only worked in this sector since 2007, forming just before the global financial crisis. The challenges that have emerged in wider society in some cases are only just playing out now. Charities to support the ageing population are present such as those starting to use sport as a vehicle in dementia support (Clark et al., 2017) or active ageing (Age UK, 2020) and addressing fitness and volunteering through working on green neighbourhood programmes, which overlap between mental health and fitness with social isolation prevention (Active Lives, 2020). New issues and agendas emerge all the time. For example, global conflicts in Afghanistan and Iraq and the time lag in military veteran in needs has recently been identified as a new target market for the industry. Sport and physical fitness projects such as Moving Forces In Manchester have be used to address mental health, isolation, and alcohol issues (O'Hanlon et al., 2020).

In considering your role and what role you can play, you need to be reflective about your position as a student, graduate, and future employee or volunteer in the sport development sector. Work in the areas of public health, social policy, youth work, and physical inactivity can be incredibly challenging. It does not also mean that there does not remain a cohort of the workforce that will work in traditional domains of sport development. NGBs in each home nation will still need elite sport performance staff, community coaching social enterprises will need coaches and managers of their programmes, and professional clubs will need designers of projects for their local communities. But, it is, I suggest, going to be an increasing requirement and skill set to understand your community, the people you're aiming to work for, and not give a project to and ask them to 'receive it'. Reflective practice is key here where you acknowledge gaps in understanding, for as the breadth of policy issues gets greater, requirement to use monitoring, research, and evaluation is assumed as mainstream and specialist theoretical knowledge is self-led not tutor driven. By this, I mean learning at university must become a vehicle for you to shape the reflective gaps in understanding as co-produced learning with tutors and peers. No longer will you have an experience led by a lecture driven solely by a tutor. They will ask for you to input from your understanding of policy as a volunteer, in multiple settings. Seminars should be supported by reflections from key industry video interview resources to reflect the very latest policy shifts. Yes, a policy document from 2015 is useful. However, an account from the latest sport minister and how it has been interpreted by the largest two to three social enterprises in the UK compared to a fairly static local authority shows how you need to be constantly reflecting like any other professional, whether nurse, doctor, teacher, or youth worker.

The future of sport development has always been short lived. By this I mean researchers that have been exploring this domain of sport and leisure policy have consistently identified that it is held hostage to the whims of government (King, 2009; Houlihan and Green, 2011; Houlihan and Green, 2009; Houlihan and Lindsey, 2013). In 1995, MacDonald called for the death of sport development (MacDonald, 1995). Others have suggested that it the purported link with mega-events and mass participation 'virtuous cycle' (Grix and Carmichael, 2012) that is the historical embodiment of sport development. However, for this researcher, it is in the communities of sport that lie the future of the profession. This is not to say that there are not multiple contested communities. Instead, as the book has identified, new communities of organisations are emerging (Social Enterprises; Community Interest Companies; Active Partnerships), new ways of delivery are taking precedence (*parkrun*, contracted out market-led social hubs, virtual delivery) and society itself is changing (ageing, dementia, patterns of drug misuse, technological shifts in sporting behaviour). The older ways of analysing these spheres of sport development policy and practice may still be relevant. The sociological, business management, and political theories of the last 40 years may be useful. Society is changing so quickly, we need to consider the areas of theory we draw upon and the concepts we use to explore and understand sport development.

To end on a powerful vision for the future of sport development, I draw on the work of Kippin, Griffiths and Stoker (2013) in their summary of a reform agenda for public service. They argue for the use of 'social productivity' as a core concept alongside social businesses and public services. Both ideas when aligned to the design of public services such as sport development give a sense of optimism around this area of public services. Likewise, the authors argue for the central process to unlock such potential as strong civic and community leadership and the co-design and co-production of public services. In the case of sport development, this perhaps is returning to some of the 'bottom up-work' of the past that aligns well with community development (Sherry, Schulenkorf, and Phillips, 2016). With a workforce that have a strong sense of interdisciplinary theoretical working, ability to be reflective and a global sense of what sport development means, this may offer an exciting future for the profession.

References

Active Lives. (2020) *About us*, available at: https://activlives.org.uk/activgardens/, [accessed on 05 June 2020].

Age UK. (2020) *Being active as you get older*, available at: www.ageuk.org.uk/information-advice/health-wellbeing/exercise/, [accessed on 05 June 2020].

Armour, K. and MacDonald, D. (eds.) (2012) *Research Methods in Physical Education and Youth Sport*, London: Routledge.

Baker, C. (2017) *Coordination of Community Sport Development in Wales: An Investigation of Stakeholder Perspectives Concerning the Organisation and Structure of Community Sport in Wales*, Gloucester, University of Gloucester.

Belfiore, E. and Bennett, O. (2010) Beyond the 'toolkit approach': Arts impact evaluation research and the realities of cultural policy-making, *Journal of Cultural Research*, 14: 2, 121–142.

Bloyce, D. and Smith, A. (2010) The emergence and development of sport policy, in Bloyce, D. and Smith A. *Sport Policy and Development: An Introduction*, London: Routledge, 29–55.

Bloyce, D., Smith, A. Mead, R., and Morris, J. (2008) 'Playing the game (plan)': A figurational analysis of organisational change in sports development in England, *European Sports Management Quarterly*, 8, 359–378.

Brackenridge, C. (1999) Managing myself: Investigator survival in sensitive research, *International Review for the Sociology of Sport*, 34:4, 399–410.

Brunton, J. and Mackintosh, C. (2017) Interpreting university sport policy in England: Seeking a purpose in turbulent times?, *International Journal of Sport Policy and Politics*, 9:3, 377–395.

Cairney, P. (2016) *The Politics of Evidence-Based Policy Making*, London: Palgrave MacMillan.

Clark, M., Murphy, C., Jameson-Allen, T., and Wilkins, C. (2017) Sporting memories, dementia care and training staff in care homes, *The Journal of Mental Health Training, Education and Practice*, 12:1, 55–66.

Coalter, F. (2007) *A Social Role for Sport: Whose Keeping the Score?*, London: Routledge.

Coalter, F. (2015) Sport-for-Change: Some thoughts from a sceptic, *Social Inclusion*, 3:3, 19–23.

Coalter, F. Long, J. A., and Duffield, D. S. (1988) *Recreational Welfare: A Rationale for Public Leisure Policy*, Aldershot: Avebury.

Collins, M. (2010) From 'sport for good' to 'sport for sport's sake' – not a good move for sports development in England? *International Journal of Sport Policy and Politics*, 2:3, 367–379.

Department of Culture, Media and Sport (DCMS). (2015) *Sporting Future a New Strategy for an Active Nation*, London: DCMS.

Devine, C. (2012) London 2012 Olympic legacy: A big sporting society?, *International Journal of Sport Policy and Politics*, 5: 2, 257–279.

Gleaves, T. and Lang, M. (2017) Kicking 'no touch' discourses into touch: Athletes' parents' constructions of appropriate (adult) coach-(child) athlete physical contact, *Journal of Sport and Social Issues,* 41:3. 191–211.

Gregory, M. and Wilson, J. (2018) Monitoring and evaluation, in Wilson, R. and Platts, C. (eds) *Managing and Developing Community Sport*, London: Routledge, 213–235.

Griffiths, S., Kippin, H., and Stoker, G. (2015) *Public Services: A New Reform Agenda*, London: Bloomsbury.

Griggs, G. (2010) For Sale – Primary Physical Education. £20 per hour or nearest offer, *Education 3–13*, 38:1, 39–46.

Griggs, G. (2016) Spending the primary physical education and sport premium: A West Midlands case study, *Education 3–13*, 44(5), 547–555.

Grix, J. and Carmichael, F. (2012) Why do governments invest in elite sport? A polemic, *International Journal of Sport Policy and Politics*, 4:1, 73–90.

Gunter, H. and Rayner, S. (2007) Modernizing the school workforce in England: Challenging transformation and leadership? *Leadership*, 3:1, 47–64.

Hartley, H. (2009) *Sport, Physical Recreation and the Law*, London: Routledge.

Houlihan, B. and Green, M. (2009) Modernisation and sport: The reform of Sport England and UK Sport, *Public Administration*, 87:3, 678–698.

Houlihan, B. and Green, M. (2011) *Routledge Handbook of Sports Development*, London: Routledge.

Houlihan, B. and Lindsey, L. (2013) *Sport Policy in Britain*, London: Routledge.

Hylton, K. (ed.) (2013) *Sport Development: Policy, Process and Practice*, London: Routledge.

James, M. (2017) *Sports Law* (Third Edition), London: Red Globe Press.

King, N. (2009) *Sport Policy and Governance*, Oxford: Butterworth-Heinemann.

Kippin, H., Griffiths, S. and Stoker, G. (2013) *Public Services: A New Reform Agenda*. London: Bloomsbury.

MacDonald, I. (1995) *Sport for All –'RIP'. A Political Critique of the Relationship between National Sport Policy and Local Authority Sports Development in London*, Brighton: Leisure Studies Association, Series edition 55, 71–94.

Mackintosh, C. (2011) An analysis of County Sports Partnerships in England: The fragility, challenges and complexity of partnership working in sports development, *International Journal of Sport Policy*, 3:1, 45–64.

Mackintosh, C. (2012) The shifting dynamics of local government sports development officer practice in England: New identities and hazy professional boundaries, in Harris, S., Bell, B., Adams, A., and Mackintosh C. (eds) *Sport for Sport? Theoretical and Practical Insights into Sports Development*, Brighton: Leisure Studies Association, 113–130.

Mackintosh, C. and Liddle, J. (2015) Emerging school sport development policy, practice and governance in England: Big Society, autonomy and decentralisation, *Education 3–13: International Journal of Primary, Elementary and Early Years*, 43:6, 603–620.

Medcalf, R. and Mackintosh, C. (eds.) (2018) *Researching Difference and Otherness in Sport and Physical Activity*, London: Routledge.

Office for National Statistics (ONS). (2017) *UK business: Activity, size and location: 2016*, available at: www.ons.gov.uk/businessindustrytrade/business/activitysizeand-location/bulletins/ukbusinessactivitysizeandlocation/2016, [accessed 05 June 2020].

Office for National Statistics (ONS). (2020) *UK business; Activity, size and location: 2019*, available at: www.ons.gov.uk/businessindustrytrade/business/activitysizeand-location/bulletins/ukbusinessactivitysizeandlocation/2016, [accessed 05 June 2020].

O'Hanlon, R., Mackintosh, C., Holmes, H.-L. and Meek, R. (2020) Moving forces: Using sport and physical activity to support men and women in the military to civilian transition, *Journal of Sport and Social Issues, forthcoming*, 1–18.

Ratten, V. (2011a) Sport-based entrepreneurship: towards a new theory of entrepreneurship and sport management, *International Entrepreneurship and Management Journal*, 7:1, 57–69.

Ratten, V. (2011b) Social entrepreneurship and innovation in sports, *International Journal of Social Entrepreneurship and Innovation*, 1:1, 42–54.

Ratten, V. and Ferreira, J. J. (2016) *Sport Entrepreneurship and Innovation*, London: Routledge.

Reid, G. (2017) A fairy tale narrative for community sport? Exploring the politics of sport social enterprise, *International Journal of Sport Policy and Politics*, 9:4, 597–611.

Sherry, E., Schulenkorf, N., and Phillips, P. (2016) *Managing Sport Development*, London: Routledge.

Smith, B. and Sparkes, A. (2016) *Handbook of Qualitative Research in Sport and Exercise*, London: Routledge.

Social Enterprise UK (SEUK). (2017) *The Future of Business – State of Social Enterprise Survey 2017*, London: SEUK.

Sport England. (2017) *Review of the Evidence of the Outcomes of Sport and Physical Activity: A Rapid Review*, London: Sport England.

Sport England (2018) *Working in an Active Nation: The Professional Workforce Strategy for England*, London: Sport England.

Sport-for-Development Coalition. (2020) *Sport for Development Coalition 2020–2024 Business Plan*, London: SFDC.

Thompson, A., Bloyce, D. and Mackintosh, C. (2020) 'It is always going to change' – managing top-down policy changes by sport development officers working in national governing bodies of sport in England, *Managing Sport and Leisure: An International Journal*, iFirst, 1–20.

UK Coaching. (2020) *We're here for the coach: Grow your coaching skills*, available at: www.ukcoaching.org/ [accessed on 05 June 2020].

Virtual Learning UK (VLUK). (2020) *Apprenticeships: Sports development*, available at: www.vluk.org/apprenticeships-sports-development/, [accessed on 05 June 2020]

Widdop, P., King, N., Parnell, D., Cutts, D., and Millward, P. (2017) Austerity, policy and sport participation in England, *International Journal of Sport Policy and Politics*, 10:1, 7–24.

INDEX

Page numbers in *italic* indicate figures. Page numbers in **bold** indicate tables.